RAW SPEED

Tai Woffinden was born in Scunthorpe in 1990, but moved with his family to Perth, Western Australia, at the age of four. He won his first speedway title there at the age of fifteen, and in the same year made his debut in the British Conference League, with Scunthorpe Scorpions. In 2007 he was crowned British Under 18 Champion, won the first of his two Under 21 titles in 2008, and went on to take the first of three successive senior championships in 2013.

He won the Speedway Grand Prix series in 2013, to become World Champion for the first time, a title he regained in 2015. When he did it again in 2018, he became the only British rider ever to win it three times, as well as being the youngest rider to have won the World Championship in the modern GP era. He is married to Faye and they have two daughters, Rylee-Cru and Calle. As a family, they divide their time between this country and Australia, as well as Tai racing regularly in Poland.

Peter Oakes is an award-winning Fleet Street journalist who was formerly TV and Showbusiness Editor at *The People* and Sports Editor of the *Daily Star*. A long-time speedway fan, he is the leading columnist for the world's top-selling magazine dedicated to the sport, the weekly *Speedway Star*. He has written or edited more than thirty books on football, speedway, TV and darts, and is co-author with speedway legend Ivan Mauger and Liverpool FC manager Bob Paisley.

RAW SPEED
TAI WOFFINDEN

MY AUTOBIOGRAPHY
WITH PETER OAKES

JB

First published in the UK by John Blake Publishing
an imprint of Bonnier Books UK
The Plaza,
535 Kings Road,
London SW10 0SZ
Owned by Bonnier Books
Sveavägen 56, Stockholm, Sweden

www.facebook.com/johnblakebooks
twitter.com/jblakebooks

First published in hardback in 2019
This revised and updated paperback edition published in 2021

Paperback ISBN: 978-1-78946-206-7
Ebook ISBN: 978-1-78946-158-9

British Library Cataloguing-in-Publication Data:

A catalogue record for this book is available from the British Library.

Design by www.envydesign.co.uk

Printed and bound in Great Britain by Clays Ltd, Elcograf S.p.A

1 3 5 7 9 10 8 6 4 2

John Blake Publishing is an imprint of Bonnier Books UK
www.bonnierbooks.co.uk

For Dad, my best friend, my teacher, my travelling companion, my father. Everything I have achieved came from what he taught me about life and how to live it.

CONTENTS

ACKNOWLEDGEMENTS

To become a world champion at any sport you need the right people alongside you, and every individual victory is because of THE TEAM.

There are so many people who have played a part in my story and I don't want to miss anyone out. They all know who they are and they will always have my grateful thanks. Those who have supported me throughout my racing life, those who have sponsored me over the years (some when I was a virtually unknown fifteen-year-old over from Australia), members of my pit crew who have worked tirelessly to ensure I went out with the best chance of winning every race, those who have driven thousands of miles to make sure both I and my machinery got to where they needed to be on time.

My thanks to each and every one of you who have, at one time or another, been such an invaluable part of TEAM WOFFINDEN.

TAI WOFFINDEN

RAW SPEED

* * *

My thanks to all those who helped jog Tai's memory and recall what happened in his too-young-to-remember days, especially all his family members, including wife Faye, mum Sue, nan Cynthia, parents-in-law Sean and Tracy, Neil Machin, Peter Adams, Rob Lyon, Steve Johnston, Andrew Skeels, Len Silver, Jacek Trojanowski, the legend Andi Gordon and Josh Gudgeon.

To list everyone else who has contributed in one way or another would risk missing someone out, but they know who they are, and life would have been far more difficult without their help and assistance.

PETER OAKES

FOREWORD

If you asked me to describe myself in four words I'd say: focused, loving, crazy and loyal.

Focused, because I have been since I decided to stop dicking about partying and concentrated on trying to be the best in the world.

Loving, because I'm devoted to my wife Faye and our little girls Rylee-Cru and Calle.

Crazy, in the sense that I could never resist a challenge, however bizarre or dangerous it might seem. If someone dared me to jump off a building no matter how many storeys high, I would probably do it without even checking what was below!

And loyal, to the people around me – I have had virtually the same pit team for a decade and my philosophy is, if it ain't broken why change it? – and to my clubs in three different countries.

That just about sums me up, and I guess one of the reasons I wanted to write my autobiography is so that people can understand me on a deeper level than just this bloke who has tattoos and a lust for racing a motorcycle that doesn't have brakes.

I want everyone to know where I have come from, what I have been through, what I have overcome along the way, how hard I have worked since I stopped partying, and what it has taken to get where I am today. I have raced, and continue to race, motorbikes for a living, and I have grasped the opportunity to do that with both hands.

I came back to Europe when I was fifteen, my dad died when I was in my late teens, I went off the rails, came to my senses, and since then have won three world speedway titles.

Not once in my career did I ask anyone like Tony Rickardsson, who won the World Championship six times, or Jason Crump, the only Australian to be a three-time World Champion, or other people at the top of the sport how I should live and what I needed to do to achieve what they had achieved in speedway.

I want to give all the kids everything I know; every bit of knowledge I have in my head I will willingly give them. I'm not worried about giving away my secrets. Why should I be? By the time they have made it as far as the Grand Prix, I will probably be retired so it's not going to disadvantage me in any way. I hope that by reading my story they will avoid some of the pitfalls and learn from my mistakes.

In some ways I have been fortunate to have had a career at all ... I must have been only a split second away from death when I was still at school, and even before that I could have lost two or three fingers after foolishly reaching down to see if the chain on my push bike was tight enough.

We had some BMX jumps down the front of our house in

Australia and I kept snapping chains, so I bought a heavy-duty chain and fitted it. Not long afterwards, riding through the park on my way to school, I reached down to check the tension. I knew there was a steel pole in the middle of the park and while I was checking the chain I looked up to see where the pole was. As I did so I must have pushed down on the pedals, with the result that I chopped off the end of the middle finger of my right hand, the blood spraying out.

I went straight to the deputy head at school, they called my mum and we went to the nearest hospital, where we sat for six hours with my finger still bleeding.

When we did eventually see someone we were told they couldn't do anything for me and that I had to go to the city hospital for plastic surgery. But although I had cut off the top of my finger at eight o'clock in the morning, it wasn't until around twenty-four hours later that they operated, attaching my finger to a flap of skin at the bottom of my thumb. It stayed like that for six weeks and then they cut my finger away from the thumb, so that the hand could function normally again. Fortunately, it has been okay ever since, but it could have ended up differently, and perhaps I'd never have been able to ride a bike again.

I was only thirteen or fourteen when I nearly lost my finger, but the biggest scare of my life came twelve months or so later, when Dad and I went out in his Holden Rodeo pick-up truck to spend the day on our motocross bikes in the bush.

In some Australian states you can get a learner driving licence when you are fifteen and as long as there is someone qualified in the vehicle with you, you can drive.

We spent all day at Lancelin, a small town at the end of State Route 60 (Wannaroo Road), where we could ride the bikes up and down the sand dunes.

On the way back, with me driving, Dad felt sleepy and then fell asleep, which you are not supposed to do if you are with a learner driver. A couple of times I momentarily closed my eyes, which I'm sure we have all done while driving when tired.

With Dad still out, I started to fall asleep, and put the window down in an effort to stay awake. The road was just a single carriageway each way, a really dangerous highway that must have accounted for the deaths of around thirty people a year.

The next thing was that I must have fallen asleep, for I drove onto the wrong side of the road and then suddenly woke to see another car coming straight for us. I yanked the wheel full lock to the left and then back to the right, hit the kerb and somehow that took the 'ute' (utility vehicle) back to the right side of the road (in Australia, like the UK, they drive on the left).

I still have no idea how the two vehicles avoided each other, but I do know that we came that close to dying. I am sure that if my eyes had stayed closed for another fraction of a second the result would have been a head-on smash and none of us would have walked away alive. After that I was so scared that I didn't ask to drive again for about a month or more, having come closer to death than I have ever been.

That near-miss taught me not to drive when I am too tired, and that it is something I can always tell the young kids to remember when they get behind the wheels of their vans on the way home after a speedway meeting. In fact, I like to think that I can use all my life experiences to help them remain focused at all times, whether they are on or off the track.

When it comes to racing, I have been loyal to all the teams I have ridden for and have only ever left any of them for specific and valid reasons.

In England, I rode for Scunthorpe, Rye House and

Wolverhampton, only leaving to join a side in a higher league to progress my career.

In Poland, I have ridden for just three clubs, Czestochowa, Gniezno and Wroclaw. I only left Czestochowa because they wanted to use a Polish junior who crashed a lot, and if he missed meetings my average was too high for me to be allowed to replace him. They loaned me out to Gniezno in the First League for a season, but that didn't end very well because the two teams raced each other in the 2011 relegation/promotion play-off, and I had an awful meeting in the first leg, only scoring four points.

As if that wasn't enough, someone at Gniezno, who isn't at the club any longer, accused me of deliberately riding badly because I was a Czestochowa rider and only on loan. I didn't ride in the second leg after being diagnosed with flu, and I also missed the Elite League Riders' Final that same weekend.

When Czestochowa couldn't fit me in the following season, I moved to Wroclaw and I've now been there eleven years.

I've had more clubs, five, in Sweden, but again there have always been good reasons for leaving.

Vargarna and I fell out over money; I had too high an average to go back to Dackarna; I really enjoyed my time at Vetlanda but it is a really unique track and I got a little bit bored with it and also, a very good friend of mine, Bosse Wirebrand, finished working with the club. I would have stayed a long time at Masarna but there were money issues, and I was at Indianerna for two seasons, 2018 and 2019. They treated me well, they paid me every week, and if I hadn't decided to cut back on my racing, I would probably still be there.

If you find a club you are happy at, why change every year?

As to the 'real me', I know I am outspoken, and that this can rub some people up the wrong way. I don't hide my feelings but I'm always honest, although quite often that lands me in trouble, and I know that some people think I'm arrogant, self-centred and selfish. Equally, sometimes I don't feel that I am appreciated in England, especially because I don't ride here any more, as I will explain in this book. To me, this seems to be an example of a particular British mentality: build someone up and then just knock 'em down as quick as you can.

I've been through it all, for there's always someone ready to have a go at you whatever you do. In that, I'm just like every other British sports person I know. The public want to see you get better and better, but as soon as you do something wrong you are knocked straight down.

Okay, you can say that the only people who turn on you are the idiots, but there are a lot of them and they can sometimes get you down after a bit. It's not two or three, it's two or three hundred a year, but I have my own way of responding: I block them all on Twitter.

I'll search Twitter for 'Woffinden' and will see every tweet even when senders don't tag me in it. If they are slating me I'll click on their profile and I'll see that they follow me and I block 'em. Anything negative, I block. When I see people slating me, it frustrates me because I think *Do I deserve this from someone sat on his arse giving me grief?* when I don't know them and they don't know me. But they are giving me a bad name, and other people will see that.

They don't know it, but these people make me hungry to win. I use all their negative comments as motivation, so it's not necessarily a bad thing. I know what they're saying, and that gives me the incentive to achieve more, to get to higher levels in the gym, better levels when I'm riding – essentially, to prove them all wrong.

FOREWORD

As this book records, there have been ups and plenty of downs, soaring peaks, deep troughs, highs and lows, but at the age of thirty I'm a three-time World Champion.

I have a beautiful wife I love with every bone in my body (including all those I have broken along the way), we have two precious daughters, we have an incredible home and a fair few bob in the bank.

There have been the black times, including my dad's death and the tragic road accident in which one of my best pals was killed, but how many thirty-year-olds have what I have?

TAI WOFFINDEN

CHAPTER 1

A DEATH AND A
TURNING POINT

What the fuck do you get as a Christmas present for someone who only has weeks to live?

What do you get your best friend, the person you love more than anyone else in the world?

What can you buy for someone who had given up everything for you?

What can you get your dying dad for his last Christmas?

I've never been good at thinking of what to get at the best of times. But this was different. The doctors had told us that Dad's cancer was terminal. He was only forty-seven and that's no age.

The funny thing was he was meant to die before Christmas (2009), so what do you buy your dad?

You don't want to upset him, so you can't really buy him something that he can use in the future.

I'm shit with presents anyway, I always buy funny or jokey stuff.

I must have spent weeks and weeks trying to think of

something that he'd like. It was no good thinking of something that would last, it wasn't as if he wanted something to keep for years.

In the end I thought of something that I knew he would enjoy.

My dad used to smoke weed, not heavy but he used to. He didn't drink, so when he used to go out to the pub where his mates were, they would be drinking and he'd go out, have a little joint and go back in.

So I bought him some weed, some Rizlas, a grinder to grind up his weed, a lighter and his favourite sweets – they were called milk bottles– so when he was stoned he could eat them all.

That was the present I bought him and I parcelled each thing up individually and put that in a parcel, then that in a parcel, and that in a parcel. So he opened the shoebox and there was his Rizlas on top of the next box that was inside of that, and then he opened that and there was something else on top of that.

He went through and through and through, and he's saying, 'What the fuck is this?'

Dad was diagnosed with cancer of the pancreas in the February or March of 2009 and I will never forget him telling us the dreadful news.

He sat me down in a room and said: 'I need to tell you something, I've got cancer and I can't stop it.'

That was all, and that was, like, a big blow. He told me in the bedroom, I walked downstairs, and out of the house to where my van was parked. I put three massive dents in the side of it then walked down the road, composed myself and came back, trying not to show any emotion at all.

I broke my knuckle on the side of the van and then the season started, like a week later.

Actually, I was lucky that I'd got to spend a year with him. It's not like he had a car crash and he was gone, so that was cool because we had that time together. He came everywhere with me, to every meeting he could.

We had never really said that we loved each other but, after he told me about the cancer, it was like every single day. I told him I loved him and he said he loved me. It just changes something.

They said that he would just fall asleep and that would be it. But it was the complete opposite of that, nothing like what they said it would be. He was sat down talking to me and having a cup of coffee. Everything was sweet, no drama. He sat up in his bed and he had his oxygen blowing in his nose, just as if nothing was wrong at all.

And then he's saying, 'Get me my pants, I feel sick.' And he was sick. He weed, he pooed and then he just started screaming. His body just shut down, like everything disappeared from it. It just chucked everything out. And then he started calling, 'Help me, help me, help me.'

We had two nurses to help look after him and we tried calling them. We couldn't get hold of them. All was confusion. Then we called an ambulance. My mum's sister came, she's a nurse. Then the ambulance arrived.

The ambulance crew refused to give him painkillers but this is like half an hour now, forty minutes, he's been screaming for me and Mum to help him. We couldn't do anything, so we're just holding his hand and cuddling him trying to make him comfortable, and he's screaming, 'Help me, help me. Sue, Sue, Sue. Tai, Tai, help me.' The ambulance reached the hospital and rushed him in. They couldn't find the vein, they seemed to spend fucking ages trying to do that and he was still screaming, screaming. They put some gear into it and then that calmed him

3

down. They got him up to the ward, then he started screaming again so I went out and got the nurse.

They didn't have any painkillers that they could give him, so I had to get it from a different ward and this whole time he's still screaming. They gave him some more and then it happened again, so I ran back out, said, 'We need some more, he's screaming again.' And again, they didn't have any, so they went down and got some more and I said, 'Grab a few bottles.' This had happened a couple of times now. It might have been the third time that it happened. And then, after the third time, he was chilled out for ages, but it was as if his eyes were on the back of his head and he was counting. He was going 'Two, four, six, eight, ten. Two, four, six, eight, ten. Two, four, six, eight, ten,' and after about an hour of that, I was like, fuck this, I'm going home – I can't sit and listen to that the whole night. I went home and went to sleep, set my alarm for eight o'clock, woke up at six. I never wake up before my alarm. Jumped, got up early, went back to hospital. Mum was sat there holding his hand. His brother Keith was there. Nan, his mum, was there and I walked in and sat down by him and held his hand and told him I loved him. And then he stopped breathing.

And my mum was obviously crying. His brother said, 'See you' to him, my nan did too, and then Mum probably sat there for an hour. I had to say, 'Come on, say your last goodbye. Let's get out.' I had to almost pull her out of the room. She would have sat there for five days. And that's that. Dad is dead, he's gone.

Dad always tried to keep up appearances, he rarely showed how ill he was to other people, but I will never forget some of those times as that horrible illness took its hold.

And it was always stuff like him coming back from chemo and that. I don't know if it was from the chemo or what, he said it was because he had a coffee and then he had Actimel or something, he was just being sick. It just kept coming up. It was just after the chemo. And the chemo actually made him a diabetic, and he knew, and before he actually died, he nearly died.

When my dad was sick, he'd have coffee with a few sugars, bottles of fizzy drinks and loads of ice cream. So if he's feeling a bit shit, he's like: 'Get me some ice creams from the shop, Tai.'

So I'll go get them, and a few bottles of pop, and he'd be eating and drinking all this. He's actually making it worse and worse, turning himself diabetic because he's piling all the sugar in.

I'd gone to Sheffield to see Ashley Birks because I spent a lot of time with Ash and Di there. Mum called me: 'Oh Tai you've got to come to hospital. Your dad is not well.'

I'm thinking, *Oh fuck off, he's just feeling a bit sick. I'm not driving all the way down there.* So I fell out with my mum that day. Then my dad called me up and said: 'Tai, it's quite serious. I need you to come and see me.' When I got there, my mum was bawling her eyes out and she thought I was a dickhead, and Dad's lying in hospital nearly dead. The ward that he was on was just a massive long room like four times the size of a normal room with only beds in it, and all the people in their beds were completely yellow skin and bones. And my dad is sat there, and I'm thinking, *No, you're alright.*

I said: 'Look at you compared to all the people in here. You're fucking sweet. Don't worry about it.'

And then they did some tests and then he had to go on the sweeteners, but he still used to have a sugar every now and then. He was like: 'Fuck that, I've only got a few more months to live, I'm having some sugar.'

There are photos of him, and my mum hates it but there's a

picture of him at Swindon, crying, with his life reduced to skin and bones.

I watched a Travis Pastrana video, and he said that to prepare himself for the double backflip (on a stunt motorcycle), he'd accepted the fact that he could be paralysed, he could die; he'd been through it in his head and he mentally rehearsed it all – that's cool, that. So then after I watched that, I did the same with my dad.

When Dad got sick, I mentally rehearsed everything. He'd died in my head like a hundred times – we'd been to hospital, we'd been to the funeral place, done this, done that, all that sort of stuff. I went through it all in my head and when he actually passed away it was as if I was playing a role because I'd already been through it so many times.

I used to lie in my bed, imagine that he died and that I went to the crem and did all that, carried his coffin, spoke at his funeral. I'd been through it like two, three thousand times, so I mentally prepared myself for it. And it worked.

A couple of months after Dad told me he had cancer, I'm laid in bed. He's in the living room with my mum and I'm going through it all. He's not here. What it's going to be like when he's not here? The things that me and Mum are going to have to do. People coming up to me and asking me if I'm alright, *Are you alright?* I imagined it all. I imagined going into the pits at Wolverhampton and my dad having just died and it's the first time I'm seeing everyone and everyone is saying all this stuff to me. I played it over and over in my head. It's really weird, and not many people understand that. But when it actually happened, it made it ten times easier because I'd been through it. I'd already done it. I'd already done it so many times.

Pulling my mum away from the bed, me saying, 'See you' to

him, was a lot easier than for Mum because it was a big build-up for her and I'm sure she didn't do what I had done. She wouldn't have imagined Dad dying like I did. People say, 'I don't know how you deal with it.' And everyone deals with it in their own ways.

It was just like routine. So that was massive. Speaking at the funeral, that was the hardest part, as I describe later. Everything else went pretty easy, but that was the one thing that got me. I think it wouldn't have mattered how many times you rehearse for that, it isn't easy when it's someone that you love.

* * *

The specialists hadn't minced their words, telling him that it was terminal, and he probably only had another six to nine months to live. For nearly six months we had to keep the news to ourselves, no one outside the close family circle and our special friends knew that he was ill, although they sometimes asked if he was okay when he was feeling tired.

We'd bought a new house in a little village called Gunness, about three miles outside Scunthorpe, that needed some work doing on it.

The first thing we did was build a proper workshop in the garden and Dad was always there doing something. He wanted to make sure the house was finished before he died and was determined to have a family Christmas there.

In August we couldn't hide his illness any longer, so began to tell people and, in a sport like speedway, news spreads quickly.

I suppose in some ways it was a relief. Dad was having chemo most of the time; it was three weeks of it and then a week off, and then another three weeks, and so on.

He was getting more and more drawn, thinner and thinner, he wasn't eating and he was always feeling sick, but he would try not to miss any of my meetings in England even though he must have felt awful all the time.

In 2008, he had also come with me to both Sweden and Poland. In Sweden I was racing for Elitserien Vargarna, a famous team based in the town of Norrköping, while my Polish club was Ekstraliga Czestochowa.

I don't think he missed a meeting at all that year, but in 2009 he wasn't well enough and never came to Sweden at all, and I think he only did one or two early-season matches in Poland.

He did as many of my meetings as he could both in England and in the Under 21 World Championship, but I remember, the U21 final in Croatia where he was with us but too ill to do anything. He was so bad that he had to go and sit on the grass banking on one of the bends with his friend Neil Machin and another close family friend, Trevor Harding, who was over from Australia at the time.

Dad never came into the pits, but he said that he could tick off one of the things on his bucket list because he had wanted to see me in a World Under 21 final.

He had always wanted to see the start of the 2010 season, that was his dream, but he never did make it.

When that happened it was kind of like the turning point in my life, in my career. It's a shame it took my dad dying for me to grow up and do that.

If he was still with us would I have been a three-time World Champion, or would it just have been a case of *What if*?

Who knows?

CHAPTER 2

FROM SCUNTHORPE TO PERTH, WA

One good thing about Scunthorpe?
It takes about five minutes from the town centre to get out of the dump and go to a better place!

Those aren't my words about the town where I was born but a random comment in an online poll to find the 20 Worst Places to Live in England.

Scunthorpe was voted the fourth worst ... behind Luton, Hull and Dover in 2018.

Another Scunthorpe local submitted the view: 'If Maccy Ds is the chav's staple diet, what does that tell you about a town that boasts not one, not two, but three of these gourmet eateries?'

Reading those comments, I can understand why my dad was so determined to get out of Scunthorpe to make a life for me.

Who wouldn't want to leave a town best known for its dying steel business for the land of opportunities?

My dad used to go to Australia every year to race (he was a

speedway racer, too) there and he loved it. He wanted a better childhood for me, so the three of us emigrated to Australia before I started going to school.

He wanted me to grow up in Perth, with the Indian Ocean on our doorstep, soft sandy beaches at the bottom of our drive, and the lifestyle you could never dream of living in Lincolnshire.

It's impossible to compare the grimy industrial wastelands of Scunthorpe with the capital and largest city of Western Australia. They are 14,484 kilometres (9,100 miles) apart by air but light years in so many other ways.

It was like one extreme to the other, wasn't it? From somewhere everyone thinks is the arse end of Britain to a new life with the beach five minutes down the road.

I can't remember anything of my life in Scunthorpe, except what I have been told by the family, although I have occasionally driven past a couple of the houses where we used to live: 38a Neap House Road in Gunness, just outside the town, and in Enderby Road, a semi-detached house that my dad renovated, fitting leaded windows and building a double garage.

My family had something of a colourful background. Mum, who was born Susan Blanch, was one of nine children, and one of the skeletons in the cupboard was an ancestor who had shot her great-great-grandmother who was lucky to escape death. He was arrested and hauled into court for attempted murder but was judged to be insane and avoided prison, although he did spend the rest of his life in an asylum!

My nana was Cynthia Gunson, who married Brian Woffinden in 1958. They had their first son Keith the following year and Dad Rob came along on 27 March 1962.

My grandad Brian was born in Scunthorpe and until emigrating to Australia spent all his life there. Him and my nan split up and he married his second wife, Molly, in 1975 and they emigrated soon afterwards.

I don't know much about my grandad Brian even though he and Molly used to live twenty minutes down the road the whole time we lived in Australia. We used to drive down there and back at Christmas and birthdays but they'd never come to see us.

We at least talk now and he came to my wedding, but until then I always felt he never made an effort with me, so he could get fucked. I never made an effort with him because of that and if my dad said he was coming around, I'd be like, 'Alright, see you, I'm going out. Let me know when he's gone!'

My nan got married again and her second husband, Jeffrey Shores, became a speedway supporter when it started up in the town. He would go and watch the Scunthorpe Saints and started taking my dad with him and Nan when he was about eleven. This would have been the early seventies, during speedway's first incarnation in the town.

Ex-riders Vic White, who later became secretary of the World Speedway Riders' Association, and Ivor Brown, whose day job was doubling as postmaster and running the general stores in the picturesque Leicestershire village of Wymeswold, wanted to be in on the boom as new tracks flourished in the late sixties and seventies with the launch of the British League Division Two in 1968.

They had re-opened their local track, Long Eaton, in 1969 but after a year, Vic stepped down, although Ivor and his wife Kath carried on.

However, they got back together again and after looking at several possible virgin venues they went across to Scunthorpe to look at the town's smart athletics stadium in Brumby

Wood Lane, a couple of miles outside the town centre. It was named after locally born dignitary David Quibell, who was elevated to the peerage after standing down as the sitting Labour Member of Parliament for the Brigg constituency in Lincolnshire. On entering the House of Lords, the building contractor took the title of Baron Quibell of Scunthorpe in the county of Lincolnshire. When North Lincolnshire Council bought the parkland from Scunthorpe Agricultural Society in 1960, they drew up plans to build the brand-new Quibell Park Athletic and Cycling Stadium in 1965, via donations from the public after a fund-raising campaign led by Lord Quibell, who died before the project was completed.

The speedway track was built inside a banked, concrete cycling circuit and attracted crowds of up 4,000 for a series of a dozen open-licence meetings in 1971. At the first meeting on Monday, 3 May, when Scunny raced against Hull in the Humberside Trophy, they had to hold up the start because of the queues.

But audiences drifted away and the Monday race night proved unpopular. When the speedway authorities blocked a switch to Sunday afternoons after Lincolnshire rivals Boston objected to two clubs in the same county sharing the same race day, even though they were 60 miles apart, the die was cast and the track closed down early, leaving the first Australian to ride for the club, a young lad called Garth Coleman, without a team place.

However, the promoters persevered after being admitted to the 1973 Second Division, but a weak team and only five wins in thirty-two matches, saw the Saints collect the wooden spoon, eleven points adrift of second bottom.

Messrs Brown and White found it impossible to attract top-standard riders, mainly because most of their rival promoters had cast-iron links with First Division clubs and, naturally, got the first pick of the country's outstanding prospects.

Twenty riders, most of whom came and went, wore the Saints' race jacket, and one of them, Brian Osborn, bought the promoting rights in an effort to keep the club afloat.

His arrival coincided with growing complaints from the athletics fraternity that the speedway bikes were damaging the running track the two sports shared. But at the end of 1978 the conflict was resolved when the local council offered Osborn a piece of virgin land at Ashby Ville.

By the time the club moved, Dad was totally hooked on the racing and, always encouraged by his speed-daft mother, he had his first bike by the time he was fourteen and had clearly inherited his maternal enthusiasm for racing, admittedly on two wheels rather than four.

Nan was the first Woffinden to race: she and Brian were members of the Scunthorpe Motor Sports Club and took part in car racing on the grass. Nan's proudest achievements came after she'd bought an old Morris Oxford – she often told me: 'That car was in a different class and so fast that I had to start further back on the grid but I kept winning and winning, and was the club's Ladies' Champion! Your dad and uncle Keith used to jump up and down, shouting "Come on, Mam!"'

Dad's family weren't exactly rolling in it and were so hard up that they couldn't afford the fifteen pence a week it would have cost to buy *Speedway Star* magazine, so Dad would go down to the local newsagent's and read it from first page to last and then put it back on the shelf.

He bought his first bike, an old Jap, for £100, and helped to pay for it by saving all his pocket money from helping on a window-cleaning round. His first 'leathers' were made from a green lorry tarpaulin sheet!

Dad had his first ride at Scunthorpe's Press Day in 1976 when he was still only fourteen and for the next couple of years had interval rides at Ashby Ville and also spent the winter practising at King's Lynn.

He was given his first second-half rides after the Saints' opening home meeting of the 1978 season, a challenge match against Lincolnshire rivals Boston, on his sixteenth birthday and towards the end of the season he made his team debut against Canterbury at the beginning of September 1978.

Mum, who went every week with her stepdad, was the other side of the fence watching. She had absolutely no idea, however, when he lined up at the start alongside teammate Trevor Whiting and Crusaders' duo Barney Kennett and Brendan Shilleto that she was cheering on her husband-to-be.

There was no fairy-tale bow for Dad, he didn't score a point and didn't finish one of his three rides as the Saints went down 31–47, one of nine defeats in front of their own fans in another dismal season. They were saved from ending up bottom of the table only because Barrow were even worse and picked up a couple of points fewer from the 38-match schedule.

Mum, one of nine children and born in Grimsby, had only recently moved from the tiny village of East Halton (population: 600) on the Humber estuary, to Scunthorpe, although she never understood why there had been such a family upheaval.

She was only fourteen and going into her final year at school, was quickly introduced to speedway by her stepfather.

Being at an impressionable age, she developed something of a schoolgirl crush on my dad but also had a liking for his teammate, Trevor Whiting. She was bold and interested enough to send her stepdad scurrying off to the kiosk to buy a picture of Rob, and used all her powers to persuade her stepfather to get it personally signed for her!

But it wasn't until early the following year that she finally got to meet her idol, bumping into each other at the Coffee Bin, a disco-style haunt for the under-eighteens, and a regular meeting place for youngsters wanting to get to know someone of the opposite sex.

She admits: 'We didn't dance or anything like that and I honestly can't remember what we actually said to each other, whether he came over to talk to me or I went to talk to him, but I know he asked if I wanted him to walk me home! I think I was probably a little bit awestruck – I most definitely had a crush on him!'

Dad's form in that handful of tail-end matches was bright enough for him to be guaranteed a chance in the starting line-up the following season, but while he showed some improvement, the team certainly didn't.

Ahead of taking on long-distance visitors Glasgow on Monday, 11 June 1979, they had lost fourteen matches in a row, eleven in the league, home and away Knock Out Cup encounters with Berwick and a home challenge against Middlesbrough.

Even changing the team nickname from Saints to Stags hadn't brought a change of luck and they were still desperately aiming to break their duck when the Tigers arrived at Ashby Ville.

Hopes were high as the Tigers had lost all of their five matches on the road, but the miracle every fan was hoping for never materialised and they went down to yet another heavy defeat, losing 27–51!

Even that paled into significance alongside two other events that took place that Monday night.

Dad broke his left leg after crashing into the fence as he tried a harum-scarum dive on the outside of Tigers' Jim Beaton, but even more soul-destroying for the club's patient fans, the Speedway Control Board suspended the club's licence to race home meetings because of safety issues.

Non-league Castleford were also barred from operating, with SCB manager Dick Bracher dictating: 'There is considerable work needed at both venues for either to meet the Board's minimum requirements. Until they are carried out we are not prepared to sanction further meetings.'

The decree saw Scunthorpe without a home meeting (they weren't actually thrown out of the league and raced six successive away matches) until Rye House visited Ashby Ville on 20 August, ten weeks after Dad's accident.

Mum was at the Tigers match with her own father and still remembers being told to calm down after she had started screaming as Dad hit the fence: 'I was there, by then I was going out with Rob, so it couldn't have been long after we'd met at the Coffee Bin.

'When Rob broke his leg, I visited him in Scunthorpe Hospital every single night for ten weeks while he was in with his leg in traction.'

The story didn't have a happy ending, as she revealed: 'When he came out he finished with me – I was devastated!'

Three years later, when she was eighteen, Mum and a friend wrote off to a London agency looking for jobs working as nannies overseas. They had seen an advert, travelled down to London for interviews and, within a month or two, she had been offered a position with a family in Canada and it looked as if that was the end of the relationship. Dad had moved on with his life and so had Mum, or so it seemed.

Seven years after Mum's unrequited hospital vigil, they both decided, totally independently, to have a night out at the Cocked Hat fun pub on Scunthorpe's Ferry Road.

'I was home for a break. I was planning to take up a new job as a nanny in Miami and was just spending a week or so at home. I didn't go to speedway ever again after Rob dumped me and us meeting up again just happened by chance,' she explained.

'We were both in the Cocked Hat the same night. I wasn't going to go that night and he didn't normally go there because he was racing for Berwick at the time and didn't have much time to have many nights out.

'I think we might have seen each other maybe once in the meantime, at a stock car meeting when I was with my family and he was also there. We just said, "Hello, how are you?" and that was all.

'There wasn't any social media in those days, we didn't have mobiles and I would never have phoned him at home.

'We got talking again and he told me he was off to Australia and then asked: 'Do you want to come?' I thought he was joking and told him I had a new job lined up in Miami, but he said he would pay for me to go with him and that I didn't have to worry about anything. I said I'd go and when we'd been in Australia for a couple of weeks, he proposed and on 21 August 1988, we got married at the beautiful St Peter's Church in Bottesford.'

The wedding, including a reception at the Bridge Hotel in Scunthorpe, for sixty guests, family and friends, cost £1,000 all in and Mum was wearing a second-hand wedding dress she'd unearthed via an advert in a local paper during their winter stay in Australia.

It had been a little bit tight when she tried it on, but she had it altered in a shop and brought it back with her. After the wedding, she sold it to one of her friends for £60 that she then used to buy a tumble dryer!

* * *

My godfather Neil Machin knew Dad as well as anyone and if I ever need to ask anything about him before I came along, or was old enough to understand what was going on, then Neil is the first person I ask.

He recalled: 'I must have first met Rob at Scunthorpe, the old Ashby Ville track, probably in 1981 when he was nineteen. We had common ground from our first meeting because we were both just about teetotal, we never drank, and we played snooker at a works-type level. We always had a battle when we met on the snooker table, he was always hard to beat, always a competitor. It didn't matter whether it was snooker – it could be ten-pin bowls, cricket or tiddlywinks, he always wanted to win.

'If I ever got the better of him on the green baize it really was a red-letter day for me. We would always play over five or seven frames and he was difficult to get the better of. I remember beating him 4–1 and I felt as though I'd won the world final!

'His life wasn't based on night clubs or boozy nights out, he just didn't do that stuff, but when I was in his neck of the woods, I'd give him a buzz and we'd go to the snooker club in Scunthorpe and play each other.

'He was never the greatest speedway rider in the world and the only new bike he ever had was the season he managed to almost take off his toes with a chainsaw. Somehow, during the winter he'd managed to get the resources and sponsorship to get a brand-new Weslake machine but the injury kept him away from the early season stuff. Finally his first meeting came round, and the time for him to go out on the only brand-new bike he ever had in his career. He was due to go out in heat two, but his teammate Mark Burrows's bike stopped on the way to the tapes in heat one and Rob runs out with his brand-new bike that he'd never ridden and offered it to Buzz. I can't think of anyone else who would have done that. Imagine, having a brand-new bike for the only time in your life and letting someone else use it before you did. That was the type of person Rob was.

'When I first met him he was still living in Scunthorpe and he did all sorts of things to earn money. One job was shunting lorries in the steelworks, moving steel from here to there. He was driving heavy goods vehicles way before he had a licence and he would do almost anything to earn a bob or two. He always had an enormous amount of energy and industry.

'Most of us grew up in frugal surroundings but it didn't seem like it handicapped Rob in earning a quid. He'd do anything from a paper round when he was a kid, to buying and selling anything when he was older – he always led a life as a wheeler-dealer. He drove trucks for various people at times to get over injuries and would do it either here or over in Australia.

'He was always looking for a chance of earning a quid, he would never sit in front of his TV and watch all day, that wasn't his thing.

'He was a great communicator and a great story teller, a big character. I always called him the hub of the wheel and, as I wrote for his funeral service, he was a networker before networking was invented.'

Dad loved Australia. He first visited when he was only eighteen to see his father who had settled in the Perth area shortly after remarrying. Neil continued: 'He went to Western

Australia when he was eighteen, that would have been 1981, to see his father Brian who was working as a mechanic in the back of a second-hand car dealer's that was owned by Paddy Roberts, who became a lifelong friend. They developed an instant rapport and Paddy looked after him like his own son. He also met Con Migro, who was the speedway promoter in Perth.

'He went back every year after that. He would always be gone by November, often taking a bike or an engine in his luggage, and ride every week for Con at Claremont Speedway.'

Located inside the city's Claremont Showgrounds, the speedway opened its doors to bike racing in 1927 and prospered for seventy-two years before eventually closing on the last day of March 2000.

'Con encouraged Rob to bring some Poms over to ride because they didn't have enough local talent to fill the programme, and for doing that Con would always give him half his fare,' added Neil. 'As far as I know he never got his full fare paid, but Rob's attitude was always that half a fare was better than nothing.

'He organised British riders to go there, riders like Ian "Egon" Stead, Wayne Elliott, Kevin Price, Wayne Ross, Ian Hewlett, and, one year, even Neil Collins rocked up. They were the guys that would go and race for the season during the British winter at Claremont for whatever Con was offering to pay them, whether it was eight or ten dollars a point.'

On his first visit, Dad didn't ride, but he did spend most of the subsequent winters Down Under and combined his working holiday with racing the monstrous 586 metres (641 yards) lap track.

Neil recalled a story from the winter trip when he first took Mum over at the end of 1987 until the beginning of 1988: 'Sue and Rob rented a place in their joint names and most of the British riders stayed with them. Everyone had to abide by the house rules and you didn't step out of line. One day Rob said he wasn't having any more pots left on the side and if he found any on the kitchen top he would chuck them out into the back garden. Well someone did leave some out and Rob, true to his word, collected them up, threw them into the garden and smashed them all, telling their lodgers they had to go out and buy a set of new pots and pans to replace them all! That was also the best trip Rob had results-wise as he won the Western Australian State Championship, I think ahead of Brit Kevin Price, who spent 1987 riding for Long Eaton and Exeter, with the top local Glyn Taylor third.

'It was the second championship in a row that had been won by a British rider, former World Team Cup champion Simon Cross had won it twelve months earlier, and the authorities restricted the field to Australian riders only the following year!

'When Rob and Sue eventually moved permanently to Australia after he'd retired from racing in 1994, he became a director of the car dealership with Paddy Roberts and that gave him his start over there.

'They were doing what's called bunkies – that's buying cheap cars at the lower end of the market, sprucing them up and selling them on. They were really good at making a silk purse out of a sow's ear and Rob had a tremendous rapport with all the main dealers around Perth. He'd go round them all in a morning, buy up their trade-ins, put on new tyres, maybe a new exhaust, clean them and get them up to spec and sell them on.'

Mum and Dad married in England in 1988 and she fell pregnant but lost the baby, who they were going to christen Luke, in 1989. It must have been so horrible for them at the time and

I know even now, thirty years later, Mum still thinks about it and says that if that baby had survived she wouldn't have had me because she was always going to have only one baby.

I came along in 1990, on Friday, 10 August, a part of the Millennials Generation, and apparently I was very quick off the start! Mum's waters broke in the kitchen at five o'clock and I popped out at 5.50pm, fifty minutes from being at home to being born, a nine-pound little one, in hospital.

CHAPTER 3

LESSONS IN LIFE

School days are to be enjoyed and I certainly had an awful lot of fun as I was growing up.

It was all about beaches, barbecues, a bong and beating the traffic cops.

We emigrated to Perth to start a new life, the beach getting closer to where we lived every time we moved house.

Dad was a grafter and while I can't remember a lot as a kid I do remember that we moved from house to house. He always wanted to improve, move up the property ladder and that's the way school life was, we lived in this house and then Dad went, 'Right, I've renovated that one, we'll sell that and buy a bigger one.'

So then we moved into the next one and I changed school, and then when that house was done, we'd move and I had to change schools again. That was my parents building for the future.

We began in a real cheap home in a place called Heathridge,

which is an alright place but not the poshest part of Perth. As you move from the bush towards the coast the houses get more expensive.

I can't remember a lot when I was a kid but I went to four different schools: Edgewater Primary School, Heathridge Primary School, Beaumaris Primary School and Ocean Reef Senior High School.

There are things that happen when you are young that will haunt you for the rest of your life. It could be a recurring bad dream you had as a kid that, no matter what happens, you can't get out of your head.

But in my case it was something that actually happened and has scarred me ever since.

My dad used to work at Formula Cars and Commercials, one of Western Australia's leading used-car dealers, on the junction of Prindiville Drive and Lindsay Road in Wangara, a suburb of Perth where there's a family-owned business around every corner of what is an active and noisy industrial area.

Opposite the car lot was the Korean Karate Association B.T.K.D. Tae Kwon Do Club where I spent some of my time.

I must have been only eight or nine and I couldn't wait to get to classes, so ran across the road from where Dad was to the club.

There was a little kid there, I can't remember his name, but I said, 'Come and play across the road at my dad's car yard.'

I asked his Mum if he could come and she said it was alright. I ran across the road and got to the other side and turned around – and he was looking straight at me and running towards me and he ran straight in front of a car.

The driver had no chance and neither did the little lad, and he died...

He went about twenty foot in the air when he got struck and I've had nightmares about it ever since, because it was my fault, wasn't it?

I told him to come and play across the road, so if I hadn't said that he wouldn't have come. He wouldn't have run into the road, he wouldn't have been hit by a car, and he wouldn't have died.

I have struggled with that. Everyone says, 'You were only a child yourself', but...

He was a couple of years younger than me, maybe five or six, and everyone said it wasn't my fault. Only his mum was there and she had another kid in tae kwon do, and the other little one was just toddling around and doing his thing, dodging about.

Everyone says, as sad as it is, I shouldn't be feeling guilty about what happened, it was a tragic accident, it was fate.

His little head was struck by the car's bumper and he had no chance. Dad struggled as well because he was the first on the scene and he was first to the little kid, seeing him the way he was. It was bad for everyone, but obviously more so for the little kid's family. The car driver and his mother, everybody was struggling with it.

It was all my fault, I shouldn't have asked if he wanted to come and play in the car yard.

There are sad things that happen in your life, they are all part of the journey you are on and that was one of the big things that happened in my life and something I will never be able to forget.

I can remember it as if it happened yesterday.

I was well into tae kwon do, and six days before my eleventh birthday I was presented with my black belt certification.

I still have the certificate and every now and then I will look at the citation, which reads:

The black belt symbolises a level of achievement. The individual who reaches this plateau understands the meaning of discipline. He or she has the responsibility to teach that it is peace, harmony and truth that is the guide to universal happiness. Under the constitution and charter of the Action International Martial Arts Association, the individual named on this certificate has achieved this goal.

There are lessons in life that stay with you for ever; little things that can shape the way you grow up and develop.

Things that you never forget that help to mould and forge the way you live.

I like to think what I learnt at that tae kwon do school has served me well over the years and I do believe I had a disciplined childhood.

Every time I stepped out of line my dad would pull me back, and lots of events that happened have remained in my memory.

I started high school at thirteen, and the year I turned fifteen I left, so I only had eighteen months or so at Ocean Reef.

I went every day without complaint and never had to be called twice to get up. But it wasn't school that was the attraction, it was the opportunity to get out on the sand dunes to smoke a joint!

I can remember while I was at Ocean Reef that I made the sickest bong, out of a beaker and a plastic pen!

I was an arsehole at school, the deputy head was calling Mum and Dad nearly every day telling them: 'Tai's disrupting class. Tai's disrupting class.'

To the point that she said: 'We don't want Tai here any more but the only way he can leave is if he gets a job.'

I've seen it said that I was expelled from high school, but I wasn't. I went to work at Warrior Motorcycles and that was the only way I could leave school at fifteen. If you got a job they let you leave, if you didn't have a job to go to, then you had to stay.

I won the Western Australian Under 16 Speedway Championship when I was thirteen or fourteen and I sat down with Dad and said I wanted to go and do the Aussie rounds because I felt that was the year I had the best chance of winning it.

That was when I was fastest and the bike was mint, everything was real good. Fast engines. Really nice bikes.

But Dad goes: 'We can't afford to do it. You've got to pick to either go to England for a season and ride over there or go to the East Coast, wherever the round is, and do that one.'

It doesn't sound a big thing doing rounds of the Australian Under 16 Championship but the final was, more often than not, held in New South Wales and that's more than 2,500 miles away.

To drive from one side of Aussie to the other, across the Nullarbor Plain, takes around two days non-stop and a lot longer when you take into account stopping on the journey. The cost of that trip would have been mind-boggling, so I could understand why Dad said I had to choose England or the opportunity to race for an Aussie title.

I had to simmer on that for a couple of weeks before deciding I'd give the national championships a miss!

I learnt to drive when I was like twelve. With Dad owning a car yard he would always come home with different cars and we would use them to travel up to the track at Bibra Lake.

I used to drive around the track clockwise, change gears, first, second, first, second, around the corners, and then third on the straights and back to second, doing laps. Then I would turn around and do it the other way, driving anticlockwise so I would be turned left all the time going one way, and right when I went the opposite way.

I just learnt how to drive at the speedway, so when I got to fourteen I started taking the cars out from Dad's yard when there was no one there.

* * *

We had a group of very close friends in Australia, mainly but not exclusively with speedway connections, and as I grew up I was surrounded by older people, who all seemed to take a shine to me.

There were the McDiarmids, Marshall and Melissa and their beautiful family. Marshall had a go on the bikes but is now one of the leading veterans racing cars at the Perth Motorplex Speedway and, at fifty, he's still top-notch having won feature races regularly.

Marshall's mother Diana used to take me to the cinema and I always looked forward to going, although there was one thing that used to piss me off so much – she would never get up until she'd read through all the credits, right down to the last line of the assistant, assistant, junior gofer. When you're five or six once the movie finishes you want to get out of there and do something else!

I know you might not think it straight away, and she probably didn't look at it like that, but making me sit there gave me that little bit more discipline

Her husband John had a taxi business for a long, long time

and whenever I went back to Australia he would pick us up and take us to where we needed to be. At whatever hour we landed, there was never a problem.

One time, Mum and Dad were at a barbecue at their friend Frank Killeen's house with a load of their pals. Frank, a Mancunian, had emigrated to Australia and was part of a small community of Brits who had gone to live in Perth. Most of them had something to do with speedway. Frank had been a rider in the mid-eighties and, from all the stories I heard he did more crashing than winning, but he was a big favourite with the fans who stayed behind to watch him racing for Wolverhampton's junior side.

I took advantage of Mum and Dad's absence and 'borrowed' a car from Dad's yard. I was driving down the coast road with the park lights on and the cops flashed me. I thought: *Fuck, I'm in for it now*, so I nailed it and tried to run away with them chasing me. I pulled into someone's driveway, turned the lights off and slunk down in the seat, but they spotted me and put me in their car and put the siren on all the way home. I got done for that.

The police called Mum and Dad and then came knocking on the door, but nothing happened to me. I got let off because Dad answered the door and said he was really sorry and he would deal with me.

The cops took a step back – and must have thought: 'Oh, this guy's actually being alright.' They just left Dad to deal with me, which he did in his own way. He didn't shout or yell but gave me the silent treatment and said: 'I'm off back to my barbecue!'

I asked him: 'Are we going to talk about it, Dad?' and all he said was: 'No.' That was the worst treatment I got because I was left to stew on it.

Two or three years earlier I'd had a previous skirmish with the law when I decided to take my Kawasaki KX60 out of the garage. I was in my bare feet, no shoes on, no helmet, no T-shirt, and I was going up and down the street, wired, sixty a tap, just as fast as I could go.

Dad and Frank were together digging out a pool by hand. Dad goes: 'I'm sure that sounds like Tai's KX60', and, when he saw it was me, he just yelled for me to get in the fucking house.

The only reason I got the bike out was because Ben King, an older kid who had broken my collarbone when I was down at the jump, had told me to do it and I wanted to be cool.

Dad got me in the bedroom, picked me up from the floor and got right in my face, swearing at me.

I'd never seen him like that before and I never saw him like that again. He was never a nasty person, he never really got angry with me and he only ever had to talk to me and warn me and that was enough, but that time he flipped.

He rang Neil Machin who was in England and told him that he didn't know what stopped him punching my lights out. He'd got me by the throat and admitted he was scared that next time he might have gone even further.

Between riding my KX60 in the street and illegally driving the car, there was another incident that has stayed with me ever since.

Dad came home with a little mini motorbike, a mini road-race whippersnapper engine thing, like a little Chinese mini moto.

I rode it everywhere, and I do mean everywhere. I decided I'd go up to Kinross, about five kilometres away, to see my mate Rob, and was riding it through a town called Iluka when the police came past me.

I thought *fuck* and decided I had to do a runner. I turned right and right again, but the bike only had a 40cc engine. No, I don't even think it was 40, more like 18cc; it was a strimmer.

I got pulled up and they called Mum and Dad to come and pick me up. They told Mum: 'Do you want to be picking your son up off the road?'. Then the police turned on me, saying things like: 'Do you know where the morgue is as that's where you're going next time?' He was giving me shit and I'm thinking, *I'm fucked here.*

The cop knew I didn't have a licence because he'd asked me if I had one and I had to be truthful. He looked me in the eye and read out the list of offences. No licence. Underage driving. Vehicle not registered. No number plate. No insurance.

I was only thirteen and he could have thrown the book at me and that's what I was expecting but, for some reason, he never did anything.

Charmed life, that was me and motor bikes and cars, because there were other days where I could have been thrown into the slammer and they could have thrown the keys away and left me to rot!

Dad had brought a go-ped, a scooter with an engine, from England and, from as young as I can remember, I would ride the go-ped everywhere. If I wanted to go to see a mate, I'd put the helmet on, get the go-ped out and ride it here and there.

Somehow I managed to convince Mum and Dad that when you get a learner's permit to drive a car it allows you to ride a 50cc scooter, so I was allowed to buy one.

There was only one rule: don't bring the police around to the house. Not because I could be in trouble but just in case they discovered what Dad was growing in the garden shed.

That was the one rule and I'd had my scooter about ten minutes and was doing a wheelie down the road when an undercover cop drove past me, pulled me up and, yet again, took me home to face the music.

I was wetting myself. I didn't have a licence, I'd lied to my mum and dad about being able to ride a scooter, and it was against the law.

We got home, the cops spoke to Mum and Dad and then left. They didn't even ask to see my licence, nothing. Again I got away with it.

Like I said, there are lessons in life that stay with you for ever, little things that can shape the way you grow up and develop. Things that you never forget and which help to mould and forge the way you live.

Another thing happened that I can remember it as if it happened yesterday.

When I was young, probably eight or nine, I was allowed a 50-cent ice cream when we went to the shops. It couldn't cost any more than 50 cents and it was the lowest-priced ice cream on the display boards.

You could have a simple ice cream in a cone, or you could have one that has a couple of Cadbury's chocolate 99 flakes, a big squirt of cream, maybe a spoonful of sprinkles, topped off with raspberry, chocolate or strawberry sauce.

I could take my pick – just as long as it wasn't any more than 50 cents.

I can remember the day it happened. I was in the back of the van and Dad's friend gave me five bucks (Australian dollars) to go and buy an ice cream. I ran into the shop, came back and gave him the change: two dollars and fifty cents.

Dad asked: 'Can I have a bite of that ice cream.' He had a bite out of it, wound down the van window and threw the rest of the ice cream away.

He never said why he had done that but as it went cascading down the road, I knew why he had done it and that episode never got spoken about again.

It was a lesson I never forgot.

Dad always said you work for your money, you don't get anything without working for it, and it would be something I never forgot in my later life when I was chasing titles on the track.

I got a little bit of pocket money and I saved up all that to be able to buy my first car, I can't even remember what it was, but it cost 400 dollars and I worked and worked on doing it up and then sold it for another 200 dollars. Bought it for 400, sold it for 600.

I did that with three different cars, and that was also the way Dad was. He would buy something, work hard to improve it, and then sell it at a profit.

I wanted a Yamaha with the Arrow exhaust system and he turned round to me and said: 'You'd better start saving then,' and that's what I did.

One of our best friends was Steve Johnston who had been one of Dad's mates for years, having first met him through the family of Dave Cheshire, another of the Western Australia riders.

Steve, who was from Perth, was a pretty good motocrosser and had been doing it for six or seven years when he first met Dad, and always wanted to end up being good enough to earn a living in the States. But when he was eighteen or nineteen, Dad somehow tempted him to buy a speedway bike so there was something to do out of the motocross season.

Johnno had never been out of Australia and didn't even have a passport. He knew absolutely nothing about speedway but bought his first speedway bike to have a bit of fun. Then he went on the programme at Claremont but didn't even know you could earn a living racing speedway in England.

He had loads of crashes to begin with but when he did stay on he would win a couple of races and Dad told him that if he came to England to race he could stay with him and Mum in Scunthorpe, where they were still living at the time.

Dad recommended Johnno to Sheffield and he first came over in 1992. I was only about eighteen months old when Johnno lived with us and he has lots of tales about how I would toddle into the big workshop Dad had built at Enderby Road and get in the way.

I was always in the thick of it and Johnno – I've never called him anything but Johnno even when I was just starting to talk – often joked about how he'd start up his bike and hear rattling because I had slipped a couple of clutch springs, or a Matchbox toy car, somewhere they shouldn't have been.

Johnno was like a young uncle and always said I was an adult before my time. When we were back in Australia, he'd put me on a booster seat and pillow on the front seat of his car and take me down to the beach.

He'd usually take a football for a kickaround, but if there was a group of girls sunbathing, Johnno, who was still single, would always send me to retrieve the ball so he could get into a conversation with them. It was like going fishing and I was Johnno's bait.

But the most disgraceful experience with him was when we all went to watch our local big-league football team Perth Glory playing a match against a team from the East Coast (it could have been Sydney).

Dad would go to every match and this day there were about a dozen of us who went in Johnno's dad's van.

There was a place called The Shed where the adults would spend the afternoon watching the game and having their fill of beer, and in front of it was an area where they could leave their kids and still keep an eye on them.

It was half-time and Perth were 2–1 down. Johnno and Carl Stonehewer, who was over from England for the off-season, were a bit the worse for wear and decided they would do a streak across the field.

I was right at the front, next to the pitch, and Johnno left his clothes with me and told me to look after them even though I was only five or six, and then he and Stoney set off.

They managed to get to the other side, Johnno leading the way and Stoney trailing him. The players were back on the pitch waiting to kick off for the second half, but Johnno had picked up the ball, and both he and Stoney ended up in the back of one of the goals with the stewards and police.

I'm told that I was pretty upset because Johnno had not come back for his clothes. They spent a few hours in a cell before being released after paying a fine of around six hundred Australian dollars.

A funny sequel to the story, which I've learnt about since, was that Johnno was racing in the big nationwide David Tapp series that was due to visit Perth a week or so later, and Tapp was so delighted with the publicity for Johnno's streak – it made all the papers and the TV news – that he suggested he could do the same thing at another big sporting event to get even more headlines!

He was lucky, mind, to get away with that fine – some years later when a streaker interrupted a cricket test match in Perth he was hit with a five-thousand-dollar fine and threatened with a lifetime ban from the venue!

Steve's remained a close friend ever since and for a long time would stay with us when he was racing in the UK, and Dad stayed with him before we emigrated.

There were so many escapes from being in deep shit when I was a kid, but the urge to get on a bike on the road has never left me. Only a couple of years ago I could so easily have been opening my Christmas present in a police cell.

I still haven't got a scooter licence and five years ago Faye, my wife, came over to Perth with the family, Mum and Dad, grandparents, and younger brother Layne who had a bit of a go at speedway,

Layne, who had been riding motocross, only got as far as National League level, riding for King's Lynn, Cradley, the Isle of Wight and Birmingham before he decided it wasn't for him and instead began concentrating on trying to build a new career in music.

I bought a scooter and we shared it so that he could get around a little bit. I only rode it every now and then but on Christmas Eve 2016, I decided I would jump on board and go down to Westfield Whitford City shopping centre in the Perth suburb of Hillarys to buy a last-minute Christmas present.

It's one of the largest shopping malls in Australia with more than 250 retail outlets, along with a cinema complex and restaurants, and is owned by the Westfield Group who have a couple of similar centres in London, one close to the London Stadium in Stratford and the other in Shepherd's Bush, close to Queens Park Rangers Football Club.

I'm cruising and causing no harm to anyone and go through the roundabout at Hillarys when a guy cuts me up. I go down a bit further and he does it again and by now I'm getting a bit pissed off with him, so I went up on the path and went round the roundabout on the path before wheelieing off the kerb through a little sandy boggy section.

Then I saw there was a cop on the other side of the roundabout. I hadn't spotted him until it was too late.

They flicked on the sirens and came round the roundabout after me, but by then I'd turned left into a park, gone through the park and up to a lookout. It meant riding over these fucking big logs and as I did so the scooter bottomed out, bang, bang, bang.

Then I went to the other side of the harbour and hid behind the bushes to see if they were still following me and pulled into the car park, only to see another cop car a bit further down.

Again I turned left to cut across the car park, but by then I had peeled off my black shirt and was now bare-chested to make it harder for them to recognise me.

I went across the car park, quite slowly and sedately, but, fuck me, the cop car was there and I have to turn right and go down to about one and a half miles away, to Hillarys boat harbour. Here there's a yacht club, souvenir places, an aquarium and plenty of other tourist attractions, including ferries to Rottnest Island and whale-watching trips.

I've got a boat down there (I go cray fishing most days), so I glance in my mirror and see them behind me and pull up near the jetty where they launch the boats.

It was like, 'Oh God', so I just get off the scooter, park it up and dive into one of the fishing tackle shops. To make it look more authentic, I bought some bait for my cray pots and, as I leave the shop, I see them driving off and, once again, I've got away with doing something crazy.

I'm still not sure how I managed to be so lucky, but perhaps they felt like giving me an unexpected Christmas present!

I've not always been so fortunate in my dealings with the law, though, and I did lose my licence in England for speeding a few years ago.

I drive like a complete twat, I'm good at driving, like Faye will be in the car with me and it doesn't scare her a bit how fast I go. I could be going down a back lane in – what country can I say that's not going to get me in shit, Germany – where I know there's no speed limit. Anyway, I'll be on the limit and I set myself targets when I drive, like, 'I'm going to beat this car to that next junction.'

I'll come to a junction on some motorway and I'll be in the van and I'll be like right, there's like seven cars in front of me, a couple in my lane, and I'm going to get to the next junction and beat those cars in front before I get to the next junction. Once I get to that junction, I'll set myself another target and I just keep going like that.

I've lost my licence once, quite a few years ago: I got caught doing ninety-three in a fifty, at one o'clock in the morning, in the van, and I had to go to court.

It was on a single carriageway roundabout, single carriageway, and roundabout, no other cars around apart from the cop car.

He was coming the other way, and then he just jammed his brakes on and turned around and I thought that's definitely a cop, so I braked up to the next roundabout and pulled out and he'd clocked me. He read me my rights and got my details and sent me on my way, then I got a court letter.

I already had three, six, nine points and then I got another three and I was on my last warning, so I had twelve and got caught doing ninety-three and got another six, so I had eighteen. So I lost my UK licence for six months and got a big fine; I could have had twelve months and a small fine, but I took the six and copped the big penalty. I can't remember exactly how much but it was in the thousands. But it actually worked out alright, because I've got an Australian licence for when I'm at home and a British licence when I'm racing in Europe. I did four months of my ban and went to Australia where I could drive on my Australian one. Then when I got back to England at the start of the next season I could start driving my van again because my six months was up.

I don't really drive that much in Australia because I'm having a break from racing so don't do any out-of-state meetings. But I did get done in this eight-cylinder V8U that was off its head. It was like nearly a ten-second car on a quarter mile, fucking fast.

I'd done everything apart from supercharge it, all the gear, and we were coming down a dual carriageway and the traffic lights went red. I went left, nailed it down to the roundabout, drifted around the next one, but then I spotted a cop car, an undercover cop car, waiting to pull out, so I drifted past him and nailed it up the road, turned left and beat the traffic lights.

I was pretty stoked about that, just did the speed limit all the way up to the next roundabout and saw he was behind me, on his radio. I looked in the mirror and thought, *I'm in the shit again here* and then one cop car pulled up and stopped all the traffic at this next roundabout, and then I was surrounded by cop cars. One on the verge, one blocking the traffic, one on the central reservation, an undercover one behind me and another one, and I thought, *Fuck what have I done here?* I bet everyone in the other cars was thinking this guy's done for.

They told me to pull over and the first cop goes, 'How many points you got?' and I said, 'Oh I haven't got any, I don't normally speed.'

There's a drag strip where you can go on a Wednesday – they

call it 'whoop arse Wednesday' – and have a burnout; it's to keep the kids off the road.

I said: 'I go to whoop arse Wednesdays and I was just being stupid, I fancied that little blast, so I put my foot down at the roundabout and did a little skid and it is what it is, sorry, no excuse.'

The cop began talking to me about 'whoop arse Wednesdays' and asked again how many points were on my licence. When I told him I got my licence at sixteen, been driving for six or seven years, didn't have any points and always went to 'whoop arse Wednesdays' he said he'd let me off but not to do it again! Great.

And there was the time that I got led off an aeroplane in handcuffs on my twenty-first birthday while flying back from a meeting in Sweden.

I was on a Ryanair flight with Davey Watt and Scott Nicholls and I was in my seat when one of the stewardesses tells me to turn my phone off, and as we were making the approach to land she demands again that I turn off my phone.

It wasn't even on, so I tell her once or twice: 'For fuck's sake, it's off.' She's having none of it and accuses me of telling her to fuck off. I was like: 'What? I didn't tell you to fuck off.'

Then she says: 'You wait here, I'm going to call the police when we land.' And that's what she did as we were taxiing towards our gate at Stansted. And as soon as the door is opened, the cops come in, grab me, pin me up against the wall, handcuff me, take me off the plane and put me up against their car.

Luckily for me, Scott and Davey, who are quite a bit older than me and definitely more mature, were telling the police that I hadn't done anything wrong.

Anyway, I got off with a warning, but a few months later I discover that it's on my record. I got pulled up for speeding on the way to Stansted and the cop who pulled me over says: 'Oh, you've got a criminal record?' and I go: 'No!' He says I'm lying to him and as I'm protesting my innocence, it suddenly hit me: I was 'arrested' on that flight a few months earlier.

I thought it was just a warning and I would hear no more about it but, no, it's on my record. Fucking hell, that's hilarious!

My nan always jokes that she's over forty years older than me and I've had more skirmishes with the law than she has...

CHAPTER 4

SCORPIONS, WOLVES AND TIGERS

Rob Godfrey knew he was taking a big risk when he offered me a team place... without ever seeing me race.

I'd not even ridden a 500cc speedway bike in competition when he told my dad that I could do what he had done in 1978... and ride for Scunthorpe.

Rob and his initial partner and co-promoter, Norman Beeney, had persuaded the council to let them build a track on the site of the former Normanby Park Steelworks, in a zone for disruptive motorsports.

The Scorpions began from scratch, started training there in September 2004 and became the twelfth team in the third-tier Conference League in 2005.

In their first season they finished in the bottom half of the table but won thirteen of their thirty matches, which was certainly an improvement on the last Scunthorpe team that had been forced to pull out of league racing after only nine matches because of poor attendances.

Maybe changing the team nickname again – they had been the Saints at Quibell Park and the Stags at Ashby Ville – had something to do with it!

Rob and Norman, who were joint owners when I agreed to ride for them in their second season, had shown they were willing to take a punt by signing several teenagers and also giving girl racer Jessica Lamb her league debut at Wimbledon.

So maybe offering an unknown, untried fifteen-year-old Scunthorpe-born Australia-raised kid a team spot wasn't such a big gamble to them, especially given Dad's history at the club.

But what they didn't know was that I almost never came over because, just before we all left Australia, I broke my right leg – my tibia (the shinbone, the second largest bone in your body after the pelvis) and fibula (the smaller bone at the back).

Everything was booked, the air tickets for Mum, Dad and me, and about a fortnight before we were due to board, we went to say goodbye to Paul Smith, the younger brother of Andy Smith, a former Grand Prix rider and the first Englishman to be British Champion three times in a row, between 1993 and 1995.

Andy and his wife Michelle had bought a house in Perth and even though he had a business, Foxy Race Products, in Europe, he would spend his British winters in the heat and sunshine.

Paul, who was also an ex-rider although he never reached the same heights as Andy, had been over on holiday with his better half Trish, and we met them at a boat harbour where there were Olympic trampolines that you could pay to go on.

It was closed this day but, me being me, I decided I would jump over the fence when I started to get bored with the adult conversation.

I was having a ball on the trampolines and would have carried on for hours but Mum shouted across to say it was time to go, and to meet her and Dad at our car, parked nearby.

The trampolines were surrounded by a safety fence, built so that if you got your jump wrong you would bounce off it and back onto the trampoline.

There was then a metre and a half gap before another fence, with electric wires running through it, I presumed to stop hooligans getting in and vandalising the trampolines, rather than ensuring that no one escaped and got out!

There was no open gate and as I'd climbed over the fence to get into the park, there was only one way to get out. Over the first fence and then over the electric fence. The mistake I made was standing on the electric fence to get more leverage. As I did so the fence sort of crumpled in on itself and I landed flat on the wires running through it.

It must have been like putting your finger into an unprotected electric socket. I was zapped and flipped over by the sudden jolt of power and landed awkwardly.

I'm flat out on the floor, and when I try to stand up my ankle goes over sideways. I knew I'd done some serious damage but there were no tears because the adrenalin was still flowing after my time performing acrobatics on the trampoline, and even though I told Mum I thought I'd broken my leg, she didn't take me seriously and just yelled: 'Get in the car.'

I hobbled over and, with every hop, I could feel my foot flapping around but somehow I managed to climb into the car.

Dad was still with Paul and Trish behind their apartment's locked gate. I was trying to call him but no answer. Mum was going frantic, feeling sick as Aunty Caroline, who is a nurse, told her how serious it was and that they had to get me to the hospital asap because she thought I had broken my leg. It was about five minutes before Dad came back to the car and off we went. They gave me an anaesthetic but an hour later they said they couldn't operate because I still had a big scab on my leg from a previous mishap and they were worried about possible infection.

I stayed in hospital for about a week, had a full course of antibiotics and then the op. Lying in the hospital bed I could clearly see the imprint of the electric wire lines burnt into my chest.

I suppose it could have been a lot worse, I could have been dead from the shock, but all I was worried about was what Dad might say if we had to cancel our flight to England.

I was discharged to go home and Aunty Caroline came round and injected my belly to thin my blood the day before we set off for Perth Airport and the flight across the world.

I was on crutches but at least I was able to travel and we didn't have to cancel our tickets, but before we left Dad had a stern word with me to say it was time I stopped messing around and took things a bit more seriously. We were on our way.

Even though I was still on crutches, I rocked up for my experience of riding the Eddie Wright Raceway, intending to test my leg to see if it was strong enough.

I think I waited three weeks when we were doing physio and I went and got a motocross boot to wear as it offered more protection than a normal speedway boot. It was stronger and stiffer but trying to get your foot in and out was painful.

We took the plasters off my leg. I've taken off every plaster I've been in and now I go private they tend not to put pots (casts) on and instead brace it.

We'd got everything set up, built up the bike and were all set for my first practice session but that didn't last very long. My rear chain came off when I was flat out at the end of the straight and I went through the fence and bust my fingers.

That's genuinely what happened. First practice, first lap. Obviously we've got no brakes so when the chain comes off it just goes. There's no engine brake or anything. I took out three fence panels. Back to hospital and I'd broken two fingers in my right hand.

In my first season I crashed so often that every week the Kevlar race suits I got off Johnno (Steve Johnston) needed stitching. My nan's cousin, Auntie Pat, brought the sewing machine around so Mum could mend them. After every meeting they were washed and then went on to the sewing machine and by the end of that first season they were literally falling to bits. Mum was having to put patches on them to keep them together.

We lived on the caravan site with Nan – I don't think we should have been because it was a residential site for retired people – and there shouldn't have been a fifteen-year-old living there.

I soon got to know my new neighbours and there was a miserable old bloke living across the road called Geoff Cundy. I actually liked him, but was he miserable. He was alright really, but he always seemed like our own version of Victor Meldrew from the TV series *One Foot in the Grave*.

He must have taken a shine to me because he used to slip me £20 here, £30 there. In a way Geoff, who died five years ago, was my very first sponsor. He would come across to see me, slip me a twenty-quid note and say: 'Go on son, get yourself a new tyre.' We didn't have any money and when he bunged me the cash, it was bloody great. We were just starting and grateful for those few quid, so I put his name on my gear and even had Geoff Cundy tattooed on my forearm.

I blew an engine one night riding at Scunthorpe; Geoff was there watching but obviously left the stadium before we did. We got home after the meeting to find £100 had been pushed through the door. There was no note or anything but I knew where it had come from and went across to his van to thank him for the money. All he said was: 'What £100?'

He was a really nice bloke, and we had a bit of banter despite our age difference, and I would always call Geoff, the old c**t!

We had bought a couple of bikes off Johnno while in Australia and I brought one of them over with me. The bike had already done six seasons in Europe and although I rode it a few more years it was quite an old bit of kit and I'd already smashed it a few times in Perth.

You were able to ride in the Conference League from your fifteenth birthday and while you did get paid – in my case it was £10 for every point I scored – it was principally a training league and what you got in the wage packet after every meeting never even went close to covering costs.

There was also a little contribution, usually, five, ten or, if you were lucky, fifteen pence a mile towards your travelling expenses.

No one would ever get rich from racing in the Conference League and that certainly wasn't on either mine or my dad's minds when we first signed for Scunthorpe.

I decided to throw in my lot with the Scorpions for a variety of reasons, all based around the town of my birth.

My mum and dad both came from there, we were, when we first came back from Australia, sharing my nan's caravan, which meant we had somewhere to stay without having to buy a house, and we could save a lot of money that way. Plus all my dad's friends were there, and Uncle Dave, my grandad Brian's brother, lived there as well. Uncle Dave got me one of my early, most loyal sponsors in Flexseal, a Barnsley-based company specialising in drainage, plumbing and water management. Their managing director Tony Leyland drank at the same pub as Uncle Dave and they backed me to the tune of £10,000 a season in 2006 and were still with me when I won the 2013 World Championship.

We didn't consider going anywhere else at the start of my career and the plan was to race for Scunthorpe but to spend my first summer travelling to as many tracks as possible to get experience and laps on my bike.

I knew that I would be a wanted man after my first season in the Conference League being voted the Planet Speedway/ Supporters' Rider of the Year at the Speedway Riders' Association end-of-season 'Oscars'.

I had to wear a suit and tie at the do, hosted by Sky Sports presenter Sophie Blake (who married but is now separated from seven times British Champion Scott Nicholls), at Coventry's posh Hilton Hotel.

I felt at home there despite the posh surroundings because my Scunny teammate Josh Auty was there, having been voted Conference League Rider of the Year by the SRA; Jason Crump was both Elite League Rider of the Year and Speedway Rider of the Year; and his grandfather, Australian team boss Neil Street, was specially honoured for his Outstanding Contribution to Speedway, so there were a few people I knew.

My mum summed up our first year back in England and gave away a few of my secrets, by telling guests: 'This year really has been amazing, a huge adventure for all of us. It was back in December last year that we decided to come over to England with Tai to give him a chance in speedway.

'We had a family discussion, sitting round the table, and Tai wanted to do it. He'd left school, he's not academic at all, and he really wanted to do it, so we just thought "Why not, let's give him a crack at it."

'He's just amazed us really. Hand on heart, I was just hoping he would see the season out and we wouldn't be picking him out of the fence all the time. I was just expecting him to get two points here and two points there, but what he's actually done has blown us away.'

I had no idea how I would go because I didn't have anything to judge myself by.

Everyone probably expected me to sign for Sheffield because of our friendship with the owner Neil Machin. As I said earlier, he was my dad's closest friend and my godfather.

Neil spent every Christmas I can remember with us in Australia. He would fly over for a month or two in Perth, recharging his batteries before returning to England to get Sheffield up and running again. Every year since I was a kid, Neil always brought something over for Christmas, a Sheffield race jacket or a speedway jacket or something along those lines. One year he rocks up with a silver helmet...

The Silver Helmet is, in various forms, one of speedway's oldest competitions and was revived in the Second Division in 1970 when Romford's Ross Gilbertson was nominated as the first holder of the new trophy and he would defend it against the opposition's top scorer in a two-rider match race.

He got the better of Ipswich's Ron Bagley in his first defence but then lost it against the same rider when the Bombers travelled to Foxhall Heath the following afternoon, a Good Friday.

Bagley then defended it at the Witches next league match and so it went on for the next twenty-one years. The competition was dropped at the end of 1990 after a couple of format changes but reinstated seven years later under the original terms.

In 1999 it reverted to a monthly defence with Leigh Lanham,

holder at the end of the 1998 season, starting off as the defending champion.

He lost out to Sean Wilson, one of Neil's stars at Sheffield, in his fourth defence of the summer, who won it five times before being beaten by Workington's Carl Stonehewer who then went on to successfully retain the title twelve times. The last occasion was against Reading in September when he left Racers' Petri Kokko trailing.

During the winter the promoters decided it was time to ditch the competition altogether and, somehow, Neil ended up in possession of the trophy. He's not sure how he came to have it but he brought it over to Aussie one winter and gave it to me, so I was literally the last holder of the Silver Helmet even though I never raced for it.

Why didn't I sign for Neil and Sheffield? There were a few reasons ... the track, my career and our long-term friendship.

Dad wanted me to be at a track where you had to learn a technique.

We had gone to Scunny first because we had the contacts there and it was the best place to get set up.

There wasn't much fuss when I decided I'd start the big English adventure at my hometown club, far from it. I don't think it was even reported in the local paper, but coming towards the end of my first season, Dad said: 'Right, well you've done Scunthorpe, which rides like a big, fast track – so you need to go to a small, technical circuit next.'

They were the tracks I struggled on, the really tight technical ones, and that's the major reason that Sheffield was never in the picture, because Dad felt I needed to go somewhere where I had to learn how to master a tricky track where you had to turn the bike.

Dad always said if I could ride a little one, I could ride a big one, and that was the biggest factor in deciding to sign for Wolverhampton and to go out on loan to Rye House.

I know Neil felt he was in a pretty difficult situation because he never wanted to create any kind of conflict within what he considered to be part of his family. He had been Dad's mechanic and they were as close as you can get. He intentionally took a step back from trying to convince me to sign for him, and because he was a friend and knew how my dad thought, he was totally supportive of the decision to go elsewhere. He understood we were looking beyond today and tomorrow and much further ahead, and knew that Mum and Dad had packed in their business in Australia and travelled across the world to give me a shot.

It would have been great for him and Sheffield if I had gone there in 2007, but we both accept it was the right decision – where would our friendship have been now if I had become a Tiger?

What would have happened if I'd ridden for Sheffield for three years and we had fallen out over something? It can affect your friendship, can't it? That never happened, we are still big buddies and Neil still comes out to us, and we can all spend Christmas Day on the beach, like we have always done.

Maybe it would have been the same if I'd ridden for him and he had been my promoter: nobody can know how it might have all turned out.

You had to be sixteen to ride in either of the two top divisions, what was the old Premier League and Elite League, and I can remember telling Neil that I wanted to ride for the Tigers on my sixteenth birthday, which happened to coincide with their match against Redcar.

He couldn't fit me in without declaring me in his team officially with the British Speedway Promoters' Association, but there was a facility at that time where you could name two young riders to share a reserve position in the side. As long as both were named then either of them could ride.

He had to pair me up with a young rider called Benji Compton who, as luck would have it, had scored eight points at Stoke on the previous Saturday, and the last thing he would have expected was to be left out the following Thursday for someone who had never ridden for the team before.

Neil told me that when Benji's mum found out, she went bonkers, but Neil's only response was: 'Look, he's my bloody godson and how many sixteenth birthdays does a lad ever have?'

So I did make my debut for Sheffield on my sixteenth, but I could have understood it if Benji, and his mum Bev, had marched into Neil's office, thrown their Sheffield body colour at him and marched out again!

I had a terrible meeting, but at least I was on the winning side even though I didn't score a point. Three rides and three last places must have left the Tigers' fans wondering what on earth Neil was playing at.

Thankfully for me, and probably Neil as well, the rest of the team covered and Benji was back in the line-up at Redcar the following night, and stayed in the side for the next five or six weeks until Neil took another gamble in the quarter final of the Knock Out Cup at Somerset in the middle of September.

But I didn't do any better at Highbridge and we all drove back to Scunny that night having got a duck again.

In my first two meetings for Neil and his Tigers, I had six rides and six last places and possibly I was responsible for us going out of the Cup because the fifteen-point gap was too much.

It didn't help that the team, with the guesting Mark

Thompson at reserve and getting a couple of points, pulled back fourteen but went out of the competition by a single point on aggregate.

Had I managed just one third place at Somerset we would have been in the semi-final, and maybe we could have ended the year with at least one medal as a Sheffield team member.

It wasn't all bad though, as Neil still had total faith that I would get it right and he handed me a third and a fourth chance to impress the fans in two late-season play-off clashes at Owlerton.

I rode against the Isle of Wight in the second leg of the semi-final and scored nine from four rides as we overcame a seven-point first-leg deficit and, a fortnight later, I top-scored with 14 out of 15 in a 52–37 win over King's Lynn.

I missed the second leg at the Norfolk Arena because of a clash of dates with Scunthorpe's second leg of the Conference League Grand Final.

So instead of the 90-mile trip down the A15, we all had to set off early morning for a taxing six-hour journey down to Plymouth. At least I could celebrate with a beer or two as we added the championship to the KO Cup we had won five days earlier against the same opponents.

But Sheffield, without me, couldn't hold onto the fifteen-point lead we had fought so hard to get twenty-four hours earlier. I felt sorry for Neil as he had seen his team lose in two finals that season, beaten by King's Lynn in both the league Grand Final and the Premier Trophy.

My season had a totally opposite ending as Scunny did the treble, the first time in their history that they had won anything other than the wooden spoon! Mum, Dad and the rest of the family enjoyed that, having spent virtually all their lives in the town.

It was also a fantastic season for me as I'd started out with a paid maximum against Newport at the end of May and had drawn down the curtain on 2006 with three winners' medals.

My dad expected to be picking me out of the fence every week, going round the country getting two or three points in the Conference League, but I proved him wrong. He was glad to see I was ready and as he had ridden for many years he had the experience to help me out massively. Everything he taught me I used.

I was also able to sort out my future before we all left to go back to Australia.

There were some people who thought that I might go straight from the Conference League into the Elite League, jumping from the bottom league to the top league without bothering to have time in the Premier League. Lewis Bridger had done that twelve months earlier, leaving Weymouth to sign for Eastbourne, and he'd had a pretty good 2006, amassing 278 points in 50 matches for the Eagles.

Going back, my first year had been one of ups and downs. I'd not even been able to take my place in the Scunthorpe team at the beginning of the season because I'd broken my leg, so had had to wait until 23 April for my first public outing, against the touring US Dream Team.

What a dream it was for me, even if it provided promoter Rob Godfrey with a headache, as he admitted he wrestled with a selection poser.

Would he keep me in the team for the next league match, or should he stick with Scott Richardson who I'd watched doing well in the early meetings?

Rob had a dilemma, telling the local press: 'We really don't know what we are going to do. We definitely do not want to upset

Scott because he's going to be a very good rider and has done so well this season. Tai would probably not be so upset if we left him out – but how can we leave him out after a debut like that?

'He was fantastic, he had the third fastest time of the day and the ride he put in in heat two when he got a 5-1 with Scott was just breathtaking. It is not an easy decision.'

I got the chop, saw my team go down to a defeat in the opening league match of the season, and that was the only time I have ever been dropped racing in England!

And I had to wait a little bit longer than I thought to get back on the track because the next five meetings, at Rye House twice and King's Lynn (where Boston were based as there was no track in the town), and home to Buxton and Newport, were rained off, another new experience for me as that was virtually unheard of in Australia!

The weather was so bad that, as a team, we had to have a special practice just to stop all of us getting rusty, although I managed to slot in some after the meeting races at various tracks.

Dad was adamant that I should sample as many different tracks as possible, so we were kept busy even if there wasn't a team meeting.

Eventually it did stop raining and I finally went out for my first Conference League race against Newport on Monday, 29 May – thirty days after my first appearance and nearly eleven weeks into the season!

Even though I wasn't taking too much notice of what was happening elsewhere, to put that time span into some sort of perspective, Jason Crump had already won two of the first three rounds of the Grand Prix and was leading the World Championship race on seventy points while I hadn't had an opportunity to get off the mark in league racing.

Finally, my career was under way and it seemed that one man who was pleased was my promoter and he told everyone who would listen: 'I think Tai could go all the way in the sport. I've seen him riding at Sheffield in the second half and I've had reports back from the other tracks he's been to and already I think he could be good enough for a Premier League place after his birthday in August when he's sixteen.'

What's that saying about pride before a fall? In my very next match, at Mildenhall, I set the fastest time of the day, better than thirteen of the fifteen race-winning times in the Fen Tigers' Premier League KO Cup quarter-final tie against Somerset that followed our event.

I came down to the earth with a bump, involuntarily lifting the front wheel off the shale in my second heat and coming down so heavily that the paramedics ruled me out of the rest of the meeting.

I had my share of tumbles but nothing as serious as what happened to the Stoke Spitfires captain Luke Priest during our visit to Loomer Road.

He was seriously hurt and left all of us with a decision to make. There was blood all over the track where Luke had crashed and he was tended to by medical staff for an hour and twenty minutes before being taken to the local hospital for emergency surgery on a broken pelvis, ankle and elbow, as well as very traumatic internal injuries.

We had a team meeting, all the riders, managers John Adams (Pete Adams' brother) and Kenny Smith, promoters Dave Tattum and Rob Godfrey, and the referee Dave Watters, to discuss whether we should call off the meeting there and then.

Some wanted it off and some felt we should carry on, but when news came back from the hospital that while Luke was in a bad way his injuries weren't life-threatening, we agreed we should carry on, the meeting restarting shortly after the usual curfew time of 9.30 pm.

Moving up into the main body of the team at the beginning of August (the top five and the two reserves are decided by riders' averages and can change on a month-to-month timescale) was another new challenge, but I never felt it would affect my performances and it didn't even though I was facing better riders in most of my races.

My reserve partner had been Josh Auty, who was also fifteen, and we signed off with twenty-eight points between us as we both had to move up into the top five for the rest of the season.

We were both on a roll and so was the team as we honed in on the silverware-deciding part of the year. Nevertheless, both Josh and I did have, one Saturday afternoon, the distraction of having to judge a beauty competition at a local Scunthorpe show. We took our bikes along and also gave away hundreds of free kids' tickets and must have done a good job as the club reported a record Monday-night crowd a couple of days later!

Josh and I pushed each other along, we were both fifteen and both probably keen to prove we were the best but it never got out of hand at any stage, although I had another spectacular crash at Rye House, getting out of shape and hitting Danny Betson's back wheel. Danny went to hospital and I had to sit out the rest of the night with concussion but the most painful thing was we lost by one point, which could have had an impact on our league title hopes.

Fortunately, it was no worse than a splitting headache, so I didn't miss the next match and we quickly got back on the winning path. We won everything, so that was cool. Sometimes I'd say to Rob: 'Pay me double and I'll touch the tapes and go

15 metres behind and give the fans something to watch!' Bear in mind I was only on £10 a point so it was only costing him thirty quid and it was worth the extra money to give the fans some excitement.

The master plan for the first year was always getting around the country, riding almost every night, just trying to get as many rides as I could at places like Belle Vue, Coventry, Wolverhampton and Sheffield, as well as at Scunthorpe.

It was a lot of second-halves just trying to get rides where I could. The target was to get a ride at every track, even if it was only two or four laps at the end of the night.

The idea was to find out about the tracks and to get the gearing right so that if I did go back to the track in 2007 I could look in my book and say: 'Last year, it was this, this and this, the track's like that', then go out and have a look and get things right.

It was my first year, so it was all one big learning curve and I lost count of how many tracks we visited, although it probably wasn't as many as we were planning because of the weather.

As we approached my sixteenth birthday we were aware that we would have clubs ringing up and trying to get me to sign for them. The grapevine can often be right but sometimes it can be totally wrong and when whispers began that I had secretly signed for Sheffield shortly after my birthday, Dad decided he had to do something about it.

A formal announcement that I had joined the Tigers even appeared on the official website of the British Speedway Promoters' Association and Dad was anxious to let everyone know I hadn't committed my future to anyone.

He put out his own statement spelling out the situation: 'Nothing definite has been decided about next year at all. Sheffield's not really a track that brings you forward, you just become a track specialist there and I think Tai would struggle away.

'I just want everyone to know that Tai has not signed for Sheffield. I was gutted that it was on the BSPA website, I even rang them up and said, "This is not true."

'We're still interested in talking to anybody about next season. At the moment, I've been trying to get him round all the tracks to put him in the shop window so he can pick where he wants to ride.

'He likes Belle Vue, it's his favourite track, and we'd love to sign for a club like that and then get loaned back to Scunthorpe.'

He then reflected how all of us were feeling, when he added: 'He's totally caught me by surprise how well he's done this year. It's shocked me and it's still shocking me, but I definitely think he needs another year in the Conference League. I don't think he's ready for Premier League yet, they're too quick and there's too much pressure, but there will be chances for him.'

He could also have added that we didn't have the financial backing that we needed if I was going to carry on climbing up the ladder.

In the end I committed my future to Elite League Wolverhampton, who agreed to pay me a £10,000 signing-on fee; the other thing that swayed me was that every time I rode around Wolverhampton I crashed. I thought, every time I have to go to Monmore Green while riding for another club, I'm gonna struggle. I didn't have a problem with any other track so if I could master Wolves, I could ride anywhere.

I crashed most places in my first year, so much that when we went on a bit of a tour, Wolves on a Monday, the Isle of Wight on Tuesday, Poole Wednesday and Swindon Thursday, we had to take two spare front wheels, two spare sets of forks and two spare diamonds. Every morning after a crash, Dad and I would wash the bikes, change the frames, forks, front wheel, put the mudguards back on, use the cable ties and a bit of duct tape and go again the next night. I knew from the start which way my path was going and where I wanted to be. It was about the process of building and growing as a rider and it was all carefully planned, a year or two in the Conference League, a couple of seasons in the Premier League and then, by 2009, when I got to Wolves, I was ready.

My first Premier League club was Rye House, signing for them before I returned home to Australia at the end of 2006 and I had a few adventures there; we had a great couple of years together. Rye House was probably the most fun, racing motorbikes and partying like crazy. Tommy Allen, Chris Neath, Steve Boxall, Luke Bowen, Robert Mear. It was quite a young team; we raced on a Saturday night so we went down the Friday evening and stayed overnight. We'd all go to the pub and hang out there: for atmosphere and having a good time, those days were the best. The whole set-up. The track was always prepared immaculately.

Len Silver, Hazal, his ex-wife and business partner, and her husband Steve Naylor and a few other people who worked at the stadium would always have lunch at the pub. Sometimes all or a few of us riders would be there, it was just a good vibe. The pub used to be owned by an Australian rider called Dicky Case, who sort of took over running both the speedway and the pub, so it had a real feeling of being a proper speedway place.

I was a menace, I was always the trouble causer in the team and right at the end of the year, they grabbed me and taped me to the start pole, poured flour on me, egged me, oh mate, I copped it.

On what I think was my first time at the Perry Barr track

in the semi-final of the Premier Trophy in 2007, we had won the first leg by a comfortable 14 points at home on the first Saturday in June. We went to the Midlands for the return on the following Wednesday, confident that we would go through to the final, but the meeting turned into one of the biggest nightmares any team could suffer.

I was out with Tommy Allen for our first rides in the third race and Tommy came down on the second bend.

The race wasn't immediately stopped, but when the red light did come on I was coming up the inside of Brummies' Jason Lyons and he turned left a little bit. My front wheel hit his back wheel, which put all the weight onto the right-hand side of the bike and as I was falling, I gave it a handful and wheelied straight into the fence halfway down the straight.

It was a wire fence so it ripped all my knuckles off, and I've still got the scars to this day. First the handlebars and then the bike went in and stopped, but when it did the seat bucked me up into the air. I think I did three somersaults before ending up on the dog track on the other side of the fence, missing a tractor by inches. I had narrowly missed hitting the pits gate as well, going between the light posts, so I was very, very lucky.

They reckoned I landed so flat, my body spreadeagled like a star pattern when I hit the ground, which spread the weight, and that's why I wasn't more badly hurt than I was. All of me literally hit the ground at the same time. Boom. My mum, who was there watching, later told me that it was like seeing a stick figure without any arms as I somersaulted over the fence.

It's a weird feeling, trying to stand up and finding you can't. Your legs won't take any weight. I could push up on my arms but when I tried to stand up my legs wouldn't do it, which was really strange.

I can't really explain how I felt because I didn't really think anything of it and by the next day, I was like *Fuck, I wonder how long it's going to take before I can start racing again?* Your body has a natural way of blanking out the detail, it blanks out the thoughts and feelings as well as the pain. I only broke my arm but my body was in shock, which was why I didn't have any feeling in my legs. I couldn't walk. I went from hitting the ground to waking up in hospital and shouting for my dad. I couldn't remember anything from hitting the dog track to yelling for Dad.

They did all the scans and X-rays and said I was alright, I'd only broken my arm. I went and had my arm put in plaster and left the hospital in a wheelchair, Dad pushing me to the van. But when I got there I couldn't walk. I couldn't put one leg in front of the other, and that was one of the scariest moments I've ever been through.

The hospital team said I was alright to go home and when we told them I couldn't walk they said everything would be okay. Dad had to lift me into the bunk bed in the van, and I fell asleep as he drove back to Scunny. He woke me up when we got there to ask 'Do you want to come to bed?' I said 'No, I'll sleep in here' and spent the night in the van. I woke up the next morning, rolled out of bed and I was alright. I could walk again!

I don't think I experienced the lack of feeling in my legs immediately after the crash, because when I landed I was rolling around on the ground, swearing. Then the medics stopped me, laid me flat, braced me, put me on a board and sent me off to hospital. I was told that I'd been drifting in and out of sleep so I must have been suffering from concussion, but finding my legs wouldn't work was one scary moment.

The following day I looked at my body armour. It has padded sections and a moulded honeycomb effect on the outside, and because I hit the ground so hard the honeycomb pattern was imprinted on my back, my elbows and my shoulders.

Things got no better for the team. Tommy had to pull out of the match with knee ligament damage, I was on my way to the city centre hospital, so after only three races we were down to four fit riders because we were already using rider replacement for the injured Ray Morton and had only started with six men.

I've no idea what the Rockets' owner Len Silver, manager John Sampford and those fans who travelled up to the Midlands must have been thinking, but it got even worse as our number one, Chris Neath, joined me in hospital after injuring his lower back in heat five to leave us with only three riders – Steve Boxall and our two reserves, Adam Roynon and Luke Bowen – with another ten races left.

In hospital, I was unaware of what was happening back at the track, and can't even remember seeing Neathie when he came in, but it meant that we had to go into each of the last six heats with only one rider. Yet even so, we only lost by nine points on aggregate.

I was still riding for Scunthorpe in the Conference League and for Rye House in the Premier League, and that was a good year both for my clubs and for me. The Scorpions had the best season ever, doing the treble – that is, winning the League, Conference Trophy and Knock Out Cup – while the Rockets won the Premier League, beating Sheffield easily in the Grand Final even though we lost the first leg at their place. On the individual front, I was both the Conference League Riders' and British Under 18 Champion, so that was six major trophies in the same summer.

CHAPTER 5

SWEDEN, POLAND AND FIRST BIG WINS

Sometimes it's worth taking a chance and seizing an unexpected opportunity – even if it costs you a quid or two.

And that's how I got my first break in Sweden. When you look at the financial pecking order, a sort of Speedway Stock Exchange, the top-ranked company would be Poland plc.

Then comes Sweden plc, with UK plc very much at the bottom of the FTSE 100.

Britain is also the easiest country to break into, simply because there are far more tracks and infinitely more opportunities than anywhere else.

This year there are twenty-four teams in the British leagues – six in the Premiership, a dozen in the Championship and another eight in the third-tier National Development League, a successor to the Conference League where it all began for me.

It would have been more but for a combination of the

pandemic and other problems, which has seen Swindon, Somerset and the Isle of Wight all pull out of league racing, at least for 2021.

In the last completed season, 2019, there were twenty-six teams in Britain -- seven in the Premiership, eleven in the Championship and another eight in the National League. Stoke, who were in the lowest level, are no longer around, their Loomer Road Stadium having been sold for redevelopment as an industrial site.

The top league Premiership side can have anything between twenty-eight and thirty-six matches a season, a Championship team can have a similar number, and in the National League you'd expect to get at least twenty-two and maybe as many as thirty-odd meetings. At least that was the case until this season when the promoters decided that the NDL should be used strictly as a training league and is now principally the home for the big boys' nursery teams with Mildenhall, the only side that isn't attached to a club in one of the two top leagues.

This season, Sweden only has fourteen sides in their two top divisions, eight in the Bauhaus League and six in the lesser All-Svenskan League. They also have a third tier, called Division One, with a minimum of four but unlikely to be more than six teams!

In Poland there are eight in the PGE Ekstraliga, eight in the Ewinner First League and another seven in the Second League, including teams from Latvia and Germany.

But the biggest difference of all is that in the UK, the majority of riders double up, especially those in the two top leagues, so, in non-Covid times, it wouldn't be unusual for someone to be doing sixty or even seventy matches a season.

In 2007, when I was still sixteen and in my first professional season in Britain, there were thirty-six different teams. I made forty-three appearances for Rye House (I also missed six matches through injury), twenty for Scunthorpe (absent for another seventeen either because of being hurt or clashing fixtures), three for Poole and two as a guest for Belle Vue and Somerset.

I raced at all three levels and also accepted bookings for a string of individual meetings. If someone wanted me there and I wasn't racing anywhere else, I would be there.

I rode in the Keyline Scottish Open in Edinburgh, the Banks's Olympique at Wolverhampton, the Ace of Herts, and Stuart Robson's Benefit meetings at Rye House, the Garry Stead Benefit at Sheffield, and the New Era Trophy at Oxford (my first individual meeting success).

I won the British Under 18 final at Wolverhampton and was in the British Under 21 Championship, winning the qualifying round at Scunthorpe and getting on the rostrum, in third spot, in the final at Eastbourne.

I also had one ride – a crash ended my night without completing a lap – in the senior British Championship, the second big event of the season at Monmore Green.

Rye House finished fourth in the Premier League Four Team Championship to give me another meeting at Peterborough and I represented the Rockets in the PLRC (Premier League Riders' Championship) at Swindon.

And I also had a couple of big events for Scunthorpe: the long trip down to Devon to lead Scunthorpe to victory in the Conference League Four Team Final at Plymouth, winning four out of four races, and the shorter journey for the league's Pairs Championship in my own backyard at Normanby Road – and I tasted victory in the Conference League Riders' Championship final at Rye House!

Additionally there was a World Championship debut as one of Great Britain's representatives, scoring eleven points in the Under 21 competition on my home Hoddesdon track as Rye House hosted a qualifying round that was won by Russia's Emil Sayfutdinov.

Unfortunately a broken wrist meant I had to withdraw from the semi-final, although there was the consolation of not having to make the marathon 27-hour, 1,563 mile trek via Dover, France, Belgium, Holland, Germany, Poland and Lithuania to Daugavpils in Latvia!

If my maths – never a strong subject at school back in Australia – is right then I did more than eighty meetings in Britain during a busy season!

Even in those early days, though, the goal for any ambitious rider was to land a team place in either Poland or Sweden, where the money dwarfs anything you can earn in domestic action in the UK.

It's not only about the money: the higher-echelon leagues in both Poland and Sweden have been for some years now considerably stronger than Britain, and to get on you have to always be testing yourself, preferably against the best riders in the world.

To give you an idea, of the fifteen qualifiers for the 2021 Grand Prix series this summer – Oliver Berntzon, Jason Doyle, Max Fricke, Maciej Janowski, Krzysztof Kasprzak, Artem Laguta, Robert Lambert, Freddie Lindgren, Leon Madsen, Emil Sayfutdinov, Anders Thomsen, Martin Vaculik, Matej Zagar, Bartosz Zmarzlik and myself – not a single one has a British club.

Yet all fifteen were contracted to a Polish club and eight of the fifteen had a place in a Swedish squad, while the first three stand-by picks are riding in both Poland and Sweden but not the UK.

I was still pretty raw and a new name in 2007 but Dad and I decided we would try and get a Swedish team place as soon as I could.

I'd already got a place in Poland, as one of Czestochowa's juniors.

The Poles had a rule that each team had to have two riders under twenty-one in their senior squad, so it wasn't quite as hard to break in there if you were young. They always study the results and statistics from Britain and as soon as you start to make any kind of impression they will get on the phone and invite you across.

Having a squad system as well makes it less of a risk and if you don't get points in Poland then there's a long line of other youngsters waiting to jump in. Basically it's a no-lose situation for the Ekstraliga clubs. If you cut it, they have a prospect on their hands – if you don't, they just cut you and you spend the season out in the cold.

Sweden don't have quite the same set-up so it's definitely more difficult to get a contract, which is why Dad and I agreed to go and ride in an individual meeting there, the Karlstad Open, without being promised a single penny!

We had a chat with a few people over there and got talking to a guy called Peter Jansson who was Vargarna's team manager.

He invited us over but warned us: 'I can't pay you any money but we will give you a bike that's got an engine in it!'

Peter's boss was called Torsten Sahlin, a multi-millionaire who started business life selling lorries. He then invested heavily in real estate and when the future of Vargarna, one of Sweden's most famous clubs, a little like Belle Vue in England, hit rocky times and was threatened with going under in the mid-noughties, he saved the day and was very much involved in the running of the club.

With his money, we were expecting a brand-new bike to be waiting there to use but when we went to Torsten's workshop the only machine we could see was a battered old Jawa. Now when I say old, it was the biggest fucking bag of shit I had ever seen.

My bikes weren't very nice but this made them look like Rolls-Royces. It didn't have an engine in it when we got there.

All we had taken with us was a seat and a pair of handlebars, and I think our own carburettor, so that at least the bike would have a feel of my own. We bolted the seat on, had to spend around three hours sorting the bike out and managed to borrow an engine that we bolted into the chassis. I think it had once belonged to a rider called Mikael Blixt who was well known at one time as a tuner. He'd spent a couple of seasons racing in England for Berwick, Peterborough and Poole in the early eighties and the engine looked as if he might have used it then!

He was a decent tuner and had used some special inlet valves that looked something like a golf ball, so we thought we could only give it a go. We put the bike on a trailer, something we had never done before because we had always used a van, our first one being an ex-Post Office Ford Escort. We moved on to a bright orange ex-RAC Ford Transit and then, later, to an old Mercedes Sprinter.

Anyway, we loaded the bike up on the trailer and towed it behind Peter Jansson's car, to the track that was around 100 miles through some real Swedish countryside.

When we arrived and unloaded this bike, all the other guys must have wondered who we were. They were all lined up in their new or nearly new Sprinters – all shining, immaculately prepared bikes and we rock up with one bike and this little toolbox!

There were some big names in the meeting: Mikael Max, who had ridden in more than fifty Grand Prix rounds, Stefan Dannö and Peter Ljung who were ex-GP riders as well.

But we fucking go out and win it. Little, unknown Tai Woffinden, who had only turned seventeen less than a month earlier, only goes out and wins it.

I got thirteen points from five qualifying races and then passed Niklas Klingberg, Dannö and the mighty Max after missing the start in the final

It was Mikael Max's home track and I passed him, I went underneath him, in the final. He wasn't happy, was he?

That was the first time Freddie Lindgren, who would become my teammate at Wolverhampton a couple of years later, had seen me riding as he was there watching.

I'd gone to Sweden to ride free of charge so there wasn't any fee involved, but I left with a big wad of cash because I'd fucking won this meeting that I wasn't supposed to win. I left the track with all this cash in my hand. (I say all the cash, it wasn't much but to me it was because I didn't get cash like that ever.) I took out something like 500 Swedish kronor (I can't remember what that would have been then but it's around £40 today) and gave that to Peter as a thank-you for organising it all.

So we were driving along the road and we were talking about how it had all happened and I couldn't believe that we were leaving there with money. Peter was laughing and my dad was laughing and I was sitting in the back, counting my cash!

I went to Sweden free of charge to show who I was and so Peter could have a look at me. I won that meeting and on the way back Peter goes: 'Ooh, do you want to ride for us next year?' and I said yes and that was it.

I'd got my Swedish team place in 2008.

Vargarna were competing in the Allsvenskan League – Sweden's equivalent of the Championship – and it had some good riders in it: Joe Screen, who had been World Under 21 Champion in 1993 and in the GPs for five years between 1996 and 2000, and Antonio Lindbäck who were both at Norrköping even though Lindbäck had spent 2005, 2006 and 2007 as a GP mainstay; Max and Dannö were still at Solkatterna, who were based at Karlstad; Thomas H. Jonasson and Peter Ljung rode for Valsarna.

I was stoked to be able to fly home at the end of the season knowing that in 2008, I had team spots in Poland, Sweden and the UK.

* * *

Everything was sweet but the year 2008 would turn out to be tinged with sadness when two close friends, Darren and his wife Sharon, were killed in a road accident.

Darren was the son of former Great Britain captain Nigel Boocock and his wife Cynthia. Nigel had been one of the England's most popular riders, nicknamed 'Little Boy Blue' because of his coloured leathers, and a big crowd-pleaser because of his spectacular style. He had reached nine World Finals between 1962 and 1972, with a top finish of fourth at Wembley in 1969.

His brother Eric, Darren's uncle, was also a famous rider and in 1970, the brothers teamed up for England in both the World Team Cup and the World Pairs Championship, winning silver and bronze.

Darren and Sharon's accident happened totally out of the blue in July when they were on the way to meet me on Darren's Triumph Spitfire motorcycle. They left their Rotherham home with Sharon riding pillion and collided with a lorry on the winding A631 between Maltby and Tickhill.

I had agreed to make a guest appearance for Coventry against Poole that Friday evening and we had arranged to meet at the Sir Jack Pub and Carvery at Bramley, close to Junction One on the M18.

We tried to phone Darren on the way to see if he was on time but got no answer. We didn't think anything about it and just thought that for some reason he wasn't able to answer his mobile. We got to where we were to meet him and tried again. Sharon's mother answered and explained what had happened.

Obviously we were all on a downer but we went to Coventry and I tried to do my bit even though it was difficult and after four rides I had to pull out.

It was one of those things, it could have happened to anyone, you have got to move on but remember them and try not to get too low about it.

They had a son, Jack, who was twelve and on a school trip in France. He returned home on the Saturday while Eric had the difficult task of phoning Australia, where Nigel and Cynthia lived, to break the awful news that they had lost their son and daughter-in-law in a road accident.

From my first day back in Britain, through his company, Ozchem, Darren had sponsored me with methanol and we would regularly link up on the way to meetings all over the country.

Later in the season I dedicated my victory in the Premier League Riders' Championship (PLRC) final to Darren, who would normally have been in the pits with me at Sheffield.

He was in my thoughts throughout that particular meeting because Owlerton was our local track and when I was interviewed after stepping down from the rostrum I unloaded my feelings to *Speedway Star* magazine.

I told them: 'I was having an awful meeting – I started off with a second in my first one behind Jason Bunyan and the next one I was third.

'Before the meeting I'd had people saying I should win it and there I was, laughing at the thought because it was going so badly.

'I've had sore throat and a snotty nose for a couple of weeks and I just can't shake it off.

'I didn't start the night off too well but I sat down and I was thinking about Darren and then I thought, *I want to do this for Booey*, and changed things.

'Thinking about him made me realise I had to get on with it. I didn't feel too well because of my cold, I coped while riding, but in the pits I was coughing and coughing, it's been a nightmare.

'I found it a little weird with Darren not being there, we used to go to Sheffield every Thursday and Booey was always there.

'I can't really explain how it feels. I have known Booey since I was born, he's kind of always been there and even when we moved to Australia he seemed to be on holiday there all the time.

'I spent a lot of time in his company and he would come to most of the meetings.

'He was a sponsor as well and that only came because he was a family friend. He was more part of the family than anything else.

'He gave us a fair bit of methanol and we have still got some of it left. We were using it on Sunday, although we are almost running out and will have to buy some from someone else now.'

Darren was only forty and Sharon thirty-nine and it was an

emotional meeting for me and even more emotional to dedicate the victory to two very special friends.

It was a tragedy and none of us will ever forget Darren and Sharon.

The win, despite the circumstances, meant I'd become the first rider to hold the titles of British Under 18 Champion (I'd won it towards the end of 2007), British Under 21 Champion, and Premier League Riders' Champion at the same time.

Winning the British Under 21 Championship and then the PLRC were two of my goals, so I was feeling pretty happy about the way the season had gone, especially as I also retained the Under 18 crown on my penultimate meet of the season.

I was able to pack my Kevlars, helmets and bikes away on the last night of October after a second place in Scunthorpe's Hallowe'en Trophy and, forty-eight hours later, I was named as the fans' Rider of the Year for the third season in a row and the Speedway Riders' Association Under 18 Rider of the Year for a second time.

I'd also ridden for Great Britain in both the senior and Under 21 World Cups and been reserve at the British Grand Prix at Cardiff, both a bonus.

I'd been automatically picked as first reserve at the Millennium Stadium after finishing third in the British final at Swindon. Scott Nicholls was the overall winner, adding another national title to those he had won in 2002, 2003, 2005, and Eddie Kennett, who was runner-up, left Blunsdon with the wild card.

Despite having to settle for being first reserve, I was shocked by how far I'd come on in such a short time. For the first time since arriving back in England I actually felt nervous going into the latter stages of the meeting.

Everything was okay and just like normal in the five qualifying races, but when it came to the semi-final, a few nerves started jangling and it was all a bit weird. I'd never felt like that before, except a second or so before I did a bungee jump!

There were plenty of crashes on a dodgy Cardiff track, but the biggest talking point wasn't the race strip or Jason Crump's win but the decisions of Polish referee Marek Wojaczek in the officials' box, which were really controversial. I spent the whole meeting being on standby for my first GP start but never getting it.

I'd captained Great Britain in a dramatic Under 21 World Cup semi-final that went down to a last heat decider. With only the top-scoring nation automatically going through to the final, we were still in with a mathematical chance of making it, but my third place behind Sweden's Thomas H. Jonasson and Filip Sitera (Czech Republic) meant we missed out and had to settle for third place overall, five points adrift of Sweden and two behind the Czechs.

Happy enough with my own performance – I got eleven points – it was a bitter disappointment I couldn't celebrate my first outing as the GB skipper by getting through to the final.

Shortly before the British GP, I'd been given one of the biggest lifts of my career a few hours before rolling up in the Welsh capital for practice after the Great Britain boss, Jim Lynch, had told me that I was in the Lions' squad for the World Cup.

He was honest enough to say I wouldn't be in the starting line-up in the opening event at Coventry but he wanted me to travel to Denmark in the squad for the later stages.

Jim admitted that he'd been convinced I was ready for it after chatting to my Rye House promoter Len Silver, who was a former national manager himself, having led GB to the gold medal in 1973, 1974 and 1975, which is still a record today.

There was even talk of being fast-tracked into the Grand Prix series as a permanent wild card in 2009, although it would have come as a big shock to me if that had happened. I admit I'd have been tempted to have a go if the invite had come along, as I did in 2010, but at the end of only my third season on a 500 I knew that I wasn't anywhere near ready and would have been off the pace. It was certainly too soon for me. I wasn't ready to make that enormous step up because there were so many other guys around who were going a lot quicker. Everyone in the GP had superfast bikes, big brand-new vans or huge motor homes while Mum, Dad and I were still driving around in an unreliable 2001 Sprinter van that had broken down three times during the year!

At the World Cup, we got there with the smallest and worst van in the pits. All the race tyres were stacked up, five tyres for each rider, and we only had three rims to put them on!

We were still doing everything as cheap as we could except for my bikes, they were what I spent my money on. We made sandwiches for away trips so we didn't waste money in the expensive motorway services and we were still living in a caravan in Scunthorpe. We had two rooms, Mum and Dad had one and I was in the other, in a room that was two metres by two metres. My workshop was a couple of miles away in a shed in Uncle Dave's back garden and meant a journey across the River Trent.

When I look back on 2008, I'm pleased that I'd kept my upward momentum and was now in a position to make the next giant step, moving into the Elite League in England at eighteen.

I'd also acquired a new car – a Fiat 126, which in the past I'd always thought was a horrible little hatchback. But I loved them because they look so wicked!

When I went to my Polish club Czestochowa, I kept saying how much I liked them to the owner Marian Maslanka and on my eighteenth birthday in August, we rolled out on parade for our Ekstraliga match against Leszno in front of about 15,000 packed into the stadium. We all lined up for the introduction of riders and they gave my mum a bunch of flowers and the whole stadium were on the feet singing 'Happy Birthday' to me in Polish.

Then this little Fiat 126 comes trundling around the track with a big ribbon around it and they say it's my birthday present.

It turned out to be a special day, as we won our tenth match in a row to confirm our place at the top of the table and made sure we would be in the play-offs, facing Wroclaw in the quarter-finals. I had a decent day all round as I scored five, paid six, points from reserve in the 56–36 win, so everyone was pleased.

I kept the car for a couple of years, but in June 2010, Kamil Cieslar, a seventeen-year-old Polish youngster on the club's books, crashed in a junior meeting. A former Polish 80cc champion, Kamil was paralysed from the waist down and his career was over.

A special Facebook auction was organised to help raise funds for his lengthy rehabilitation and I handed the car back to the club, asking them to include it in the auction so that it might help someone who needed some urgent financial support and it went to a special cause.

CHAPTER 6

GRAND PRIX?
'NOWHERE NEAR READY'

Tai,

I love you heaps, you have been a mega son for me. I have enjoyed every minute with you. I have tried to take you everywhere with me, we have had some wicked times together. I don't know how bad I am but it must be getting close to the end. I seem to be really struggling to breath [*sic*].

When you get down a bit just sit down. And have a minute thinking about something what we did. I'm sure you'll find a giggle or two. If you look back it's been amazing. No one can take that away from us. Will write more tomorrow as I think...

Those are the words in the letter that Dad wrote me days before he passed away. It was quite a nice letter and personal.

I can recite the words by heart, every capital letter, every word, every comma and every full stop.

They were the last thoughts and words of my dad, shortly before he passed away on Saturday, 30 January 2010.

They are the words of a father to his son, of the love and bond between the two of us, and they will always be a part of me, no matter how long I live.

I have kept the letter; it's in a little frame upstairs in our new home.

The words are also tattooed on my back, alongside a portrait of my dad as I will always remember him. It took two six-hour sessions with a tattooist called Ronnie Goddard from Boston. Someone tweeted me saying I should get him to do the ink and I hit him up and said can you do it? He's won loads of awards for his work and he would drive the fifty or so miles across to the house and I'd pay him for a day's work.

We did this in two sittings, the first to do Dad's face and the second the actual wording of the letter. Another reminder of Dad is the tear I had done halfway through 2016. I see it every day and it reminds me of what I have been through and how bad times were, but also, on the flip side, of how strong a person I have become and how I will never go back to that place I was in.

We have a great relationship and seeing what I do to keep fit inspired Ronnie to train. He was overweight and I told him about my training stuff and what I eat and he went back home and started doing some runs. The next time I saw him he was like a kid, he'd lost weight and said how much better he felt for it.

Faye bought me an Ashes-into-Jewellery necklace as a wedding present and I used to wear that all the time, but it was beginning to lose its colour because it was in contact with water, so now it's hanging at the side of our bed. I can see it every morning when I wake up and that's another permanent reminder of Dad.

Sometimes I sit there and think, *Would I have won world titles if my dad was still here?* I can only answer that question with honesty – I don't know!

When Dad was still here I used to go out and party with the boys.

If he had been here, would I have still been doing that every night? Would I have made that important step and become a professional athlete who watched what he ate and what he drank?

Or would I have been one of those riders who stayed at that level and carried on partying, living the dream, as they say?

I don't know. Who knows?

As I explained earlier, Dad got diagnosed with cancer in 2009. He got back from the hospital and told me what was going on and said: 'I've got nine months to live or something.'

It was kind of, in a way, nice that we knew and it wasn't like a car accident; that would have been really fast and you have lost someone straight away.

The hardest thing I ever did was read Dad's final, final words just before his committal at his funeral at Woodland Crematorium on Thursday, 11 February. The crematorium is in Brumby Wood Lane, Scunthorpe, almost opposite, a couple of minutes' walk, maybe 100 yards or so, from where Dad had seen his first speedway meeting at Quibell Park, so there couldn't have been a more appropriate setting for someone who had spent most of his life involved in speedway. Dad's parents would have driven past the crem to go watch the Saints during their eight years at Quibell Park and all that was missing were the bikes warming up in the pits ...

There were so many of our friends there – Steve Johnston, Marshall McDiarmid and Russell Johnson flew in from Aussie to carry the coffin, and everywhere you looked in the chapel there were friends who had a long-standing relationship with Dad, not just from the time when the family moved Down Under but before I was born. All of them had one thing in common: they all had a lasting influence on my life as I was growing up.

Others came from all over Britain and Europe and included people who had ridden with him and against him throughout his speedway life.

I am still not sure how I managed to stand up and read his letter, not the private last letter to me but the words he wanted all his friends to hear, the last words we would all ever hear from him. I had to choke back the tears as I read it, word for word as he had written it, as he bravely faced his own death.

I've maybe left this a bit late to write, but here goes.

We're here today to say goodbye to me. So goodbye. Ha-ha. I'm sure there will be plenty of tears but that's not what I want. I would like you to go from here thinking that we all had a good time. My life has been cut a bit short... but I wouldn't change it for the world.

I have tried to take my family on a lifetime adventure and that I have done. We have had a mega time travelling the world and Tai has had a mega upbringing with his schooling in Australia, a whole new experience from what he would have had if we had stayed in the UK.

So don't be sad. Let's all leave this building and get on with what we have to do. S.Y.F.L.

* * *

In 2010 they offered me a wild card and I took it. My dad was always right and I should always have listened to him. Before he passed away, he begged me: 'Don't do the GPs, Tai, because you are not ready for it.' I had different views. I'd gone from a nobody to a somebody, meeting every challenge along the way, and, like most nineteen-year-olds, I thought I knew best. As I discovered, he was spot-on.

That year was really hard, I wasn't enjoying it because my dad wasn't there; I wasn't ready for the GPs, so that was knocking my confidence on my league racing. The whole thing spiralled out of control and I was partying as hard as I could to block it all out.

That was my getaway, getting smashed in the bars after races. I just wanted to have a good time and at the end of that year's racing, I was going to finish speedway.

All my mum and dad did all their life was overpay their mortgage to get it paid off. They paid it off, and twelve months later my dad went to the doctors and was diagnosed with cancer. So they never had the opportunity to enjoy their life together mortgage-free. It kinda changes your outlook on life when something like that happens. I look back at those moments now and that time made me the person I am today.

My dad was only forty-seven when he died. He would have been fifty-one when I became World Champion for the first time, he would have been fifty-nine this year (2021).

I wish he was still with us ...

* * *

It's every sportsman's ambition to be the best in the world.

That's what you dream about when you are growing up and whenever anyone asks you about your ambition you always give the same answer: I want to be World Champion.

I was no different to the hundreds, thousands of other young hopefuls, but I was fortunate enough to achieve that ambition.

Speedway is different to most other sports because each year only fifteen riders are offered that chance.

In the years when Dad was racing, he had the same chance of being World Champion as Ivan Mauger, Ole Olsen and all those other ambitious hopefuls who set out on their path. Each country would hold its own qualifying rounds and, by a series of elimination meetings, the sixteen to race in the once-a-year World Final would be discovered.

All that changed in 1995 – four and a half years after I was born – when the one-off World Final, which used to attract 90,000 fans to Wembley and over 100,000 to Katowice in Poland, was binned by the world governing body, the FIM (Fédération Internationale de Motocyclisme or International Motorcycling Federation). Instead they launched the Grand Prix series, with the first round at Wroclaw in Poland, on Saturday, 20 May 1995 and everything changed.

The representatives of the various federations had actually voted for the biggest upheaval in the sport's history at their autumn congress in Ohio, USA, in October 1992, despite opposition from three major and influential nations: Denmark, Sweden and Great Britain.

It was easy to see why they didn't want to end the status quo, as they were the three countries that had staged the majority of the money-spinning World Finals.

Great Britain organised the first sixteen World Finals, all of them at Wembley, the sporting mecca for any sports-loving supporter, whether it was football, rugby league or speedway.

Australia's Lionel Van Praag had been the first officially recognised World Champion in 1936. The 1939 World Final had to be cancelled a few days before it was due to be held because of the outbreak of the Second World War but once the competition was re-introduced to the international calendar in 1949, when Tommy Price was crowned as Britain's World Final winner, Wembley was the championship's spiritual home.

All that changed when Sweden hosted the first World Final outside England – at Malmö in 1961, then Gothenburg in 1964, and then the big night rotated between the two countries until Poland came on to the scene in 1970.

Once Britain and Sweden lost their stranglehold as the two hosting countries, it was inevitable that some of the smaller speedway nations would want to get in on the act and I'm told that was one of the main reasons there was a groundswell of opinion voting for the launch of the Grand Prix series with five rounds to begin with.

If five different countries could hold a 'mini' World Final, then surely that was the way to go?

Britain, Sweden and Denmark didn't think so and tried to veto the plan, but they were outvoted by ten countries: Austria, Czechoslovakia, Finland, Germany, the Netherlands, Hungary, Italy, New Zealand, Poland and the United States.

Poland had staged six World Finals but of the other nine nations, only Germany (in 1983, 1989 and 1993), the Netherlands (once, a two-day meeting in Amsterdam in 1987), and the USA (at the Los Angeles Coliseum in 1982) had known what it was like to put on a World Final.

You can understand why there was such support for the Grand Prix concept and even though its opponents managed to delay it for a year (the first GP season should have been 1994 but it was delayed for twelve months), it has survived and flourished.

The FIM also scrapped the all-can-qualify format and, for the first time, the challengers for the world title were chosen by the world governing body.

They plumped for the top ten finishers in the last World Final, which was at Vojens, Denmark, on Saturday, 20 August 1994.

Another five picks were based on the results of the 1993 World Final at Pocking, Germany, on the grounds that they had been promised a spot in the maiden GP series but had been denied that when the first round, scheduled to start on Sunday, 22 May 1994, was scrapped after bloody turmoil in which the British authorities threatened to boycott the series and ban their riders from taking part. It took the next six months or so for them to be dissuaded from opposing what many people felt was progress and simply moving with the times.

Obviously, I was oblivious to all the behind-the-scenes politicking and by the time I was ready to follow the dream of being a speedway World Champion, the GP series was firmly established and I have never known any different.

I'd never been to a packed Wembley for a World Final, I'd never seen a crowd of 100,000 waiting for the new World Champion to step onto the box, so for me it was all a matter of trying to do well enough to become a Grand Prix competitor.

Ole Olsen, the Grand Prix race director, rang me at the end of October 2009 and first broached the subject of going into the series as one of the four regular wild cards.

My Wolverhampton team manager Peter Adams had been close to Ole during his racing days and had been his personal manager. He'd guided him to his world titles in 1971, 1975 and 1978 and had kept in touch with him ever since they first got together. Ole had also worn Wolves' colours for six seasons in the seventies, so had an affinity with the club.

The GP chiefs were anxious to have at least one, if not two, British riders in the 2010 series because no one had qualified outright.

GRAND PRIX? 'NOWHERE NEAR READY'

Chris Harris and Scott Nicholls had finished fourteenth and fifteenth in the rankings in 2009, which meant neither of them automatically stayed in the series for another year. Scott had been a regular in the GPs since 2002 but had only made the top eight cut-off twice in eight seasons, finishing seventh in 2003 and eighth in 2007. And Bomber had qualified for the first time in 2007, won the British GP in spectacular fashion at Cardiff that June but still missed the cut three years in a row!

The GP didn't want to go into the new season without at least one Englishman, and preferably two, so Ole called Pete to ask if he thought I wanted to be in it.

I met up with Pete at The Belfry Golf Centre in Sutton Coldfield one Thursday night and had one of their carveries, which is legend. He explained that he'd had a call from Ole about me being in the Grand Prix but that I shouldn't accept because I was nowhere near ready, mechanically, financially or mentally. I didn't have the experience at that level to cope, he said, but he did add that I should do what I wanted and he would support me. Pete was seriously advising me to tell them I wasn't ready, but I said I'd talk about it with Mum and Dad and let him know. I had a chat with them and spoke about a lot of things, and I made the decision that I WAS ready for it and DID want it.

The next day I rang Pete back and said I wanted to give it a go, and he was finally able to call Ole, who'd kept pressing Pete, asking him if he was sure I wanted to do it. He told him: 'Yeah, I'm sure, I'm sure.'

Then Ole rang me and he didn't pull any punches, and despite what Pete had told him he kept asking me if I really wanted to do it. He only wanted riders who were totally committed and not someone who said 'that would be great' but weren't desperate to have the chance of being in it.

Pete said I wasn't ready. As I mentioned earlier, Dad told me I wasn't ready, it wasn't my time. He was really ill by then; we had a hospital bed in the house and we would gather around it and have discussions about things, and at that point he was still saying I wasn't ready, that I needed a few more years before I would be good enough to be in the GP.

But, in my eyes, I was ...

I'd started in the Conference League at Scunthorpe, I'd gone to Rye House in the Premier League and then joined Wolverhampton in the Elite League.

I'd gone from reserve to heat leader and won titles in all the leagues and I just assumed that in 2010 I was going to keep climbing the ladder.

It never entered my head that I wouldn't make the next step and everything wouldn't carry on the way it always had been, on the up.

It didn't help that there was no British riders around who could have done it with a real chance of doing well. If there was it would have been a whole different story but there wasn't and with a British GP at Cardiff they needed a British rider and they wanted more than one. so me and Chris Harris got permanent wild cards.

The decision to do it was purely based on what I wanted to do. A few other people around me, apart from my dad, were saying I wasn't ready and maybe that made me get the bit between my teeth and want to do it. If someone tells me I can't do something, I want to piss them off and show them I can and that was also a reason behind saying yes.

Even in league racing, in the British League, riders were showing up with new vans but we still had an old Mercedes Sprinter. I'd gone from a Ford Escort to a Ford Transit, ex-RAC bright orange thing. I thought I needed something a little bit better, but even so the upgrade was only to an old white Sprinter, it wasn't anything flash. I also had a van in Poland that my club, Czestochowa, had bought me.

All the GP riders were turning up with these big motorhomes. Guy Nicholls, who owned the Trucks 'R' Us business in Ipswich, sponsored us for half of that year and supplied us with a motorhome that we put the bikes in to drive to the GP rounds, but I just used it for GPs and still used the old Sprinter for league racing.

I remember being in it at Rye House one weekend for an individual meeting at the start of the year and getting into trouble because I emptied the toilet into the River Lee that runs alongside the back of the pits. I didn't know any better and just thought it was piss and shit and it would disappear like the water from the showers. But all of a sudden there's this huge pool of blue chemical floating on the top of the river and someone complained to the speedway, and the promoter Len Silver went barmy!

I'd been at reserve at Cardiff in 2009, and I had to admit when I went to my first Grand Prix at Leszno in Poland I wasn't professional. I was still the young kid living the rock and roll lifestyle, partying with the boys.

I think I went out on the Friday night after practice, into town, into the clubs with a big group of people. I was probably feeling a bit seedy when it came to the following day's meeting. I definitely would have been slaughtered – whisky, Jack Daniels and Coke.

That's all I'd done in the previous years and I assumed I could keep doing what I had always been doing and progression would keep coming. Why should it be any different? I was a kid who had grown up in Australia where we used to party pretty hard, at weekends, Saturday night, Sunday night, any night; that was all I did in Australia and all my mates did too.

I came over to England and, okay, I was a kid getting paid to ride a motorbike. I had the best job in the world. At Scunny I went from reserve to heat leader and partied; I didn't change anything the following year, and at Rye House I went from reserve to heat leader and partied; at Wolverhampton I went from reserve to heat leader, I was enjoying myself, having fun and partying.

Why would I change? That's all I'd known, so just crack on, do what you normally do, it would work. Why wouldn't it? Why wouldn't I do what I would always do? Drink, party, drink some more, party some more and keep scoring points and earning money.

My lifestyle had never stopped me improving: every season I was getting better, beating bigger names, claiming scalps and going higher and higher.

I was sure it would work as it had done at Scunthorpe in 2006. I'd made my debut at home to Newport at the end of May and been unbeaten by an opponent in my four races. It didn't matter that every other rider had also been unbeaten in what was a fifteen-race whitewash and the biggest win in Scunthorpe's history – I had started with a maximum, one of nine that first season.

I'd got another max in my second match for Rye House – away against Newport – in 2007, and in my first meeting for Wolverhampton in the Elite League in 2009, I'd got seven, paid eight, out of twelve, and beaten both Rory Schlein and Oliver Allen who were both established top-flight riders at the time.

It would be something similar in the next level, or so I thought.

But I was wrong.

Obviously I got my arse tanned in the GPs, but as far as league racing, I didn't take a knock, I plateaued. It wasn't that bad but you can't spend most nights partying, race in the World Championship and be competitive.

I thought I was ready but Dad was right, 100 per cent. And Pete was right.

By the time I got to Leszno for the first round, the European GP, Ole Olsen had stepped down as race director and Tony Olsson, a former Swedish international, had taken over.

Poland had been plunged into mourning a fortnight before the meeting when the president Lech Kaczynski died after a Tupolev Tu-154M jet plane crashed while making its approach to a Russian air base, killing all ninety-six passengers and crew.

Racing in Poland had been suspended, so many of the riders had been short of track time, which should have worked in my favour as I'd already had nine tough league matches for Wolverhampton so had an advantage over some of my rivals.

But it had been hard. I wasn't scoring the way I thought I would and in those early matches had never got into double figures. In my first three years in England I was winning everything and everywhere and this was tough, it hit me like a ton of bricks.

Trying to treat my first GP like a normal meeting was the way I felt I could keep pressure off myself, but I wasn't making any starts and you find out that it isn't as easy to pass people the way it can be in a league match.

I finished last in my first two races, ended as the lowest scorer, with only the one point from five races, beating Bomber in my third outing.

The British promoters didn't help me either and I almost

fell out with Neil Machin, who was running Sheffield, in one argument. I was racing in the Swedish Elitserien, their top division, for Vargarna on a Tuesday night, and in the build-up to the second GP of the year, at Gothenburg, I was lumbered with a schedule from hell.

Wolverhampton had a match against Coventry on the Monday, I flew to Sweden early Tuesday morning and rode for them at our Norrköping track against Piraterna on the same day, then had to fly back to England on the Wednesday. I had a night at home before a British Championship semi-final at Sheffield on the Thursday night and then was back at the airport at the crack of dawn on the Friday morning to travel back to Sweden for Friday's practice and Saturday's meeting.

The logistics were a nightmare, so I asked if they would let me switch to the other semi that was at King's Lynn the following Wednesday. But the promoters dug in their heels and insisted I turn up at Sheffield, which left me flying more than 3,000 miles and racing in three meetings in four days, hardly the best preparation for a GP.

With a little bit of consideration I could have had one flight and four nights' sound sleep before the Swedish GP.

Neil, who was on the five-man British Speedway Promoters' Association Management Committee that made that decision, defended it even though he did publicly admit that it was terrible timing for me. His argument was that they wanted to have a GP drawcard in each of the semis, but I couldn't understand why they couldn't have made it easier for both Bomber and me to be in the same qualifier and I certainly thought I'd got the raw deal.

And that was before the week ended disastrously for me, through no one's fault except an airline!

I always believed in organising my diary well in advance and once the Grand Prix calendar was confirmed in the previous October, I arranged my travel to get me and my bikes to Gothenburg for the round. I had everything booked to go to Sweden on the Tuesday and planned to stay there for the rest of the week.

Then three weeks before the trip to Sweden, they made the draw for the British Championship and I had to undo everything that was already firmly in place.

I must have spent nearly £1,000 re-arranging everything, I had to cancel the hotel and couldn't get a refund and had to rebook a different flight, and the only way I could get there in time was to fly from Humberside Airport, near Grimsby, to Amsterdam's Schiphol Airport and then from Holland to Gothenburg.

I didn't have any bikes left in England – there was no way I could use them on the Thursday night and then get them to Sweden in time for official practice – so I borrowed some machines from my pal Steve Johnston for the Sheffield event.

There was an unholy row as the Sheffield British Championship semi-final turned into a farce. A rainstorm flooded the track and forced referee Dave Dowling to call it off after only twelve heats.

Because every rider had taken three rides it was decided that the result would stand. I missed out, having had a stoppage and two second places in my three races that left me a point away from qualification.

Even though I was riding strange bikes I was still confident I could make up lost ground in my last two heats but the decision – the wrong one in my eyes – was taken that the meeting wouldn't be re-staged.

I wasn't the only one complaining and, to his credit, Neil did want to run the meeting on another night as there was still five weeks to go before the British final.

That was bad enough, but it wasn't the end of a dismal story because my flight from Humberside was delayed for a couple of hours and I missed most of the GP practice even though my machines and mechanics were there and ready to go.

It was just a complete nightmare, I missed out on the British final, couldn't practise properly and was a grand out of pocket, and it was something that could have been avoided if the promoters had shown more consideration towards me.

The Swedish GP almost went as badly as Leszno and, again, I was bottom of the pile with only four third places as Kenneth Bjerre became the twentieth different rider to win a GP round.

Missing practice wasn't to blame for my performance, I still got in around eight laps, which was enough to give me the feel of the shape of the track.

It seemed as if the whole world was against me, I'd lost my dad before the season started and everything was turning to shit. My mood wasn't helped by a totally false rumour going around that I was on drugs.

Things couldn't get much worse and thankfully they did begin to pick up in Prague at the Czech Republic round when I won my first Grand Prix race. I made some mistakes but I went away knowing what I had done wrong and it's always better to do that than to leave any meeting scratching your head and wondering what's happening.

There were still eight rounds to go and plenty of races to prove I was right and Dad was wrong about whether I was ready for the biggest challenge of my career.

I was fairly happy with the way things went at the Danish GP – I scored another five points and beat Tomasz Gollob, Jason Crump and Nicki Pedersen, all World Champions, in the same race.

Torun was another improvement as I reached my first semi-final; it was the perfect pick-me-up going into the British GP at Cardiff.

Ivan Mauger, one of speedway's legends and one of only two stars who have won six world titles – Sweden's Tony Rickardsson is the other – joined those who felt my GP chance had come too early and that I was too young to mix it with the big boys.

Still I didn't think that was the case and was determined to keep going.

I was nineteen and had gone from Conference League to Grand Prix in only four seasons and there hadn't been many who had gone from the bottom to the top in such a short time span.

It was amazing how fast it all happened, virtually going from being a nobody to almost a celebrity, and I have to admit I did struggle to take it all in.

I'd never thought about being a speedway rider when I left school at fifteen and here I was getting ready to race in front of 40,000-plus screaming, horn-blowing fans wanting me to win what was, in their eyes, my home Grand Prix.

Already I had been reserve twice at Cardiff, but to actually go to the tapes was something else and it's still a place that sends tingles down my spine every time I walk out on parade.

Chris Holder, my partner in the Australian 125cc Pairs Championship when I was only twelve, gave me something to be pleased about with his first Grand Prix win, in an Aussie one-two ahead of Jason Crump, Jarek Hampel and Hans Andersen.

I'm sure it was a great night for Chris and Australia in the city's Walkabout bar once the meeting was over, but I can't remember anything about it because it was the meeting where Michael Lee, my engine tuner, and I parted company.

The rest of the GP season was much of a muchness and I

knew that I didn't have any realistic hope of picking up enough points to get into the top eight and book myself a second season in the series in 2011.

After Cardiff we had the customary mid-season break for the Speedway World Cup, and helping Great Britain go direct to the final in Denmark was a bit of a boost to us all. Even though I smashed into the fence trying to get around Rory Schlein in my second ride, we gave our own fans something to cheer about and had a three-point lead over Australia after the twenty-five races. I also had the satisfaction of beating Chris in an important late race.

I was in a bit of pain on the night and had to keep taking short, sharp breaths while out on the track because I'd taken a real whack to my ribs. The track medical people thought I might have cracked one of my ribs.

The final was something of an anti-climax. But for a typical Vojens downpour on Saturday night who knows what might have happened?

Referee Craig Ackroyd managed to get through only four races before the meeting had to be abandoned. When it had to be called off we were in second place, three points adrift of Sweden but ahead of both Poland and our Danish hosts.

When we all reassembled at the track on the following afternoon it was a different story as we never got over a stumbling start that saw us pick up only two points – I was excluded for a starting offence – from the first four heats.

At one stage we were in with a shout of either a place on the rostrum or even the gold medal, but we missed out completely in the last heat when Andreas Jonsson finished in front of Lee Richardson to clinch third spot behind Poland and Denmark.

Peter Johns took over tuning my motors and I have to admit

that at one point I had started to think I was a superstar because I was in the GPs.

I began to do more work myself, starting straight after the last race at Vojens. While everyone else had packed up and left the track, I was still there washing down my bikes and then heading off to Calais and the P&O cross-Channel ferry.

I drove straight to Johnsy's house in the village of Bishops Itchington, which is about seven miles from Junction 12 of the M40, to sort out a problem we'd had in the Speedway World Cup and quickly got to the bottom of it.

The rest of the GP season went as I might have expected and my engines were awesome although I was having to learn set-ups on the job.

I finally felt I was fast enough and was okay to concentrate on the important thing, my racing, rather than be overpowered by the behind-the-scenes stuff that led to the eventual bust-up with Michael Lee.

I knew my only hope of staying in the series was to get another wild card but I was beginning to have doubts about it. I'd had three years where I just went up and up and I thought the fourth season was going to see that continue but things levelled off.

I'd had a difficult year, especially with my dad passing and all the shit that was going on. At times the last thing on my mind was racing and that's no good for anyone; it always needs to be the first thing you are thinking about.

I felt the final six weeks or so of the season went much better even though my GP scores never reflected that and I ended my first year in the series the way I had started, without fanfare and not enough points to satisfy my ambitions.

The last round of the season was at Bydgoszcz in Poland and, in some ways, it became a farewell party.

Britain's Tony Steele refereed what was a record thirty-seventh Grand Prix – he had taken charge of his first one in Prague in 1999 – and did it as he always did – smoothly and without any fuss or letting ego get in the way.

Tony was one of the best, if not the best, official on the circuit, but he was being bumped off the list because he had reached and passed his fifty-fifth birthday a few weeks earlier. Why a referee is considered too old at fifty-five, I have no idea – we had the ludicrous situation where Greg Hancock was fifty in June 2020 and was still fit enough to ride at the highest level, and was only prevented from doing so because of his wife being treated for breast cancer, yet a referee only five years older is deemed to be past it and no longer fit for purpose. It's not as if he has to run around the track keeping pace with the riders or is on a football field where highly-tuned athletes can sprint with a ball at twenty miles an hour!

At least Tony wasn't completely lost to track racing as he has stayed involved and is now an important figure as vice chairman of the British Auto-Cycle Union, the Speedway Control Bureau and on the Track Racing Commission of the FIM. He's a good guy and I'm glad he's still involved in the sport.

The Bydgoszcz meeting was like one big birthday party for the Polish fans, with their top rider Tomasz Gollob, who had been ever present since winning the very first GP in 1995, finally crowned World Champion. He was only the second Pole to win the title – the relatively unknown Jerzy Szczakiel had been the first when he caused one of the biggest upsets of all time by beating Mauger in a run-off at Chorzow in 1973 – and there was no bigger sporting idol in Poland than Tomasz.

He was apparently Poland's biggest earner, his signing-on fees, points money and commercial earnings outstripping even the best-known footballers. One of these, Zbigniew Boniek, who played in three successive World Cups and moved to Italian giants Juventus at the height of his career, would be a familiar figure in the pits when Tomasz was riding. Not that I knew who he was – but the Polish boys in the pits were pretty excited!

They were the two best-known figures in their hometown of Bydgoszcz and even when he went on to become head of the Polish Football Association, Zibi was still around.

Tomasz carried on in the GPs until the end of 2013, making the last of his 164 appearances as a wild card in the first meeting at the awesome PGE National Stadium in April 2015, with a sell-out 58,000 crowd giving him a hero's reception and send-off.

He carried on racing in his domestic Polish League for Grudziadz before suffering life-changing injuries when he crashed while on his motocross bike in April 2017, almost two years to the day after his final GP. How crap is that? He races in thousands of speedway races and comes through it all pretty okay – and then towards the end of his career he does that riding motocross.

It was actually Boniek who revealed to the Polish people that his close friend Tomasz had been airlifted to Bydgoszcz Hospital and was undergoing emergency surgery on severe spinal injuries. He has never ridden again. He was paralysed from the waist down and has spent most of the time since the accident either in bed or in his wheelchair. However, perhaps there is hope as, in an interview with the Polish TV station nSport+ in January 2021, he revealed: 'There is a big difference between what was four years ago and what is now, I feel there are things that are happening positively. I can feel my legs, feet, toes very well and this is something I didn't feel four years ago.'

I don't want to be negative about Tomasz but he did piss me off one time, when I ran into him in the Scandinavian Grand Prix at Stockholm's Friends Arena in 2013, because he could so easily have ended my chances of the world title.

It's an absolutely great venue but is normally only used for football and concerts, so they had to build a track every year they had a GP.

You never know what the race strip is going to be like, and, for me, practice is a big thing. I'm on a mission, trying to get the bike as fast as I can, setting it up, changing one degree on the ignition and telling my pit crew to make it a little bit softer so I can pull a little bit harder into the corners. I'm always searching for that perfect set-up, I want as much grip as I can get.

We were practising and Tomasz is out on the track and he's got his manager and a couple of mechanics out there as well, the way he used to. He's doing laps and is coming off the corner at quarter throttle and half throttle and looking at his guys and shaking his head as if to say, 'I'm not happy with this.'

Whenever I go to practice I do it to get my equipment dialled in for the track and the conditions. Then, in the meeting, Tomasz pops out of the start in front of me but I had more speed going into the third turn because I had everything set up correctly and was getting all the grip I wanted.

I caught him up and when he locked up I couldn't do anything and went into him.

We came together, I was thrown into the fence and did more damage to a broken collarbone and Tomasz was knocked unconscious, had to be strapped onto a spinal board and taken to hospital and that would be his last race as a fixture in the GP series.

I felt bad, because he didn't deserve that and in some ways it was just a racing incident, but people will look at that crash and have no idea what had happened at practice the day before

I'm not saying it was his fault that I ran into him, but I was in control of my bike, I'd set it up to go as fast as I could and I felt that if we had both gone around the corner at the same speed there would have been no crash for either of us.

However, I respect the bloke, to do what he did in his career is amazing. He's a legend.

I went back home to Australia at the end of the 2010 season and while I might have had the best intentions, things didn't work out the way I wanted!

I had told reporters that I was going to be training with Steve Johnston, and I was determined to lose weight. I'd insisted that I could lose 12 kilos (nearly two stone), no matter what.

But as soon as I got back home I went off the rails a bit.

Australia was more my dad's thing than Mum's and it was hard for her to go back to where they had been with Dad not being there, but she said if I wanted to stay in the house I could do so.

I lived there for three months, it was a two-storey Mediterranean house, five bedrooms, two bathrooms, and it was just like open house for all my mates and their friends. Whoever wanted to party and whoever was willing to party any time of the day except for the odd night off and first thing in the morning.

At that point of me being back in Australia and partying and not thinking about anything except partying, I couldn't give two shits whether I went back to England or not. I wasn't interested one bit in in racing, I didn't know whether I wanted to race in the UK any more.

Dad wasn't there. It had been me and Dad all those years, growing up, and then I didn't have Dad any more.

I couldn't ride at the level of the World Championship at that time and I didn't really enjoy my league racing because everywhere I went there were people coming up to me and saying, 'Sorry to hear about your dad.'

I heard that every time I went to a meeting: fifty to sixty people, every race meeting. I'd had a gutful, I just wanted to do my own thing, but you can't hide away when you do a job like being a speedway rider.

I had a bit of a breakdown, just because I hadn't really had a chance to mourn the death of my dad. I was there for my mum all the time, just trying to be there for her, and I didn't really cry or anything when I was in England. That was the hardest part for me, I was just trying to get on with my racing at the same time as being there for my mum. I bottled it all up but when I got back to Australia, I was really struggling to accept what had happened.

It was a really tough time, to the point where I was fifty-fifty as to whether to pull the plug on speedway altogether and just sell everything and get a job in Australia.

I had started working with a sports psychologist, Mike Garth, when I was struggling, we did all this stuff and he said to do something so simple – he told me to write a few things down and compare them, to note the pros and cons of staying in Australia and not riding speedway or going back to England and racing.

That A4 piece of paper told me everything I needed to know, the story of it, how my dad passed away, how I was going to quit, then started riding again, the progression over those two years, to get myself in a spot where I got another wild card for the Grands Prix and then went out there and just killed it, broke my collarbone twice and still got on with the job.

It showed there were better things to come out of going back to England and continuing with speedway than staying in Australia and trying to get another job, so I decided to give it another crack and stick with it.

I'd never turn down a drink or the chance to party in either Australia or the UK, but I realised if I was going to make the best of my racing that I had to live a calmer and less boisterous life and that is what I did.

As I have said, I don't actually like the taste of alcohol so that made it a little easier for me, as did realising that I would be throwing away what talent I had if I didn't change.

CHAPTER 7

DAD IN HOT WATER

I *never saw Dad ride in his prime but he can't have been that bad as he had a lengthy career.* Everyone I have ever spoken to says he was okay and good enough to hold down a team place in the Second Division in Britain for around fifteen years.

When I started, he would come out on the track with me to show me the best lines to take, so I could see that he must have been a decent standard in his younger days.

As I mentioned earlier, he started at Scunthorpe, his hometown team. He went on to also ride for Middlesbrough, Rye House, Boston, Birmingham, Berwick, Edinburgh, Stoke, Milton Keynes, Sheffield and Exeter, so later on when he was taking me around we'd always be bumping into people he either rode for, raced against, or knew in passing.

He never made the breakthrough to the First Division where he would have been mixing with the big names like Ole Olsen,

Hans Nielsen, Bruce Penhall and Erik Gundersen on a week-to-week basis, although he did have one match for Halifax in 1981 and then a handful for Sheffield six years later.

He was the lifeblood of speedway, getting on and doing his job. However, he did have a few brushes with authority over the years.

There was one incident at Boston in 1983 when he was thrown out of a race because the ref said he had both wheels over the inner white line. He didn't take too kindly to the decision, ran up to the referee's box, and to the astonishment of everyone in there and the fans close enough to see, he dropped his leathers. He had to be restrained by security staff and was detained until police arrived and they arrested him for indecent exposure.

That was bad enough, but he was again in hot water when he was banned for two years at the beginning of 1991 having failed a drugs test a couple of months earlier. It was at a time when social use of hash was, if not rife, then certainly not unknown, among riders, and the behaviour of some of them was causing a bit of concern and anxiety to the authorities.

American Shawn Moran had won the bronze medal at the Overseas Final of the 1990 World Championship at Coventry and been tested after the meeting. He went on to win the Inter-Continental Final weeks later and then finished runner-up to Per Jonsson in the World Final at Bradford's Odsal Stadium.

But, some four months after he'd ridden in the Overseas Final, the Speedway Control Board (SCB) finally revealed that he had given a positive sample and he was subsequently banned for twelve months by the world governing body, the FIM, although half of that was suspended.

He was also stripped of the silver medal and, for the only time in the history of the World Championship, official results still record that the Swede Jonsson – who, sadly, is now in a wheelchair after being paralysed in a racing accident in Poland – was the 1990 World Champion and Australia's Todd Wiltshire was third, but there was no second-placed rider!

Within weeks of them announcing that punishment, it leaked out that another rider had given a positive sample, in a domestic meeting.

It was Dad. He had been pulled aside by the testing team from the Sports Council after what was only his second meeting for new club Milton Keynes at Long Eaton a couple of days before the end of August. This time the British authorities weren't quite as lenient as the FIM and he became the first second-tier racer to be punished for a drugs offence.

Others, including Gary Havelock and Mitch Shirra, had been found similarly guilty but, unlike Dad, they were all allowed to come back before their ban had expired. The SCB were tough in those days; they'd hand out punishments rather than slaps on the wrist or token fines.

At the same February hearing, Dad's former Stoke teammate Eric Monaghan was also hit by a year's ban after taking two over-the-counter cold remedies, Night Nurse and Day Nurse! In his case, the beaks were at least a little more forgiving and allowed him to continue riding by delaying the suspension for two years.

Dad missed two full seasons because he was made to serve the full sentence after being unable to afford to pay the punitive £600 costs. To give you an idea of how savage their decision was, at that time a National League rider would have only been earning around £15 a point.

I was only three weeks or so old when the test took place, so can only imagine how difficult it must have been for my parents when he suddenly lost a large part of his income, but more than that, was denied doing something he loved.

Dad had flown to Australia and was not there for the hearing because his father Brian had had a mild heart attack, but he was represented by family friend Neil Machin, who argued that my dad hadn't been smoking but was a victim of passive inhalation during a night out.

Neil always had faith in Dad and was the first to offer him a lifeline, the day the ban ended. He had often helped in the pits where Dad was riding, putting the methanol into his bike and helping him drive all over the country, but in 1992 he did a lot more as with his partner Tim Lucking he saved the Sheffield track from shutting down.

The previous owner, Cliff Carr, had seen crowds drop after the Tigers went down a level following thirty-four continuous seasons in the top-flight and the fans didn't like it. They turned their back on the club and Cliff ran into the inevitable financial problems that came with more money going out than was coming in.

Neil and Tim took over in the middle of 1992, inheriting the team.

Dad's name was one of the first they announced as they built up their own side in the winter, ahead of the start of the 1993 season.

Neil explained to the Sheffield fans: 'While he's been out of action, Rob has had the chance to take a step back and look at things. He's always been helping out in the pits and he's convinced that he can still do a job despite not having ridden, save for a meeting in Australia, over the last two years. He is one of those extrovert characters who, we are sure, will appeal to the public as well as help build team spirit.'

DAD IN HOT WATER

Dad seized on his lifeline, lapping up a second opportunity, and spent two successful seasons with the Tigers before finally retiring at the end of 1994. Neil has remained close to us all, and as well as being my godfather he is one of those loyal friends who have played a huge part in my career.

Dad learnt the hard way and so always discouraged me from taking drugs, even though a lot of people found that hard to believe, after I'd started racing.

I smoked a bit of weed when I was a kid in high school but nothing more.

I was more into drinking, but the funny thing is I don't even like alcohol – I hate the taste of it!

Life truly was a party for me. The partying really started at Ocean Reef Senior High School, when I was fourteen or fifteen I used to get on the piss with my mates all the time – before school, after school and everywhere we could get away with it, during school.

I used to go into the bush across the road from where we lived and have a few drinks and then go to school. My mate's mum would go to work, she worked nights, so I used to rock up at his house and get on the piss and crank the music up and have parties.

It was all wild. It was wicked. I hated school. I didn't want to be there. I used to surf before school. I used to surf after school nearly every day. Me and my mate Ryan Richford went down for surf weekends, down at Margaret River, a two-hour drive south in the wine-growing region close to where the Indian Ocean and the Southern Ocean meet. It was a popular resort for everyone and we used to surf and party a lot.

When I came back to England to ride, I'd go back home to Australia and I'd party solid for three months, like every day, just out of control. And then probably a month before the season started again, I'd fly back to England, have a bit of a detox and then start riding again.

Before my dad died, I could go out and get on piss all night and get really, really drunk and it would be fine.

I was alright until my dad died. When that happened, obviously things slightly changed. When my dad died, I started fighting when I got drunk. So I kind of like learned my lesson not to drink any more because I just turn into a dickhead when I'm drunk.

CHAPTER 8

TUNER MELT

Michael Lee has seen it all, done it all and, as the saying goes, got the T-shirt.

I'd never heard of him when I first met him after signing to race for Rye House in the Premier League in 2007. In fact, I didn't know any speedway rider at that time, and there is a story about how I went to one Grand Prix where they were introducing this American guy and someone asked me who it was and I had absolutely no idea.

It turned out it was Bruce Penhall, who won back-to-back world titles at Wembley in 1981 and Los Angeles Coliseum in 1982. He retired on top of the box and went on to appear in a major US television series, *CHiPS*, about the Californian Highway Patrol. The production company that made the popular series and Bruce had signed a contract before the World final came around and the script was written in such a way that he would announce his retirement at the meeting. He was probably instantly recognisable anywhere that had speedway or

American TV crime dramas, and I didn't have the slightest clue who he was!

I've never been interested in the history of speedway, and at that time the only riders I knew were those who raced in Western Australia, because I'd seen them riding, as well as, naturally, those former riders who were Dad's friends, some of them having also moved to the Perth area for the better life.

My dad had ridden for the Rye House team in 1985 when his boss was Len Silver, who was still running the Hertfordshire club twenty-odd years later when I went to Hoddesdon. Michael Lee was doing the engines for most of the riders, and I quickly discovered that he was a lot more than an engine tuner, or a retired rider who had built up a business servicing motors to stay involved in the sport while making a living.

You had to be in awe of him when you discovered what he had done on the track. British Under 21 Champion, British Champion and then World Champion. All by the age of twenty-one! How could I not have wanted him in my crew? I thought I could learn so much from him, and so did my dad.

But our relationship turned really sour, and I wouldn't cross from one side of the pits to the other to say hello to him now. My mum has not spoken to him for about eleven years, and I don't think she ever will again because of what happened in 2010.

Michael had had what you might want to call a chequered career during his own racing days, and published his own autobiography in 2010 (*Back from the Brink* by Tony McDonald), in which he talked quite openly about his demons, especially drugs.

He had been England's Great White Hope when he first started, coming into the sport a year later than I did because, in his day, you weren't allowed out on the track competitively until you were sixteen. He had been practising regularly, though, particularly at his local track, Mildenhall in Suffolk, and from his times in training and exhibition races it was clear to everyone that he was an exceptional talent and heading for the heights.

He made his debut for Boston in the Second Division and ended his first year at the top of their rankings, scoring nearly four hundred points and averaging more than nine points a meeting, which was phenomenal for a sixteen-year-old. Even more impressively, he also rode for First Division King's Lynn in 1975, and in 27 matches for the Norfolk side scored 182 points; again, an astounding result for someone in his first season.

In his first meeting for the Stars, he arrived at the track expecting to be riding in a couple of nondescript second-half races but was plunged into the team and ended the night having beaten the England skipper, Ray Wilson, passing him from the back!

The next year he concentrated on the top-flight, was among the top twenty riders in the country and became the youngest-ever works rider after being headhunted by Weslake Engineering, who were providing bikes and engines for a handful of the world's top stars. He was more a shooting star than a rising star, and was only nineteen when he qualified for his first World Final and still a few months short of his twenty-second birthday when, in 1980, he became England's second youngest World Champion.

Michael had the potential to have become speedway's first millionaire by the time he was twenty-five, but he started dabbling in drugs, marijuana. He hit the front pages of the national papers in England after a 130-mph police chase on the M1 ended with cops searching his Porsche and discovering a pipe and a small quantity of hashish in the glove compartment.

He was often the subject of controversy. He was excluded mid-race for a starting offence at King's Lynn and then returned to the pits in the wrong direction. At the subsequent hearing he was banned for five years for endangering the lives of riders, even though the three other riders and the home promoter gave evidence that he had posed no danger. On appeal he was cleared of this but suspended for just twelve months, meaning he was eligible to race again at the start of the 1985 season. He retired midway through 1986.

Towards the end of 2007, the first year he worked with me, he was in court, having admitted growing £3,000 worth of cannabis plants at his Suffolk home.

His lawyer successfully argued that all the Class C drugs were for personal use and he escaped gaol, receiving instead a fourteen-month supervision order to help end his addiction.

I knew about Michael's colourful past when I first met him, although at first certainly not in detail, so I can't say that I was unaware of some of the things he had done. So far as I was concerned, however, that was in the past.

When we first came over – or back – from Australia my engines were prepared and tuned by Glyn Taylor. He had a long family association with speedway through his father, Edwin Taylor, whom everyone knew as Chum.

Chum, who came from Perth, was one of Australia's top riders in the fifties and sixties and for quite a few years was the hotshot at the Claremont Speedway. He won the Western Australian championship a few times and, even though he was coming towards the end of his career then, was Australian Champion in 1966. He had come over to Britain when he was in his early twenties to ride for Ashfield Giants in Scotland, and then moved to Wales to join Cardiff Dragons before signing at different times for Bristol, Swindon, Southampton, Oxford, Poole and Cradley Heath.

So Chum Taylor had been around the block a few times and knew all about engines, and that rubbed off onto his son Glyn, who had actually been born in Cardiff when his dad was living there.

Glyn must have learnt so much from his father, and followed in his tyre treads when he began riding at Claremont as a seventeen-year-old. He signed for a promotion company called Allied Presentations, which owned and ran a handful of speedway clubs with a different director having charge of each one.

Initially he made his UK debut for Peterborough early in 1973 but he was then shifted up-country to Crewe, probably because Allied thought his experience of riding at Claremont, which was one of the longest tracks in the world at 586 metres (641 yards), might see him more suited to Crewe, which was the longest track in Britain at 403 metres (441 yards). It had been longer (429 metres/470 yards) when it was first opened four years earlier, and at one time the track record-holder, Barry Meeks, was in the *Guinness Book of Records* as the fastest speedway rider in Britain! Glyn wasn't that quick and he was never one of the top guys but, like so many, he had a decent enough career and usually found a team place, riding for nine different teams.

My dad had known Glyn from the first time he went to Australia to race in the winter, and they were also teammates at Sheffield the season Dad came back from his two-year ban.

When he retired from racing Glyn started tuning engines, so it was no surprise that Dad felt he was the right person to look after my motors when I first came back from Oz. He prepared my engines for the first few seasons, but when I joined Rye House in 2007, which was where the Michael Lee connection came, it made sense to change tuner. Michael was always at the track and seemed to be preparing engines for most of the riders there. We didn't have any problems for the first couple of years and I thought we had a sound relationship.

He told my dad, on his deathbed, that he would look after me. Dad had always told me to look after my mechanics and they would look after me. They are such an important part of everything. In the end I reckon I was shelling out something like £10,000 a month to Michael because I was having so much work done on the engines to make them go better. I was testing and testing, practising and practising, trying to extract the best performance from both bike and myself.

I am happy to pay big money to get the engines I want, as would any other top racer.

I was also paying all Michael's expenses. I'd been offered a place in the GP series in 2010 and the first half of the season I spent nearly 30,000 quid on engines!

I think I had fifteen Jawa engines at one time – to give you a comparison, I now have six engines. I was advised 'you need an engine for this track, you need an engine for that track, you need an engine for slick tracks, you need an engine for grippy tracks.' I relied on Michael's advice.

I was riding in Poland that year at Czestochowa, and I was spending whatever I earnt over there and in England buying more engines. I was always paying invoices, every time an engine was changed.

About a week before the 2010 British Grand Prix, which was at Cardiff fairly early in July, I told Michael, 'I'm going to get another engine, I feel like I'm riding okay but I'm getting nowhere. I'm going to take one of yours to Ipswich and one of Johnsy's.' Johnsy was Peter Johns, another former rider who had a reputation when it came to tuning motors, and I was keen to try one of his to see if there was any difference. At the time, I was the only rider using Michael's engines in the GP series and I felt that was holding me back, but, after I'd told him that, I sensed that the way he was with me had changed.

Riders did switch between tuners so it was hardly unheard of; Chris Holder, for example, used engines from both Peter Johns and Jan Andersson. There were plenty of experts skilled in coaxing that extra grip and speed out of an engine and Johnsy was one of the best, along with the likes of Ashley Holloway, Brian Karger and Flemming Graversen.

I'm not sure whether Michael had had one of his clients in the GPs before, but I was certainly the only one using him in 2010. I was spending thousands of pounds with him, and me wanting to try a Johnsy motor became a big issue.

When I spoke to Johnsy I took him my three best engines from Michael and told him I needed him to do me a couple to try out at Ipswich. A rider always owns the engines and just takes them to whichever tuner he wants to use, so it was no big deal to let him have those Michael had previously prepared for me.

I put everything into 50-litre plastic boxes, all the flywheels and cams (for those who don't know, camshafts operate the valves in a 4-stroke engine, and different tuners use different cams to produce different power characteristics). I've still got the boxes sitting in my garage, because when Johnsy saw everything he just said, 'Holy fuck, I'll do you one engine for all the tracks.' I'd been using different engines for different tracks, so when he said that I was like 'Fucking hell, just build one good engine I can use,' and that's what he did.

At that time one of my mechanics was Jonathan Birks, the brother of Ashley Birks, a motocross rider who had just taken up speedway at Scunthorpe. Jonno, as he was known, was friends with Michael, and Cardiff, the biggest week of the year in so many ways, was the week when everything went pear-shaped. Jonno was different with me that day at Ipswich, as well.

We got to the track at Foxhall Heath and we tried the Johnsy engine. I got seven points, and that was the first Johnsy engine I had. On the following day we rocked up to Cardiff, and Michael was so off. He was like, 'What engines are you using?' and I said 'I'm going to ride yours.'

He came down to the pits and asked again what I was using, and again I said 'I'm using yours,' but he just left. I didn't think anything of it. He sat in his car and after the GP, when my bikes were parked next to the motorhome I was using, he got out of the car, came over to me and told me he quit. There and then. He didn't give me any explanation, and then Jonno quit as well.

My motorhome was in the pits. So I went 'Fuck it all' and loaded up the bikes on my own, punching a hole in the side door of the vehicle.

Michael had quit, and then so did Jonno. Additionally, Louis Carr, another of my mechanics who had been with me for a few years, had quit some weeks earlier, saying he didn't want to get involved in any more of it, so he left.

So I am sat there with a motorhome and my mother, who had come with me to Cardiff. Jonno's quit, Michael's gone, and Louis is gone, even though he went separately. So I said 'Fuck it, Mum, we'll just go and get hammered.'

There's an Australian-themed bar, the Walkabout, on St Mary's Street, Cardiff, and it's only about a hundred-yard walk from the Millennium Stadium where the GP had been held (it is now known as the Principality Stadium). It's a favourite haunt of off-duty riders, and there are scores of them who regularly go to the British Grand Prix, especially because there is usually a big meeting across the Severn Bridge in Somerset on the Friday night.

If you want to get a rider's autograph, the Walkabout is the place to go, but you will have to get in there early because it has an awful lot of customers!

It's one of the watering-holes in the Welsh capital where a lot of the riders go before and after the GP, and to say it is lively is an understatement. They serve drinks until three o'clock on a Sunday morning. I've no idea what time Mum and I left that Sunday morning, but I do know that we both got absolutely slaughtered.

But not even a hangover could distract me from the situation I was now in. I'd started the season with two mechanics I trusted, and an engine tuner I trusted, and there I was, an hour or so after the British Grand Prix, having finished twelfth with six points; with no mechanics and no engine tuner. Then, just when I thought things couldn't get any worse, they did.

On the way home to Scunthorpe on the Sunday, I had a phone call from Guy Nicholls, who had provided me with the motorhome through his company Trucks 'R' Us. He wasn't happy with the way things were going. The contract was finished and he was not going to continue sponsoring me for the second half of the season. On top of that, I would have to take the motorhome back to Ipswich, where his company is based.

I was frustrated, so frustrated at the time, and I think someone from Guy's company called to say the motorhome had to be dropped off. I told them it was sitting outside my mum's house and I'd leave the key hidden on the front wheel. When I woke up early the next morning it was gone ...

Michael was producing the best engines he could for me, but I wanted something better for racing in the Elite League and competing against the best riders in the world in the Grand Prix series. I was better than a Second Division rider, and I needed to be on the best gear possible to compete at GP level. I wanted to go out and beat Greg Hancock, Jason Crump, Tomasz Gollob or Nicki Pedersen, riders who were all World Champions and still at the top of their game. They had the best engines and employed the best tuners. I wanted to be – needed to be – confident that I was competing on level terms.

Mike had been a tremendous help to me when I was at Premier League level and when my dad was alive. But once Dad died – that was it.

There was a spell at Czestochowa when I was using a Marcel Gerhard-tuned engine and I was riding with Greg Hancock, who was also having his motors prepared by Marcel, a former long-tracker and the first Swiss rider to win a track-racing gold medal when he was FIM World Long Track Champion in 1992.

Greg and I used to get 5–1, after 5–1, after 5–1 – we just used to boom together. I wasn't at that point in my career when I should have been getting maximums with Greg, but once I got that Gerhard rocket underneath me I was away.

I was riding Jawas, who were sponsoring Michael as a tuner. The famous Czech company, which made the bikes and engines of that name, had a long and proud history. It had been founded in Prague by Frantisek Janecek, who was born in a small village in Bohemia, which became a part of Czechoslovakia and is now part of the modern-day Czech Republic.

Janecek was a mechanical genius who obtained a degree from the Berlin College of Engineering, and patented more than sixty inventions before buying the motorcycle business Wanderer from the German manufacturer Winklhofer & Jaenicke along with the tooling and designs for a new 500cc motorcycle. He named the new company Jawa – combining the first two letters of his surname with the first two letters of Wanderer – and the first Jawa motorcycle was produced in 1929; their machines were familiar sights at the Isle of Man TT races in the thirties.

Janecek died in 1941 and over the ensuing years the company was nationalised during the Communist era before going back into private ownership. In 1962 it merged with another Czech motorcycle company, ESO, which had manufactured a speedway machine that was raced principally behind the old Iron Curtain in Russia, Poland and Czechoslovakia. They began to gain more prominence and when Barry Briggs won the third of his four world titles in 1964, they were desperate to get him to use their machines and so gain a foothold in the West.

The partnership produced mixed results but, more often than not, if the engine lasted four laps, Briggo would win the race and he was impressed enough to start thinking about his future. So when he was invited to defend his title on what was still called an ESO, he struck a hard bargain, insisting that he would only do so if he was appointed the sole UK concessionaire for speedway machines, engines, spare parts, etc.

The manufacturer agreed, and even though Briggs missed out on the rostrum that year, he regained his title in 1966 and became the first rider to become World Champion on a Czechoslovakian bike.

The ESO brand name was changed to Jawa, and it became the machine that everyone wanted. Jawa bikes became the mount of choice for speedway riders, with Ivan Mauger and Ole Olsen dominating the World Championship between 1968 and 1979, when they won the World Final nine times between them, Mauger on six occasions and the Dane in 1971, 1975 and 1978. Poland's Jerzy Szczakiel, Swede Anders Michanek and Britain's Peter Collins were the only other winners during that decade and more, and of the five of them only Collins wasn't a Jawa rider.

But, as with everything, the dominance of one particular engine is cyclical and by 2010, of the fifteen permanent GP riders, only Kenneth Bjerre and myself were relying solely on Jawa engines, while my Wolverhampton teammate Freddie Lindgren had both the in-vogue Italian-made GM and a Jawa-powered machine in his pits bay.

There is a reason why there weren't sixteen riders using Jawa at that time, but that doesn't mean you couldn't win races or meetings with the Czech-built engine. But it had to be on pace in particular with the Italian GM, the brainchild of a former speedway rider named Guiseppe Marzotto.

Egon Müller became the first prominent rider to take a GM to a World Final and after having the engine specially tuned, he was crowned World Champion in 1983. His success launched a new era, with Jawa gradually being left behind and the GM taking over as the power unit of choice among the top riders, including Denmark's Erik Gundersen, who succeeded Müller as world number one; like the German, he was mounted on a GM.

I had taken another step forward in 2009, for I had gone full-time at Wolverhampton and was riding in the Elite League. I was also riding in the Polish Ekstraliga for Czestochowa and in the Swedish ElitSerien with Vargarna.

Michael's gear wasn't going fast enough for me in Poland or Sweden or the GP. You've got to remember that when my Dad was alive I was the only person in professional speedway who was actually running Jawas, but nobody was making starts in front of me, right from day one.

One day I was at a meeting in Poland and had just beaten Tomasz Gollob and all the big boys off the start. Gollob acknowledged me after the race, even though I had blown him away. I mean, Tomasz Gollob was everybody's hero. The bloke everybody wanted to beat, and I did it on the Jawa with a Jawa clutch. One of the mechanics at that meeting actually came over to ask if I was using a Jawa clutch and were they any good? My dad was able to say: 'Haven't you just seen him get out of the fucking start on one?'

After the Cardiff drama, Michael rang my mum and told her that I didn't put 100 per cent in, I didn't train, and I didn't do this and I didn't do that. She was furious and told him to leave it out, reminding him that my dad had died that year. From that it all escalated out of hand, and ended with Michael telling Mum: 'Well, it's been six months, he should be over his father by now.'

What a disgraceful, heartless thing to say about someone's husband, never mind my father. Mum hung up on him and has never spoken to him since, and that's eleven years ago now. She told me the whole story at the time, and how he wanted to blame me for everything, but it was all shit.

My mum never usually uses the word hate, but when Michael Lee's name is mentioned, it is clear that she hates him and hates what he put her son through.

I just felt it was more than all that, though ... to me, it was about the pledge he made to Dad on his deathbed, the commitment to take care of me and have my back.

Speedway's something of a small community. There aren't thousands of riders, there aren't even hundreds of tuners, so it's almost impossible not to bump into someone on the circuit sooner or later.

I've seen Michael at Mildenhall and just nodded at him. Hating someone that much, if they came up to me and said hello, I wouldn't be able to walk away and not say anything – that's not who I am. But he didn't come up and try to talk to me so I just nodded. If someone nodded at me I couldn't look the other way, I would have to nod back to them but he ignored me.

Three years after our split, Michael was back in the dock at his local magistrates' court in Bury St Edmunds, and was found guilty of possession of cannabis and amphetamines, for which he was fined £600. He also had his promoting licence at Mildenhall suspended by the Speedway Control Bureau, and for a time he was actually barred from entering the pits at any track in the country.

CHAPTER 9

WORLD CHAMPION

There were two days and two events, 163 days and 1,053 miles apart, in 2013 that changed my life.

On Saturday, 5 October I crossed the finishing line in heat five of the final Grand Prix of the season at Torun, Poland, to become the new world speedway champion.

On St George's Day, Tuesday, 23 April, I'd sat down in Nando's restaurant close to Nottingham's Trinity Square on my first date with Faye Cupitt. It was the day before her eighteenth birthday and the gorgeous girl sitting opposite me was going to be my future wife.

I'd stumbled across Faye on Instagram a week earlier and I thought she was beautiful. We got into some general chit-chat and messaged each other for a couple of days before I had the opportunity to go and see her.

Neil Machin used to have a little game we played when we went out in Perth: we'd be walking along the road or sat in the boat harbour or on the beach, and he'd see a young girl and ask me: 'How many out of ten is she, Tai?' I'd answer a six, maybe a seven or, if she was a real looker, an eight.

Faye is definitely a ten!

I had started the season as a wild card in the Grand Prix, someone who had no chance of winning the series, a 500–1 outsider with the bookies. An unattached, single man enjoying a single man's ways.

I've kept a diary of everything Faye and I have done together since I 'stalked' her on Instagram. The diary chronicles how our relationship blossomed as I chased the world title, Faye watching me for the first time at the British GP, our first holiday together between GPs, her being at Torun when I sealed the World title, celebrating together in Las Vegas at the Monster Energy motocross event.

I can look back to 2013 and read through it and relate to my emotional journey to become Britain's first speedway World Champion since Mark Loram won the title in 2000, the sixth season of the GP series.

Mark won it without winning any of the six rounds and showed that consistency over a season is more important than any individual victories.

I managed to win only one round – at Prague's Marketa Stadium in the Czech Republic GP – but the important thing is to make the semi-finals, which means scoring enough points in the five qualifying races to be in the top eight.

I did that in ten of the twelve rounds. The only places I missed out were at Cardiff in the British GP where I ended up in hospital with a broken collarbone, and in the penultimate meeting, the Scandinavian GP, at the Friends Arena in Solna, a suburb of Swedish capital Stockholm. There, I crashed with

Tomasz Gollob as I mentioned, and re-broke the collarbone I'd fractured badly at the Millennium Stadium but I gritted my teeth and rode on to pick up seven valuable points before pulling out of my last race because of the pain and discomfort.

I've been World Champion three times in eight years and also on the end-of-season podium three times: second in 2016 and 2020, and third in 2017.

The only times I missed out on a medal were in 2014 when I was fourth after losing a run-off against Nicki Pedersen after missing a round, and again in 2019.

In 2014 I had tied with Nicki in the overall standings despite sitting out the Gorzow GP of Poland with a broken hand. Had I been fit for that meetings and scored one point I would have been third in the final standings.

I know if I ask people how many GPs I won between my first, disastrous stab at it in 2010 and the end of the 2020 series, most of them would get it wildly wrong.

The answer is eleven – and that's not a lot over the course of ninety-six rounds...

My first victory came in 2013, four rounds in, in what was my fifteenth GP, discounting a couple where I was a non-riding reserve, and by then I was feeling far more comfortable and confident than I had done at any stage in 2010.

I was pretty much ready at that point, and didn't really have much thought about it when I was told I could have a wild card again.

Two years had gone by and I'd won the British Under 21 Championship for a second time, in 2011, and had a decent year everywhere in 2012.

I went round to Peter Johns's Warwickshire workshop, and talked to him to see what his thoughts were, and obviously I'd had a chat with my team manager Pete Adams. Everyone around me was saying, get on with it.

I thought I was ready and this time I knew I was right. Obviously it was my first year back in it and it was all new again, but it was like a second chance and that's the way I looked at it.

I didn't want to be one of those riders who gets a wild card year after year, after year, so I started getting everything prepped up and sorted.

I'd grown up in every way in the intervening years, I'd stopped partying and I'd started training and eating properly and it was paying off. As I boarded the Ryanair flight to Prague, one of the world's most popular stag-night venues, for the fourth round, in May 2013, the only thoughts in my mind were of building on my fourth place in the standings.

I couldn't have checked in in better condition or better spirits. I'd won the British Championship at Wolverhampton, my home track, earlier in the week, and Faye and I had seen a lot of each other. I spent every spare bit of time I had at her family's house and I'd met, and got on with, her brothers, Layne and Myles.

I'm pretty chilled out before a race and having Faye around is brilliant. Because of her personality she calms me down. If I am in a bad mood she'll get me out of it, although generally I'm pretty chilled out anyway. I'm not sure if that's because of my upbringing in Western Australia where when we used to go surfing, I'd race, and then I'd watch the clock to see when it was time to go surfing again. When you drop into the wave and you're sitting in the barrel and you're carving up and down in there, it's so smooth and you haven't got to think about anything, it's just happening there, right in the here and now. That's where I'm at on the track.

Keeping calm and cool, no matter what happens, has, I'm sure, helped me achieve what I have done. It certainly helped in 2013 when I had to overcome all sorts of what could have been fatal setbacks in my quest for the world title.

I can look back fondly at my twin-campaign, winning both Faye's heart and the world title – my Twelve Steps to Heaven:

ROUND 1: New Zealand GP, Western Springs Stadium, Auckland, New Zealand, Saturday, 23 March

I knew I was on competitive machinery compared to my first GP season, but any optimism I had wasn't shared, with some bookies offering 500–1 against me winning it.

I'm not a gambling man, I didn't even look at the odds as I don't bet much, if ever, and it was only what people told me later in the season. Maybe I should have had a flutter.

It was a nice first round. I always like to get the first one out of the way, it's good just to get back in the groove. Usually whoever wins the first Grand Prix isn't there at the end of the year so, for me, the opening round isn't that important. It's a long season and if you peak too early you will run out of steam; normally those who start well, struggle at the end of the season.

I was seventh, my best ever display, but I finished fourth in my semi-final.

It was great to head out and do a GP on the world stage rather than just in Europe, and it was just about getting some points on the board to show that I wasn't just there to make up the numbers.

The biggest highlight for me was a 20,000-feet tandem sky dive outside Auckland, that gave me such an adrenalin rush.

RAW SPEED

ROUND 2: European GP, ZKS Polonia Stadium, Bydgoszcz, Poland, Saturday, 20 April

This is where I had a really good race that's still on YouTube. I must have watched it so many times since. In heat fifteen, I lined up against two-time World Champion Greg Hancock, Russian rocket Emil Sayfutdinov, and the Polish wild card Krzysztof Buczkowski.

I was last into the first corner, third coming out, and then passing Greg. A few laps later, Emil and me passed each other three or four times and I got him on the line. It's great to be in battles like that regardless of where you finish, going handlebar to handlebar, and knowing the guys you are racing against are safe.

The two commentators were going mad during the race. Kelvin Tatum, a former British Champion and skipper of England's last World Cup-winning side in 1989, was screaming: 'Fantastic speedway, you won't see a better speedway race anywhere in the world. Fabulous racing out the front, fabulous stuff from the young Brit out in the front. The way he did it and the style he did it, and the moves to come back on the inside coming out of the last corner, truly world class. Fantastic speedway. Woffinden having an absolute stormer.'

And Nigel Pearson, equally vocal, was on his feet, yelling: 'That young man, Tai Woffinden, has come of age and announced his arrival on the Grand Prix scene.'

I felt the same as I reached my first GP final, scored fourteen points and got fourth overall. The big haul of points lifted me four places in the standings behind Tomasz Gollob, Darcy Ward and Jaroslaw Hampel.

After the meeting I was told that I was the highest-placed Brit since Mark Loram was World Champion in 2000.

I was doing everything I could, my engines were good, I was training hard, I was eating properly – and it was paying off.

ROUND 3: Swedish GP, Ullevi Stadium, Gothenburg, Sweden, Saturday, 4 May

There was one race where I came on the back straight and passed Nicki Pedersen like he was standing still and I got into the semi-finals again, scoring another twelve points. In the semi I had a big off with Nicki, the first of a lot of crashes with the Dane who isn't my favourite on-track opponent! It was just a first corner where we got tangled up and we both went into the air safety fence. I had a bash on my face and was quite lucky to be able to walk away. It was a pretty nasty crash and I think Nicki hurt his arm, but he was back up for the re-run and beat me into second place so I missed another final.

Emil won a second round in a row but it must have been a tough and emotional night for him. He was crying on the rostrum as he dedicated his second successive GP victory to his father Damir who had, like my dad, lost his battle against cancer.

I knew how Emil, who had flown to Salavat to be with his dying father before travelling to Gothenburg, must have been feeling and, after accepting his trophy, he admitted: 'The last days have been very hard for me, but I decided to go back to racing, that is what my father wanted.

'The words of encouragement I had from riders and fans from around the world, knowing that they were with me, was very important.

'When I was at home, I said to my dad: "I'll win this for you." I did that. My family will feel much better for this hopefully.'

RAW SPEED

ROUND 4: Czech Republic GP, Marketa Stadium. Prague, Czech Republic, Saturday, 18 May

I was on a nice little high going into Prague because I had won the British final the previous Monday and that was the first massive meeting that I'd come away from with a victory.

I'd wanted to be British Champion for a few years and had twice been third, in 2011 and 2012. I'd been leading when the race had been stopped and then missed out in the re-runs.

The whole GP was spot on, I had good speed from the start, my bikes were good and the track was good, and I did what I needed to do by getting to the final.

What a week, British Champion and then five days later a GP winner and, three days on, Faye and I made it official that we were committed to each other. I was on a mission.

What will be will be because you put 100 per cent in and if your 100 per cent is better than their 100 per cent, it's all good, but that's not always the case.

My mechanic Jacko (Jacek Trojanowski) says he knows when I'm going to have a good or bad meeting when I walk into the pits, but anything can happen on a speedway bike.

This was my first GP win and the nineteen points lifted me into second place in the World Championship, a single point behind Emil, the new front runner.

It was an amazing feeling to get my first win and I was reaping the benefit of my new lifestyle, fit in body, fit in mind.

I couldn't have asked for a better warm-up with the British GP next on the calendar and it was the first time I'd been on the box in a GP and everything seemed to be working.

There were a few people at the start of the season who doubted me, but I was slowly starting to win them over.

ROUND 5: British GP, Millennium Stadium, Cardiff, Saturday, 1 June

The British GP at the Millennium is a whole different level to any other event I've been to. It's like somebody has flicked the switch, there's thousands and thousands of people in the streets; it's like something completely different.

And I wanted to do something different, not to prepare in a different way but to raise the most money I could for Cancer Research UK by doing a bike ride from Wolverhampton to Cardiff, which was really cool.

Wolves fan and cycle speedway rider Mike Baugh of Ace Ultra Cycles came up with a £2,000 Merida Ride carbon-fibre lightweight bike for me to use and James Dunn, the MXGP rider, did the first bit with me. I think I surprised him because he didn't expect my legs to be as strong as they were.

David Goodchild from James Easter's Ipswich-based Travel Plus Tours, who organised supporters' trips to all the GPs, was behind the wheel of James's Land Rover and drove alongside me the whole time to make sure I remained safe. The last thing I wanted was to get involved in any sort of accident on the way to Wales!

Obviously you can't jump on a bike, do a four-hour day, and feel all right; you have to rest. I'd arranged the ride, in memory of Dad, so that I had the Thursday free to rest, and after the ride I had a couple of ice baths just to chill out and make sure I was going to be okay for the meeting.

Cardiff was a special occasion for me for another reason – Faye was going to be there at her first speedway. As I said, Faye and I had first met in April, when I'd jumped in the van for the 90-minute drive to Nottingham, and after lunch I'd gone back to her house and met her parents Sean and Tracy, who'd invited me to stay for dinner before I drove back to Scunthorpe.

That route, the A18, the M18, the M1, the A610, I got to know every road sign, every roundabout, every speed camera, as I made the same journey every day when I wasn't racing.

As the season developed, so my relationship with Faye developed, and I even coped with the spicy chilli that her mum cooked on that night I first met them. I don't normally eat spicy food and I had to make sure I drank plenty of water, so that was interesting, to say the least, because first impressions are important!

At first Faye didn't even know what I did as a job and she didn't know anything about speedway, although she did have some knowledge of motorcycling competition because her brother Layne was a motocrosser.

We had made it official that we were committed to each other towards the end of May, less than a month after our Nando's meal, and Faye decided that the British GP would be the first speedway meeting she would go to.

None of us expected it would end the way it did though.

There was a massive build-up to the meeting, everyone talked about me because of where I was in the standings, and practice was good. There was no hangover from the bike ride and I was ready to rock and roll that Saturday.

I had seven points from my first three rides, a win and two seconds, and going to the tapes in heat fourteen I was actually ahead in the World Championship, one point in front of Emil!

Life couldn't have been any better, top of the world and the girl I loved in the stands watching me race for the first time.

But everything would dramatically change. My world came crashing down in the time it takes you to read this sentence.

I was on the inside gate, Nicki Pedersen in blue, Martin Vaculík in white, and Freddie Lindgren on the outside.

I had to pull the clutch in to avoid going into the tapes, which meant Nicki got the jump on me. I was second going into the third bend when Freddie dived underneath me, took my left foot away and sent me careering towards the fence, clipping Nicki's back wheel on the way. We both came down and with Vaculík also falling behind us, Freddie carried on alone while referee Krister Gardell immediately switched on the red lights to indicate he had stopped the race.

I knew straight away that I'd broken my right collarbone, landing with some force on the track and into the air fence, and also, I think, was hit by my own bike. It was an injury that is commonplace in speedway and was either the fifth or sixth time that I had done it. As I lay on the track in pain my first thought was that my season was over. I was thinking: *I have done so well so far and now I'm injured and I will have to miss a round.*

The next GP was only a fortnight away and the whole stadium fell silent, as if everyone knew it was serious and it could be the end of any chance of having a new British World Champion.

I needed oxygen and air; the ambulance came onto the track and I was helped into it and taken to the University Hospital of Wales.

My mum and Faye came down from the stands and saw me in the ambulance while it was waiting in the bowels of the stadium and I can remember that I told Faye, 'I love you' before I was taken away for X-rays.

Often you can look at a quick return to racing if your collarbone has only a hairline crack or a clean fracture, but mine was broken in four places and that's not something that heals as quickly as I needed it to.

I discharged myself from the Cardiff hospital on the same night but I can't remember how I got home – maybe my English mechanics dropped me off – other than it was Faye's house because, by then, that was my home as I spent all my time there with her.

As soon as I could I called David Clark, the consultant orthopaedic surgeon at Nuffield Health Derby Hospital, an award-winning private hospital about twenty miles from where Faye was living. He said I would be first on the operating table on the Monday morning and that I should just take painkillers until I'd had surgery.

Mr Clark plated the splintered bone, put a screw in it and told me that with metal in, my collarbone would be as good as new and if I had a week off I would be able to go racing again!

Faye went down to Bournemouth to spend a week's holiday with her nana and grandad. Her mum took me to all my appointments for laser and other treatment and it felt so normal to be part of the family.

Because of the plate holding the bones together, I could, in theory, actually have ridden the day after the op, but that would have been taking an unnecessary risk. Instead I went and opened The Pods, a sports and fitness complex next to Central Park in Scunthorpe!

I wasn't in Sweden that year and I missed the following week's Polish league race with Wroclaw to give myself more time because all that mattered was to be okay for the next GP in Gorzow.

Despite everything there were positives to take from Cardiff: I was still second, although Emil had surged ahead of me to move eight points clear, and we weren't even past the halfway stage – there were still seven rounds to go.

ROUND 6: Gorzow GP of Poland, Edward Jancarz Stadium, Gorzow, Poland, Saturday, 15 June

I could definitely feel the plate holding my bone together but the pain wasn't in the bone, more in the scar tissue that was pulling away from the plate and the actual scar that still hadn't fully healed. There was a lot of pain coming from that but I couldn't complain because I was back in the hunt and I hadn't missed a GP, so I had another chance of getting some points which I wouldn't have done if I hadn't started the meeting.

Anyone who has ever broken a bone and tried to do something will know the feeling, it's hard to explain exactly and the important thing was I was there.

In the first three races I was finding the right set-up so had only two points and looked like missing out of the semi-finals.

After those first three rides I just felt like burying my head in my hands and screaming, but then I got it together in my fourth ride and won my last two qualifying races and the first semi-final – and there I was, racing and in the final and third with a broken collar bone. That wasn't too bad!

Any podium in a GP is awesome but this felt so good, even though, of course, it hurt. I wasn't sure how I'd feel but it was pretty painful, I could feel it all the time.

I really didn't expect to be doing seven races. I just wanted to get through my five rides and collect a few points.

The dozen points ensured that I was still with the pacesetters, although Emil extended his overall lead to eleven points.

RAW SPEED

ROUND 7: Danish GP, PARKEN, Copenhagen, Denmark, Saturday, 29 June

Darcy Ward was back after being out for two months and missing three GPs with a broken shoulder, and him, Chris Holder and me let off a bit of steam.

After practice we jumped on a little Honda 125 and were having a ball. It was a good way to relax and it didn't seem to do any of us too much harm as Darcy returned to action with nineteen points to win the round, Chris was third and I added another eleven points to my total.

I wasn't 100 per cent – I struggled to sleep on the night before the meeting and must have been suffering from something as my tonsils were swollen, plus my collarbone was still giving me a little bit of pain – but I was happy with my performance.

There were more injuries: Andreas Jonsson was taken off to hospital with a broken shoulder and he was soon joined by his Swedish teammate Freddie Lindgren with a broken arm.

Overall it wasn't a good GP season in that respect as, at one time or another, Darcy, Chris, Emil, Gollob and myself all experienced nasty injuries.

AJ and Freddie had to pull out of the Speedway World Cup as we headed into the month-long summer break while action switched from the World Championship to the team competition. That wasn't the happiest of experiences for me as Great Britain finished bottom of four in the Race Off at Prague.

I scored half of our twenty-eight points and Ben Barker shouldered the blame for our dismal overall showing, admitting: 'I was terrible, I was trying too hard. I was riding with balls instead of brains.'

Faye's mum and dad came to watch our opening round at

King's Lynn, the first time they had seen me racing live, so it wasn't all bad. At least they'd seen what their future son-in-law did for a living!

The break in GP action also gave me a welcome respite from the usual routine of airport, meeting, airport, meeting, and at the beginning of July Faye and I flew out to Spain to spend a week in Murcia, a place she used visit with her family every year. Our life was sweet.

ROUND 8: Italian GP, Olimpia Stadium, Terenzano, Italy, Saturday, 3 August

The heat was on at Terenzano, it was so hot, but by the end of the meeting I knew that I was chasing a medal instead of eighth place.

Niels-Kristian Iversen won the round, I was second and Emil was third – but I got eighteen points, five more than Niels and a massive eight more than the series leader.

I knew it was going to be tough to chase him down, but from Terenzano onwards I started to pull the pin and get my head down to claw it back and claw it back. It takes a strong bloke, round after round, to be chasing, it takes someone really mentally strong to do it and I knew that could be me.

This was the meeting that lifted me, I could almost taste it, so I vowed that I was going to work so hard over the next few months and to put in everything I'd got.

I'd be staying at Faye's a lot.

ROUND 9: Latvian GP, Lokomotiv Stadium, Daugavpils, Latvia, Saturday, 17 August

The pressure was on and I was pulling Emil back and it only takes the tiniest mistake to ruin your night and ruin your championship.

He had a little crash in his last ride and maybe you can put that down to pressure, you just have to keep cool and keep cruising.

He'd been leading the race since the fourth round in Prague and had spent thirteen weeks on top of the pile, but when someone won't go away the pressure builds and builds.

Emil had seen his lead disappear and now he was doing the chasing and I had a three-point lead. You can't count your chickens before they are hatched and crazy things can happen. You don't think about getting hurt and being injured, but you do know it's always possible.

Emil and myself were engaged in a round-by-round fight and I think it had got to the point where several of the contenders were starting to think about second or third rather than first, which is natural isn't it?

Obviously you're stoked to be leading the World Championship but you can't go saying, 'I'm the best' until it's all over.

ROUND 10: Slovenian GP, Stadion Matije Gubca, Krsko, Slovenia, Saturday, 7 September

I finished second but I scored more points than anyone else at Krsko and within twenty-four hours of opening up a twenty-point lead, I had disabled my Twitter account.

I did it because I didn't want people sending me premature messages congratulating me on being World Champion!

Showing how precarious speedway can be, Emil had crashed

in the Polish Ekstraliga play-off semi-final and suffered arm and knee injuries that kept him out of the Slovenia field.

I didn't want to be distracted or start believing that the title was already in the bag – I'm happy to read about me being World Champion, but only when I've achieved it – so I told my followers that I wouldn't be tweeting again until the title race was officially over, and that probably wouldn't be until the last round in Torun. Switching off from social media also gave me more time to relax, otherwise you can spend hours on it.

Pete and I talked about what we should do and what I should say and we were on the ball with everything. Slovenia was just get my head down, focus on the job and only think about going out and enjoying riding the bike.

Krsko was a key GP in the championship. I didn't win it but I finished second with the most points and was really consistent throughout the night.

I never look at the points, I still don't now, I don't follow anyone to see what's happening in speedway when I'm away from the track; it's just part of how I think and the way I work and it has worked for me, although it might not work for anyone else.

Pete, who has a saying that the other riders are all fires and I have to put them out one by one to finish in first place, would probably have told me where I was in the standings and the boys in the pits will speak about it to me, but at the end of the day it doesn't matter how many points you are leading by – it wasn't won yet. All the fires weren't put out.

ROUND 11: Scandinavian GP, Friends Arena, Stockholm, Sweden, Saturday, 21 September

Stockholm frustrated me so much because, as I mentioned earlier, I crashed into Tomasz Gollob and it wasn't really my fault.

I heard a crack and I knew I'd done something to my collarbone, but it was weird because I could still lift my arm, and while it hurt I managed to get a few more races in and scored seven points in my next three rides before deciding there was no point doing what was possibly another three rides.

I dug really deep and kept riding because I knew I had to. I felt like pulling out, but given what was at stake, I did the right thing in carrying on. I dug so deep, and those seven points were the toughest points I've ever got in my life. I was struggling to hold onto the bike but adrenalin is ten times better than any painkiller.

Yes, I was worried. Basically, the plate the surgeon had put in was acting as my collarbone and the actual bone was just moving in between. Every time I rode, the damage was getting worse and at the time I hurt it again in Stockholm, he said, it would only have been about 60 per cent healed.

If I hadn't had the original fracture plated, for sure I wouldn't have been able to score any points but would have been on my way to hospital. That plate saved me – if it hadn't been there it could have been a hell of a different story and it's only when you look back that you realise how different your life might have been.

No matter what, you can't ride if you have an injury preventing you doing so. The plate prevented the bones coming apart and I knew what I had to do in Sweden as soon as I could – call Mr Clark and tell him what had happened. His first question was: 'How long till the next round?' I said two weeks.

I went in and saw him when I got back to England and me

and Faye sat down at a table. He had a look at an X-ray and said: 'If you can ride with it now just leave it. What's the chances of crashing on it again?' When I told him if I went over that side of the bike, I would always go on my shoulder, he told me: 'Best to leave it and once you've done the last round we will repair it and get it back to normal again.'

I always knew I'd be able to ride, no worries, but I'd be lying back trying not to move my right arm because I knew it could pop out.

ROUND 12: Torun GP of Poland, Marian Rose Motoarena, Torun, Poland, Saturday, 5 October

After the Scandinavian Grand Prix, I did an interview with TV and said: 'You have heard lots of national anthems this year – in a fortnight's time you are going to hear "God Save the Queen".'

It was just saying how it was: at that point with one round to go, I was sure I was going to be World Champion.

The boys in my pit crew had T-shirts printed that proclaimed Tai Woffinden as the 2013 World Champion and they wore them as soon as I'd scored the points I needed to win the title.

I'd no idea what they'd done, but it showed they had belief in me that matched my own belief that, at the end of the penultimate round in Stockholm, I was going to win the World Championship.

I woke up on the morning of the meeting and I didn't feel any different to normal, it was just another day at the office – I didn't feel anything.

I did some stuff with the fans at my hotel and then I just kept a low profile and kept my head down. I had some lunch with my team and my family and that was it – I didn't do anything different to what I normally do. Why change something that's working?

I went to Torun knowing six points would be enough, even if Jaroslaw Hampel, who was the only rider who could overtake me, won all seven of his races to claim a maximum twenty-one points.

I got one of those points in my first ride, five to go, with Hampel in my second race. I won it, he was third, so that was it, I was World Champion, the youngest since it became a Grand Prix series in 1995.

'God Save the Queen', celebration T-shirts? A lot of people think I'm arrogant but I guess if you know you're going to achieve something and you are confident you're going to do it, why not say so?

I knew I was going to win the title and I did, but I didn't realise I'd won till I went down the back straight.

I saw the TV producer Steve Saint hanging over the fence showing me the number-one sign, saying you have done it. I knew I'd won my race but I assumed Hampel came second.

I'd known when I went to the start line that if I came last and Hampel won, I wouldn't have been World Champion but I didn't work out all the other possibilities and everyone else in the stadium knew before I did. I must have been the only person in the whole speedway world who didn't have a clue when I was given the chequered flag at the end of heat five!

You can't explain how it feels. Being the best in the world is special. You are the best of all the people in the world, that's pretty crazy.

There was a lot of hard work and the years of living in England in a caravan, just the whole thing. All the ambitions from starting to ride a speedway bike, a 125. You want to be world champion.

That's why 2013 was the best one, you just don't know, you

don't know what it feels like and when it happens, there's a huge build-up of everything. There are tears of joy, you are happy, you are excited, you are ecstatic, it's a weird and just crazy feeling. It's different.

You can't compare winning a world title – that's my profession – to marrying your wife, to having a daughter; that's another feeling, it's just different.

I don't really know how to explain it, even now. One hundred per cent it's the greatest feeling in your career.

* * *

After it had sunk in that I was World Champion, I could look back with a wry smile.

One of the teachers at Ocean Reef Senior High School had said I would do nothing with my life, so I sent her a postcard after I'd won the title!

The world title was mine, but I didn't stop. I pretty much did two or three press things a day for the first couple of weeks and even after that, when it slowed down, I was still doing one or two a day – magazines, newspapers, TV, radio, everything.

I flew home from Torun on the Sunday and BSI (Benfield Sports International), the organisers of the GP series, had arranged for me to go on the BBC TV morning *Breakfast* show.

They put Faye and me up in a hotel in Salford Quays the night before. We had an early-morning call because I had to be in the BBC 5 Live radio studio at 6.30 am and then on the *Breakfast* sofa an hour later going out live to their 1.5 million viewers.

The only downside of it was no one had told the presenters about speedway and it seemed the main thing Susanna Reid, who has since moved from the Beeb to ITV's *Good Morning*

Britain show, was interested in was my appearance, remarking: 'The stud in your ear is almost as big as your medal.' The show's sports reporter Sally Nugent did talk a little bit about the racing, then wound up my slot, with the last thirty seconds devoted solely to my tattoos!

I never turned down a press request, I didn't say no to anything, and although a lot of the stuff I did wasn't of any benefit to me, I thought it would help British speedway.

The promoters could have done more to stress the fact there was a British World Champion, and I did feel there should have been someone there who could brief the *Breakfast* team about speedway rather than having them talk to me about tattoos and ear stretchers!

CHAPTER 10

PETE, MOSTLY

Pete Adams has a saying: 'I've taught Tai everything he knows... but not everything I know!'

We have a laugh about it and I could always turn round and say: 'Well, you've been around much longer than me, Pete!'

A lot of people have said that Pete is my second father after Dad died at the beginning of 2010, but that's not the case. He's not a father to me; he is an older male figure that I look up to.

I always look at the guys I'm racing against and the only other guy my age that I saw had older figures in his pit crew was Emil Sayfutdinov.

He had his father Damir, as well as his adviser Tomasz 'Susi' Suskiewicz, who has been working with him for as long as I can remember, and when his dad died in 2013 then Susi must have become even more important to him.

You look at some of the other riders and they don't have that older figurehead in the pits. It's hard for the Aussie guys, especially, to have that because their fathers are still on the other side of the world. It's not usually possible for someone to give up their life and their job to come across to Europe to be at their son's side all the time, so I've been fortunate to have had my dad and then Pete.

But sometimes it isn't healthy. I've seen so many times when a rider and his dad have fallen out at the meeting and had a blazing row. You have to have the right relationship for it to work. I had that relationship with my dad and I also have it with Pete.

He's been around so long, and he's been around world champions for most of that period. The first was Ole Olsen and that was in 1971, that's half a century ago this year. Pete was in Ole's corner throughout his career and when Ole retired with three world titles, he went on to help Bruce Penhall win his two world titles.

Later he was alongside Erik Gundersen and Sam Ermolenko when they won the old one-off World Final in 1984 and 1993 respectively.

I knew when I discovered what he'd done that he would be the ideal person to have with me after my dad died.

Oddly enough, the first time that Pete ever saw me ride wasn't in my first season in England but in the 2007 British Final at Wolverhampton.

Pete has since told me that he couldn't wait to see me in action, but he didn't get much of a look as I only lasted three-quarters of a lap before I hit the fence and had to pull out of the rest of the meeting!

Pete had only spoken to me a couple of times before, when I first came over, and I know he was expecting a prima donna, but he's since said that his first and lasting impression was of me walking into the pits with a big grin on my face, taking everything in my stride. He admitted to me: 'I thought you had a great attitude and a great temperament.'

Wolves finished bottom of the Elite League in 2008 and they needed to do something to put things right the following year. Pete thought I was ready to step up even though I'd only had one full season in the Premier League with Rye House.

To build a successful team in the UK, because of the points limit every club has to work to, you have to look for someone on a ridiculously low average who can end up having a very good season.

I'd been top of the averages with the Rockets in 2008 and Pete knew I would come into the Elite League with a 4.68 figure and thought I could improve on that.

Other clubs were courting me, it wasn't only Wolves, and I think it's fair to say everybody wanted me to ride for them in 2009.

We linked up at what must be his favourite meeting place, the Village Hotel just off Junction Ten on the M6. It was the night of Wolverhampton's Olympique, an individual meeting in which riders were handicapped according to their results in each race, and I had been invited to ride in it.

I turned up with my mum, dad and mechanic Jonno (Jonathan Birks). We'd arranged to meet at three o'clock in the afternoon and Pete's first words were: 'Look, Tai, you don't know me from Adam but in an hour's time you are going to! I want to tell you what I have done and what I can do for you.'

He went through the spiel, what his history was, the riders he'd worked with (Ole, Bruce, Erik, Jan O. Pedersen, Lance King, Simon Wigg, Sam, the Karlsson brothers), and why he thought I should ride for Wolves.

We just sat there and listened as Pete told us he didn't want a decision straight away but he didn't want us to leave it too long because it was halfway through October and he needed to get on with his 2009 team building.

We broke up, got back into our van while Pete got into his car and we followed him to Monmore Green Stadium in Wolverhampton to get ready for the meeting.

It was about six o'clock by then and my dad got out of the van, went up to Pete and told him: 'We have had a chat and Tai wants to ride for Wolverhampton and he wants to start next season.'

In 2009 we won the league, beating Swindon in the Grand Final. As we were approaching the crucial matches in the play-offs, he told me he wanted me to ride at number four in the team, which I didn't much like. I'd been at number three most of the season and was used to it but Pete explained that if you looked at the race format, number four came out in heat 14, the next to last race. He then gave me a reason to accept that he was right: 'When we go to Swindon, you are going to win heat 14 to clinch us the title and you will be a big hero.' And that's what happened – we only had a sixteen-point lead from our home leg before we went to Swindon for the return. That's just a little example of how Pete thinks and works, he knew I would respond. I did win heat 14 at Blunsdon and we did win the Grand Final, although Pete wasn't completely right with his forecast as Freddie Lindgren's victory in the previous heat meant we were definitely the 2009 champions!

Pete is shrewd, a serious thinker, someone who always wants the best out of his riders, his teams, but above all he wants to see speedway appeal to the masses.

He originally came up with the idea of rewarding teams who did well away from home with a point. He also got his fellow administrators to vote for a points system of two points for a home win and three points for an away win, with any away side that ended within six points of the home side getting a 'consolation' point for their efforts.

That has stood the test of time, and with some slight changes has now been in operation since 2009.

But where he has shone is in getting the best out of the riders in his particular camp, whether that was as a team manager at Coventry (for three years between 1978 and 1980), Cradley Heath (1981–83) or Wolverhampton (since 1984), or acting as a private advisor to individuals.

His record at club level is unparalleled, with nine top-flight league titles, back-to-back in 1978 and 1979 as the Bees' boss, two in three years with the Heathens in 1981 and 1983, and five in thirty-five seasons at Wolverhampton where he has been owner, promoter and/or team manager since taking over there in 1984.

That makes him the most successful manager in the modern era but he still isn't satisfied and always insists he won't think of handing in his licence until he's got ten league titles under his belt and helped riders win ten individual world titles.

I think I'm playing my part in Pete reaching his target because he's been in my corner for my three winning World Championships and I was in his Wolves team that won the Elite League in 2009 and again in 2016, when I was persuaded to cut short my temporary retirement from racing in the UK and was in the team that stormed into the play-offs and got the better of first Poole and then Belle Vue in the Grand Final.

It has been a successful partnership but there have been fall-outs along the way and that's something I have never talked about before. I didn't want to ride in the UK in 2014, but Pete said I couldn't turn my back on British speedway after having just won the World Championship.

I only rode for Wolves in England for Pete and I shouldn't have done so at that time. In my head I was sure I'd had enough of racing in the UK and even though I agreed to sign a new deal with Wolves it was the wrong thing to do at that time. I didn't want to be there, I didn't want to be at Monmore Green every Monday night, and I certainly didn't want to be travelling to Birmingham, Coventry, Eastbourne, King's Lynn, Lakeside, Leicester, Poole and Swindon!

I'd had enough of the travelling and some of the rubbish tracks, and some nights I'd rather have been anywhere else. My mental state showed itself, because I rode like shit. I didn't ride like a World Champion, I didn't even ride like the Wolves number one, and I wasn't.

My average went down by nearly two and a half points and I turned in some pretty poor performances, scoring fives and sixes at places like Coventry, Leicester and King's Lynn.

My lowest score in 2013, when I was chasing a gold medal in the world title chase, was eight points at Belle Vue and I got double figures in twenty-one of my thirty-two Elite League matches.

It was a totally different story in 2014 when I wasn't motivated the way I had been the year before, and I was into double figures in only eleven of my twenty-five league meetings. We were third in the table in 2013, got into the play-offs, but were overturned by Birmingham, as I was ruled out of both semi-final matches after re-fracturing my collarbone in the Scandinavian GP two days before the first leg.

But we weren't even in the shake-up in 2014, and ended the season third from bottom of the league! I knew one of the big reasons for that was me. I had it in my head that I didn't want to do it, but I just did it for Pete, so it is what it is.

But it wasn't as if my form was solely about being somewhere I didn't want to be. It was the same in the Grand Prix series where I wasn't the rider of 2013, although I can't say that was all because I was racing in the UK. I finished fourth, so I was a fair few points behind the new World Champion, Greg Hancock, and the surprise runner-up, Krzysztof Kasprzak.

Nicki Pedersen and I were on the same points – one hundred and twenty-one – and he defeated me in a run-off for the bronze medal. It's almost certain that I would have been third if I hadn't missed one round through injury, but I wouldn't have deserved to be any higher in the pecking order because both Greg and Krzys had also missed one of the GPs.

But what I can say is if I hadn't been riding in England, I probably wouldn't have got as tired in the middle of the year and wouldn't have crashed at Eastbourne in our league meeting there towards the end of August. I wouldn't have broken my hand and missed a round as well. If I hadn't done that I would have been in that round at Gorzow in Poland, so who knows.

I had planned to take my place in the meeting even though it was only a week after the crash at Arlington. I had daily physio and did everything I could to be there. I had ice treatment, I had special softer handlebar grips to help, I had a different clutch set-up to make is easier for me to grip and get off the start, and I even had a local anaesthetic in the hand to help dull the pain.

But it was no good, I went out there at the practice and after a couple of laps, I knew I couldn't do it. I wasn't in control and it was too painful to even think about riding the following night so, between them, the two reserves, Adrian Cyfer and Lukasz Kaczmarek, took my programmed rides and my world title slipped away from me.

You can't look back at the past at things like that, can you? There's no use looking back at what might have been, it's done and gone – and I learned lessons from it – and you take that forward.

* * *

I'd first met Pete and we had a short chat when I came over to the UK in 2006 when the plan was to ride everywhere to learn about the different tracks and decide which would be best for me – and that's what we did.

I didn't see him for a few years as I was at Scunthorpe and Rye House but we met, had another chat and he told me: 'You're ready to come to Wolves, and that was just about it.

Pete admits he hadn't seen me ride that much but he always kept his eye on riders' results and for the years I was riding for Wolves, our relationship just got stronger and stronger. Dad was still around and we talked a lot about my career, when it was time to step up from the Conference League to the Premier League and then from the Premier League to the Elite League.

I've become great mates with Pete because obviously we've been together a long time and when Dad passed away I did the GPs in 2010 and, as I've already explained, really struggled that year.

I wasn't going to come back and then I did, and in 2011 and 2012 it was about enjoying my speedway.

In 2012, I had a good year and then in 2013 the GP came along and obviously Dad wasn't there, so I'd talk to Pete about all the things I'd have spoken to Dad about.

At the end of 2012, Ole Olsen rang Pete, as he had done in 2009, to ask about me and this time he had a totally different answer insisting: 'He's more than ready.'

Pete even told Ole, who still had influence among the Grand Prix people even though he was no longer race director, that I would do an Emil! The Russian had burst onto the scene in 2009, the year before I made my ill-fated entrance, when he won his first GP at Prague and had gone on to claim the World Championship bronze medal.

Maybe that was a lot to live up to. I had gone against Pete's advice for the first time over a spot in the GPs and, as he will remind me every now and then, I'd fallen flat on my face. I wasn't going to make the same mistake again, although it was a lot easier to say yes the second time!

Ole had his reservations and was adamant I wouldn't get the wild card unless my behaviour improved. He wasn't too impressed with me riding up and down the pits on a mini-bike as I had done in 2010. 'The only way for Tai to get a place is if you are with him at every GP to keep him in control,' he demanded of Pete.

Pete ordered me to a pow-wow at the Odfellows Wine Bar in Market Place, Shifnal, and laid it all on the line: 'I have some news for you. You are going to be in the GPs and, what's more, I want to do them with you.

'If you want me to be on your shoulder, two things have got to happen. I'm going to advise and develop a strategy and every time I say something I'm always right. I remember three years ago when I told you not to touch the GPs with a bargepole, you thought I was wrong. That was your tester, now you know I'm always right. You agree and I will be an item. I will develop the whole routine and you will keep to it and do what I say.'

Pete was all about finding the right button and he's convinced that mine is money, not in a mercenary way, but I want to know how I can make money work for me.

Between practice and six o'clock on a GP weekend so many riders wander around, some will sit in their hotel rooms playing on Xbox, worrying about being on gate four in heat eight. Pete and I have zero discussion about speedway, we don't mention it, we don't talk about it. We talk about everything but speedway and the meeting. That's a lot of time to fill and Pete uses it to educate me about financial matters. He will teach me what gearing means, but only in financial terms!

We dream up money-making projects that I have then got involved in, fund-raising for charities. We have a briefing meeting with the rest of the team at breakfast, 9.30 am each GP, which lasts till eleven. Then the team go to the track to get the bikes ready while Pete and I have a sit down and talk about how I might make money. He'll tell me all about stock. He teaches me things about net worth and how much to save and what to set up, all the stuff I need help with as I have no experience of what to do with everything I earn and how to plan not only for the future but also for today.

Pete is very, very superstitious and I'm like the sorcerer's apprentice. We were in the old town of Prague and bumped into Freddie Lindgren and I won my first Grand Prix that day. It then became a requirement to find Freddie before a meeting and we did. Pete insisted we always had to see Freddie during our walks before getting to the track. It was like *Where's Wally?* The year, 2015, when Freddie wasn't in the GPs, it became a bit of a problem.

From 2009 to 2014, when I rode at Wolves every season for six years, I grew to like the man: I enjoyed his company, he gave me guidance and I listened to him and trusted him to give me the right advice.

I'd talk to him during the winter, I'd talk to him in the season. He'd pick me up from the airport and I'd stay at his house, so a friendship grew. It was a friendship rather than anything else; it was never about him being my boss or my riding for his team.

After what had happened in the GP series in 2010, I didn't know if I was ready for 2013, so I said to Johnsy, my tuner that I'd been offered another wild card and did he think I should take it?

He said: 'Of course, why wouldn't you? You're ready,' and then I had the same conversation with Pete.

'Do you think I'm ready?' I asked and we spoke about it and then I said: 'Let's go for it!' He said he would come to every Grand Prix with me and from there the friendship developed more and we had a great time.

As I've already talked about, I'd not ridden in Sweden in 2013, so I wasn't quite as busy as I had been and I managed to put everything into the GPs and won the World Championship.

As soon as the season ended we started to think about 2014 and, in my own mind, I'd decided that I couldn't do Britain, Poland and Sweden even though I had good offers from clubs in all three countries. I didn't want to race in England but Pete was very influential in my changing my mind because he thought it was a bad idea.

He's very biased towards England. Pete loves British speedway and when I said I wanted to go back to Sweden again, he said I shouldn't do it as I was taking too much on.

So I said: 'I won't ride in England then' and his reaction was immediate and definitely not what I wanted to hear. 'You can't do that, not to the fans and British speedway,' he told me.

Long story short, I did all the leagues, Wolverhampton on a Monday, Elit Velanda on a Tuesday and Wroclaw on a Sunday, because I didn't want to upset Pete.

By August, I was burnt out, I was fucked and I had that crash at Eastbourne, which only served to convince me that I had been right not to want to do so much.

We came to 2015 and I told Pete 'I'm not riding in England', and we fell out a bit but he said he would still come and do the GPs with me.

That series wasn't the same as in previous years and I could feel that; there was a different atmosphere when we were together in the pits. I believe that was because of our disagreement about my riding in England. It was a lose-lose situation on my part.

I said to him: 'I've got to do what's right for me' and I had a frank conversation with him and said: 'I'm fucked, I'm totally drained. If you cared for me you'd understand why I don't want to ride in England. There's too many meetings, the tracks are shit and, you know, this is based on my health. I want to feel better, I'm not happy in myself.'

Everything he was saying, trying to persuade me not to shelve racing in Britain, did not feel right to me. I felt he had put too much weight on the benefits to British speedway or Wolverhampton, so we fell out a bit but he said he'd do 2015.

It just wasn't the same even though I regained the world title to become only the third British rider to win two championships.

Liverpudlian Peter Craven, who died in a racing accident at Edinburgh's Old Meadowbank Stadium in 1963 after he had deliberately chosen to turn into the safety fence rather than run over a fallen rival, had been the last to achieve that feat, in 1955 and 1962 and, before him only Welshman Freddie Williams had done it, in 1950 and 1953.

I was proud to join that very select group of riders, but when I flew home to Australia in the winter, was still convinced that I was doing too much and wondering how long I could keep going without my form suffering.

When I got back, Pete and I met up in a pub to discuss a few things. As I said, he's a highly qualified financial adviser away from speedway and he was always there to help me with some of my money decisions.

That meeting didn't go the way either of us would have wanted and Pete issued me with a difficult ultimatum, demanding: 'I'm either all in or all out! If you ride for me at Wolverhampton I'll come to the GPs with you and I'll do all your financial stuff – but if you don't ride for Wolves I won't be coming to the GPs or doing any of your finances.'

I was open and didn't hold back, telling him how I felt in 2014, how it made me tired and sick and how I'd crashed and broken my hand at Eastbourne, all because I was tired and because of the state of some British tracks.

He didn't really say much about it and didn't waiver from his demand. 'That's my offer and that's what I'm sticking to.'

I left the pub and when I got home I messaged him to say that I was disappointed and that he was like a father figure and I couldn't believe he'd do this and I told him to forget the GPs. I'd just get someone else to come.

I think I spoke to him twice throughout that year. I had a chat with him and arranged to meet up with him at the Village Hotel at Walsall. We met up there before I left for Australia for the last GP of the year at Melbourne's Etihad Stadium. We had a coffee together in the lounge, I asked him how things were and we had a good catch-up. Admittedly it wasn't like old times but it was good for our relationship because we'd got to a point where we were upsetting each other.

That year he did as he said and stopped looking after my financial affairs and I noticed the difference because I didn't put any money away for personal tax. I got to the end of the year and the taxman says, 'You owe me... ' It was the first year of me trading as a company, I was paying myself dividends but I was spending it all instead of putting it aside for tax. Come January and the brown envelope drops through my letterbox and it's my tax bill, which I have to pay.

If Pete had still been doing my stuff he'd have told me to put the tax away.

I'd bought my first house in Sheffield in 2010, or maybe it was as late as 2011, when I got back from my dad passing away. I spent 130 grand on a fully renovated, ground-up rebuild and Pete said do this, do this and do this, and two years after I'd taken out my mortgage I walked into the bank and told the manager that I wanted to pay my mortgage off.

They said: 'That will be £440', so I had to explain to them that I wanted to pay it all off. I put my card into the machine and paid it off. That was all down to Pete and his advice.

I'd missed him and I'd missed his advice and I was keen to get back to where we'd been before our split.

A lot of people have assumed that my friendship and working relationship with Pete was the main reason I went back to Wolverhampton towards the end of the 2016 season, but in truth he had no part in that decision from my side of it.

I had made the first move by calling Wolves owner Chris Van Straaten to tell him that I was interested in going back and I imagine he would have had a chat with Pete to see what he thought about it.

In a way that chat broke the ice between Pete and me, that's where we started to talk to each other again because he's the team manager, but before that we'd literally only spoken to each other twice during the year.

I missed his company. Because we fell out, he didn't come to any of the GPs in 2015 and instead I asked Peter Karlsson to be with me.

I'd known him for a while and he'd been in the Wolves team when I first signed for them in 2009. He'd been around since the late eighties and had the experience of being in the GP series for seven years, between 1997 and 2003, and was still good enough to get wild card picks for his home GPs in 2007 – when he was approaching forty!

I thought PK was ideal to take over from Pete and he was cool, a real good guy, but it wasn't the same.

I felt like at the GPs, it should be me and Pete.

PK did a great job, but he's a rider so has his opinion on set-ups, and it was totally different to mine and at times it confused us. We had to figure out what I wanted him to do and what I didn't want him to do. We'd – that's me and my chief mechanic, Jacko – say we don't want you to tell us the set-up but keep an eye on the track, how it's changing during the meeting, and what they are doing when they are watering it, that sort of thing. We'd give him specific jobs and the set-up had to be taken out of it because it was confusing Jacko and me.

Pete never had any input on changing gears or that side of it. He'd tell me I needed to win a race and get three points to get into the semi-finals, that sort of thing, and he kind of kept everyone calm because Jacko gets stressed.

Pete's more like me, laid-back, and that's why we get on so well; we've got the same sort of personality, except that I've got a sense of humour!

It's important to me that we have a happy camp when it comes to going racing. If your head's not in it you're fucked. You can ride a bike but when your head goes, it's gone, isn't it?

I lost my head in 2016 with four rounds to go, thought I was going to miss out on a medal and only just got myself together for the last round – and got second. I'd started off well, qualifying for the final in Slovenia, winning the round at Warsaw, Poland, despite a dislocated shoulder, and getting on the box again at Horsens, Denmark.

I was joint leader going into the fourth round and it was at Prague's Marketa Stadium where things had always gone well. This time it didn't, and I was excluded for bringing down Bartosz Zmarzlik in the semi-final and only ended up with nine points, losing the overall lead.

When I got to Melbourne, I started training and eating well. I'd started the year like that but it's hard to keep it up.

Jason Doyle won that Czech Republic GP and would probably have gone on to succeed me as World Champion if he hadn't got banged up in the penultimate round without completing a lap. Jason, who had been around for a few years and had never looked like a potential World Champion for most of his career, suddenly became an overnight sensation after being barred from racing in both the Elite and Premier Leagues because of visa problems in 2014.

Instead of moaning about the decision, Doyley got down to his job and developed from an ordinary performer to a Grand Prix qualifier, with his second place in the 2015 GP Challenge in Italy.

There were some who probably thought he would be out of his depth as a permanent GP competitor but he coped more than well, with sixth place overall.

And he showed that he was a world-class competitor in his second season, seizing top spot in the Czech round for his first GP victory.

Following that up with three GP wins in a row, at Gorzow, Teterow and Torun, he was the heir apparent to my title going into the tenth of eleven rounds at Torun in Poland.

Disaster struck and reminded us all that we are only an accident away from the totally unexpected, as he was the innocent victim of a horror crash in the third heat of the night. Freddie Lindgren and Chris Harris had a coming-together in the first turn and Bomber bailed out, his bike hitting Doyle and sending him flat-out into the air fence, which appeared to lift off its anchorage with the force of the impact.

His title dreams were over and while the meeting carried on, admittedly in a somewhat subdued atmosphere, Jason was in the operating theatre as surgeons attended to a dislocated shoulder, a fractured elbow, and, most serious of all, a badly punctured lung.

Jason had gone into the meeting holding a five-point lead over his closest challenger but within twenty or thirty yards of the start line his season, and his World Championship, was over.

Doyley tried everything he could to make the final round in his native Australia, even telling his pit crew to get his bikes ready and ship them out with everyone else's machinery to Melbourne. But he had to eventually admit defeat when doctors told him he was grounded because the danger of being a passenger in a pressurised cabin was too great a risk.

His world title ambitions had to be put on hold ... but only for twelve months and he went on parade at Melbourne a year later knowing that only another catastrophic evening could deny him becoming the third Australian to be crowned World Champion in the new Millennium, joining Jason Crump and Chris Holder on the roll of honour.

Jason needed a strong mentality to recover from the trauma of 2016, and that side of it is so important. When Doyley was on a mission that season, no one could stop him and that's sometimes the way it is.

I don't care who you are, it's demoralising for anyone when you are having a tough time, you get into totally the wrong frame of mind, convince yourself you can't win, so just fucking cruise.

So would, or could, I have been World Champion in 2016 if Pete had been there at every GP?

Like I've said about 2013 when he was with me all the time, I don't know, but it didn't seem the same now. There was something missing, the chemistry wasn't quite right, but once we were able to meet up, talk again, it was a foregone conclusion that we would team up again.

Publicly, we'd never had a bust-up and neither of us ever said anything about it to anyone outside the bubble, but privately we had. It was all about what he'd said to me about 'all in or out'...

We'd had a complete year off from each other and we cleared the air between us.

When we spoke ahead of the 2017 GP series, I said: 'What are you doing next year, Pete? Are you going to come to GPs again?' and he replied that he would do so. He had a couple of conditions and I had only one, which was that I didn't want him to talk to me about riding in England. That was the taboo subject and it still is.

I have to confess, I wasn't always truthful with Pete – I could never tell him how I really felt about British speedway, it was just too awkward. I'd say something and Pete would always say:

'Well, at least Chris [van Straaten] pays you straight away.' There was always an answer and he'd shut me down. When he asked: 'Do Poland give you your pay cheque every Monday morning?' I couldn't help thinking: *No they don't, but they pay me six times the amount I'm getting at Wolverhampton!*

The little fall-out was good for me and now I am always totally honest about my ideas. I don't talk to him about my feelings, I'm not that sort of person. My wife Faye is the only person I will do that with but even she says she has to get it out of me. She tells me everything but says I keep things in, don't tell her things, and then I will blow up.

Pete doesn't need to give me confidence, but he notices things and can read me like a book. I'm strange in that when I'm under pressure I perform, and Pete noticed that when even I hadn't. He can press the right button when he needs to.

Pete will say: 'Tai, you've got to win this race,' and I will go and do it. I don't know if something changes in my head when someone says you have to do it. Pete doesn't blow smoke up my arse. We just have a joke and a laugh and are ourselves. It's like having a weekend away more than anything.

I have to keep asking Pete how many league championships has he won and how many times has he helped turn someone into a world champion.

He doesn't keep telling me he's helped ten World Champions and wants to win a tenth league title, but I know that's one of his ambitions. He wants ten and ten but he might not be able to have everything he wants!

Fans ask me if I will ever race in England again and I can't say I won't because of a promise I made to Pete: I told him if he helped me win the World Championship I'd help him win league titles.

I don't know if that will happen because a lot has happened since then, but it would be nice to be able to do it if it's ever possible.

There's one thing about him that gets on my nerves though: he smokes all the time. I've been trying to stop that. Faye and I told him that we were taking him for lunch one day and when he rocked up I told him he had a doctor's appointment for a full check-up.

I was worried about him. Pete doesn't eat very well, he's a diabetic and his diet is not very good so he's a bit overweight and you know he's got this issue with his knee.

We went into town another day and got his eyes tested and he's fucking blind as a bat. He'd been driving and the woman said if he didn't get glasses that day she'd take his licence off him; he's that blind. We'd be driving along the motorway and he would say to me: 'What does that sign say?' It would be the bloody exit sign!

I do care about him, he's been there for me, so I try to do the same for him. Every now and then I have to arrange things for him, like going to the opticians, because he's too stubborn himself.

It's like with the ring he has worn since he was eighteen, it was totally moulded into his finger. Cutting into his finger and so tight there was no way he could even get it off. So I arranged for him to go to the jeweller's to have it cut off and resized and now it fits him properly.

He was always complaining about having toothache, he never stopped for a whole year and I'd say go to the fucking dentist, mate, but he wouldn't. All he kept doing was saying: 'Last time I went I nearly died.' I have to try and help him out a bit.

Would I have been World Champion for the first time in

2013 if Pete hadn't been there? What do I say? I don't know. That was one of those years when everything was happening like bang, bang, bang. Pete was there and if he hadn't been would it have been different?

Like I said before, if Dad was here, would I even be World Champion? I don't know. Would I have been doing the same stupid shit I was doing when he was around? I don't know.

Pete takes time out of his life to help me at the GPs and he's never asked to be paid for his time, advice or help. He never threw that back at me, he's told me how much he's spent because he's so good with his books and everything and it's a lot of money. Airfares, his time. He writes everything down and knows to the penny what he's spent on the whole series, even down to every cup of coffee. He even itemises the time missed at work, you know, his daily rate. He can work out what it's cost him.

I've always offered him the money but he always said he'd pay for himself; he has never wanted money off me.

How many people would do that? He's the only one apart from Mum and Dad.

CHAPTER 11

CLASHES AND COLLISIONS

Sometimes everything you touch turns to gold, and 2015 was one of those years, on and off the track.

In the Grand Prix, it didn't matter what everyone else did, they were never beating me and I knew, with three rounds left, that I had the world title in my hands after I'd moved twenty-five points ahead of Greg Hancock.

And, in my private life, my relationship with Faye just grew stronger and stronger, almost by the week.

We got engaged on her birthday. Faye was at Torun to see the culmination of all the hard work we'd put in together over the season. Then, on 2 November, I officially proposed to her in the most romantic way I could think of.

We had flown to Australia for the final GP of the year and I had to engage in a little skulduggery that probably irked Faye a little to begin with.

I took her by boat to an idyllic spot off Perth called Little Island. You have to go by private craft because the island is a nature reserve and you aren't allowed to land on it and have to moor up about five metres from the shots.

With a picturesque, sandy beach, home to seals, I couldn't imagine a more romantic backdrop for a proposal.

I had to go out of the house to make a morning phone call to ensure nothing was going to go wrong and it was clear she was being a bit arsey, asking me what I was doing, who I was talking to on the phone.

Keeping a straight face, I had to tell her we were going snorkel diving. My plan was to dive down into the sun-kissed blue waters and place the ring on a coral or rock, but I had to abandon that carefully thought-out strategy when she said she didn't want to go diving.

I had to revise my plan and instead suggested that we went onto the island, but I'd clearly upset her by the way I was behaving. The ring, with a black diamond, was in my shorts and whenever she tried to put her arms around me, I kept telling her to leave me alone because I didn't want her to find the ring.

Somehow, she agreed to sit on my shoulders as I walked onto the beach and then I went down on one knee and asked her to marry me!

Earlier in our relationship, I had her bought a ring, a sort of unofficial engagement ring, a promise ring Faye called it, that was similar to her mum's, which she'd always admired, sometimes taking it off Tracy's finger and putting it on her own. I'd found a jeweller's and got one of the same design with a similar shaped and coloured diamond. But that morning on Little Island – the most captivating scene you could envisage – was when we became officially engaged and we could start planning for the actual wedding.

We had to leave Australia and fly back to Europe for the FIM Gala Awards in Jerez, Spain, but we were back in Perth early

December and we could begin making arrangements for the day Faye Laura Cupitt would become Mrs Woffinden – Saturday, 17 December 2016.

I knew that Faye was going to be mine – like I knew the 2015 world title was going to be mine as I drove out of the pits after the Slovenian Grand Prix.

Greg won the round but, after a little bit of eavesdropping and some kidology, I knew that only a catastrophe could deny me a second spell as World Champion.

I'd gone to Krsko with a healthy twenty-five-point lead over Nicki Pedersen, with Greg Hancock a further three points behind.

Me and Pete Adams sat down to chat about the action plan, call it our golden blueprint.

He was as straight to the point as always: 'Tai – now is the time to show them who's the boss, it's time to step it up.'

That's exactly what I did and I knew I had them fucked because of two things.

Greg was pitted next to the makeshift TV studio, where riders are called up, usually after a race win. I deliberately moved closer to the microphones and earwigged as he stepped up to do the interview and I heard him saying: 'I think we need to start thinking about silver and bronze because I don't think we're going to catch Tai.' I knew when I heard him that Greg's head was gone as far as catching me was concerned.

And that I messed with Nicki's head even though very few people even recognised it and thought that I had made a horrendous mistake in the semi-final.

What Nicki always does when he's got first choice in a semi, is to turn around to the rider stood next to him and go, 'Oh, what gate do you want?' It's his way of playing his little mind games and Pete and I decided it was time to turn the tables on him.

The two top scorers are automatically kept apart in the semis, which meant that I had the first pick of gate position ahead of my two Danish opponents, Nicki, and Niels-Kristian Iversen and Troy Batchelor.

So what I did was turn to Nicki and ask: 'What gate do you want?'

His reply told me everything because, uncharacteristically, he blurted out: 'It doesn't matter because you'll pass us anyway!'

And then I went out to show him who the boss was, passing him on the line after going from last to first.

I missed the start, was last into the first corner but quickly passed Troy Batchelor. It took me a couple of laps to get past Iversen because when I pulled off my tear-off, I pulled the goggles off my face as well. I just scraped my goggles going down the straight and then hunted Nicki down, overtaking him on the line.

Greg went on to win the final, I was second and Nicki missed out on additional points, so by the time the presentations had been made and the champers sprayed all over the top three, Greg was twenty-five points behind and Nicki trailed me by twenty-nine!

I'd done what Pete wanted – we'd started to pull the pin and get stuck into my two closest rivals and I'd seen, at close quarters, their heads drop.

We leave Slovenia, me thinking, with some justification, 'I've got them, they're done, their heads have gone. They know I'm gonna be World Champion.'

And I was, I had so much speed that year, I was quick as fuck.

What made Krsko even more enjoyable was that I'd had a migraine attack before the meeting but I was the one who left my rivals nursing their own headaches.

I had been a little bit stressed out for some reason but I took some paracetamol and that helped to clear it. I do get a lot of headaches and I get nose bleeds as well. I think it's from all the flying I do, the pressurised cabins.

Afterwards, Greg was back in his usual forward-looking mood, telling reporters: 'A lot of people would just take their hat off to Tai now and say thank you and congratulations, but I'm an optimistic sort of guy. I won't give up until there is no chance. Right now there's still a chance.

There was no pressure on my shoulders at all.

'The only thing I could wish for right now is to be giving Tai a bit more of a run for his money.'

He might have said that, but I knew what his real feelings were!

I've got an awful lot of respect for Greg, to lose to him is no shame, but how did he keep so motivated at his age?

The GP is not the same without him, and I can only hope that his wife Jennie makes a complete and full recovery from the breast cancer that forced Greg to take compassionate leave, and eventually decide it was time to hang up his gear for good. It meant I had one serious rival less, but I'm sure I speak for every rider in the GP series that we would much rather have had 'The Grin' lining up alongside us on the pre-meeting parade.

* * *

I'd stayed in England during the 2014–15 winter and didn't go to Australia, and instead Faye and me just had a two-week holiday in Bali, a favourite holiday destination for my family, where we did the tourist things, elephant rides and island-hopping, before I got back in the gym, working with Kirk Gibbons in Derby.

I did a bit of work on my house in Mill Street, and had a big traditional British Christmas dinner, the first I can remember, with my mum, Nan and Faye's close family, a big night for me.

Faye and I went to London, again as tourists, for a couple of days to spend a bit of time together and then, just before the season started, we boarded a Jumbo again, this time a Jumbo jet, to spend a week Down Under at a mate's wedding.

I was so confident before the 2015 season even started that I sat down with Nigel Pearson, who was handling my press stuff, and gave him a pre-season interview claiming: 'I'm going to win the World Championship this year.' I was that convinced that it was going to be my time again and there was never any period during the summer when I ever felt I wasn't going to be holding that precious World Championship trophy at the end of the GP season!

I was so confident, it was unreal, like it was borderline arrogance but it wasn't, it was that I felt so confident.

Faye even had to tell me to tone it down a bit and not let the interview go out and Nigel complied, and I don't think it came across as bad as it might have done.

I knew from the start, before I'd even seen my bikes, that I was gonna win. You obviously can't know, for sure, you are going to do that, but you can believe and I believed in my ability, I believed 100 per cent from day one, I was just, like, This is it!

And I knew in 2018, but I don't know why I feel like that. If I knew why, how, I'd be World Champion every year.

While I was recovering Faye, who had certainly never said anything previously, told me she knew I wouldn't win it that year (2019) even though I was saying I would and told the guests the same thing at the RAC Torrens Trophy lunch. She says it's all mental with me; if I'm 'in' mentally, I'll win, no problem. But she spots things about me, she'll say maybe I'm not as eager for that season, she's such a good judge of character. She didn't think my head was really in it in 2019.

Left: Wedding day for mum Susan and father Robert on 21 August 1988 at the Church of St Peter ad Vincula, Bottesford, Scunthorpe.

Right: Buried alive – Johnno (Steve Johnston) plays on the sands of Western Australia's Scarborough Beach when Tai was only four.

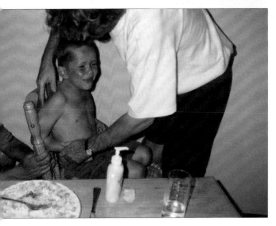

Left: Dad Rob and family friend Neil Machin try to extricate Tai after he was trapped by the arms in a kitchen chair when he was seven.

Note: unless otherwise stated, photographs are from private collections.

Above left: School portrait taken in Tai's first year at Ocean Reef High School, aged thirteen. Everything about Australia suited him.

Above right: Pilot Johnno takes Tai, aged two, on a ride around the back garden at Enderby Road, Scunthorpe.

Below left: Six-year-old Tai (driving) and lifelong friend Tyrone Zampogna enjoy the fresh air at Lake Joondalup in Perth's Yellagonga National Park.

Below right: Boy wonder – Tai gets his tae kwon do black belt certification, a week before his eleventh birthday in 2001.

Left: Sheffield star Sean Wilson, dad Rob, Tai and the Silver Helmet.

Right: Twelve-year-old Tai's all set for the 2002 Australian Under 16 125cc Championship at Victoria's Mildura track.

Left: A young Tai with Vargarna's Peter Jansson, the man who opened the doors to racing in Sweden.

Above left: You can just about see the blue motocross boot that protected Tai's broken right ankle ahead of his first season at Scunthorpe in 2006, when he was fifteen.

Above right: Rye House promoter Len Silver joins in the celebrations after Tai's victory in the British Under 21 Final in 2008.

Below: A big night and a big prize: Tai admiring the Jawa machine he won as the 2008 Premier League Riders' Champion.

Winning . . .

Top left: The first trophy of many: proud Tai shows off the reward for winning the 2005 Western Australian Under 16 Championship.

Top right: Another big step – Tai won the British Under 18 Championship in both 2007 and 2008.

Centre right: Tai is the first speedway rider to be presented with the RAC's prestigious Torrens Trophy, in this case by nominations committee chairman Barrie Baxter, March 2019.

(© Royal Automobile Club)

Below left: A dream fulfilled as Tai becomes World Champion for the first time in 2013. *(© Andi Gordon/Monster Energy)*

Left: Flat out, and leading the way – a superb shot of Tai in full-throttle mode.

(© Andi Gordon/ Monster Energy)

Right: The view of Tai that most of his opponents are familiar with . . .

(© Andi Gordon/ Monster Energy)

Left: Tai during the Warsaw GP of Poland meeting, May 2019. In the following month he broke his back in a crash during a meeting at Wroclaw.

(© Andi Gordon/ Monster Energy)

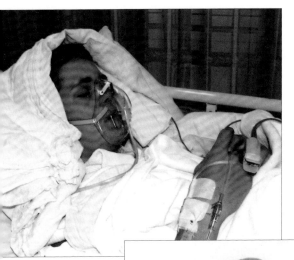

Left: A couple of weeks before leaving Perth for the UK and there are worries Tai won't be able to make it after breaking his leg at the trampoline centre.

Right: The Woffinden family – Tai, Faye and Rylee-Cru.

(© Author's collection)

Left: And then there were four: Faye with daughter Calle, born in December 2019.

(© Author's collection)

Above: World title number three at the Torun GP of Poland on 6 October 2018. *(Andi Gordon/Monster Energy)*

Right: Tai in hospital after breaking his hand during a race in Gorzow in October 2020. The injury forced him out of the Speedway of Nations Final.
(© Author's collection)

Left: Unlike his race bikes, this one had brakes. Out shopping in Wroclaw, where Tai and family lived throughout the 2020 Covid-19 pandemic.
(© Ana Bartkowska)

But 2015, we were on a mission and no one was going to stop me.

The season had got off to an embarrassing start, embarrassing for speedway, in the most striking venue of all at Poland's National Stadium in Warsaw.

I ended up on five points but that wasn't quite as disastrous as it might look in the history books, because the showpiece opener had to be called off after only twelve races in front of the Polish president, Bronislaw Komorowski, the ex-president, Alexander Kwasniewski, and Lech Walesa, the dockyard electrician who became leader of his country and a Nobel Peace prize winner.

When all the riders got together and forced the organisers to cancel that Warsaw meeting it was the best thing we ever did. We were lucky that no one was seriously injured and we had to threaten to refuse to ride after Andreas Jonsson twisted his knee, Troy Batchelor crashed twice in three outings, and 2012 World Champion Chris Holder smashed into the fence while riding unchallenged in his third race.

Thomas H. Jonasson and Nicki Pedersen were the only two riders to practise on the Friday and the track staff worked throughout the night to try to improve track conditions.

Chris 'Bomber' Harris and Nicki Pedersen went out on the Saturday morning and both of them seemed to think it was okay.

Bomber would probably have loved the conditions because that's when he's at his best, but Nicki came back into the pits and said, 'I'm sorry, boys.'

When we did start the meeting he had a shit race.

We delivered an ultimatum after twelve races and, sensibly, referee Jim Lawrence and the FIM jury called it off before someone got badly hurt.

In fairness to everyone involved, since that night, the standard of the temporary tracks, those built in stadia that don't have a permanent circuit, has improved massively.

I went into the lead in the second round in Finland, finishing runner-up to Nicki Pedersen but had a bit of a scare when my shoulder, which had been a problem for a while, popped out in each of my last two races.

That lead was never surrendered and when Greg Hancock trailed at the back in the semi-final at Torun, it was all over.

The Marian Rose Arena has been kind to me over the years – I've won each of my three gold medals there – but it's a track that I can't seem to get hold of in October when it's a bit cold, a bit wet and has a bit of moisture in the surface. I really seem to struggle there, yet take me there in the summer in the league, and I'll score fifteen points.

My confidence at the beginning of the season and again in Slovenia had been justified, although it was an anti-climax, sealing the title after my worst GP of the season!

I celebrated my 2015 victory with my mates in Australia and I used the three weeks in between to enjoy myself, putting on six kilograms. I was eating food that I wanted to eat, not food that I have to eat to stay fit and alive. I gorged on Indian, Chinese, pizza, all takeaway, all the stuff I shunned during the season.

I slid down once the job was done and when I weighed myself – I take a set of scales in my kit bag – in my hotel room at The Crown in Melbourne, it was like, what? I'd gone from sixty-eight to seventy-four.

* * *

The big talking point of the 2015 Australian Grand Prix for me and most of the riders was when wild card Sam Masters got stuck in after he became the latest rider to clash with Pedersen.

Sam was banned for twenty-eight days and fined 600 euros (the equivalent then of £460 or so). Maybe if they didn't suspend you we'd see a lot more fights, and I'm not too sure whether that would be a good or a bad thing. Everyone spoke about that incident, captured dramatically on TV, and it made all the headlines in Aussie.

The seeds of my 2015 success had been sown in 2014. I learnt a lot from that year, I learnt from my mistakes and it paid off big time.

After winning in 2013 I thought, this is a great opportunity for me to build my image and get my name out there a bit more, thinking that it would bring in more sponsorship.

I took on everything, and when I say I took on everything, if it was a podcast, magazine, a newspaper, whether it be the local Glasgow paper or the one down in Poole, I was doing everything I could. Didn't say no to anything. A guy in Scunthorpe wanted to put my photograph on a bus – went and did that. I was like a kiddie in a sweet shop, I wanted everything you could imagine and I forgot what I did in 2013 to get me to where I was.

I started the 2016 season on the back foot, I wasn't ready for it, I was bit all over the place.

I was about three and a half kilos heavier than I was the year before. I started training too late so I was playing catch up.

I went to the first GP in New Zealand on crutches after I'd crashed twice during Wolverhampton's early season Elite League visit to Leicester, returning to the top-flight for the first time since 1983.

Having shunned business class, unlike some of the other, more sensible, guys, when booking my ticket to Auckland, I tried to get an upgrade at Heathrow, but there was no availability and I had to endure the long flight in standard class, an uncomfortable experience when you have hip, back and foot injuries.

I was dreading the journey, filled myself with strong pain-killers, and it was a long way from the ideal preparation at the beginning of my title defence. Perhaps symptomatic of the way the campaign was going to go.

I suppose it says a lot when I can be so unhappy with a season that saw me fail to get on the rostrum for the only time since becoming a regular GP performer in 2013 – and that was in the very last race of the series. I'd have made it that year too if I hadn't had to sit out the Gorzow GP of Poland after ploughing into the fence at Eastbourne a week earlier. Not surprisingly, I didn't come away from the accident unscathed, breaking one finger in my left hand and dislocating another.

My intention was to ride with a specially adapted clutch lever but after having a jab and ice treatment I couldn't hold on during practice and reluctantly withdrew from the round, the first I'd missed.

As the world number one, I always harboured the desire to successfully defend my crown but 2016 saw Greg Hancock finish ahead of me, and the following year Jason Doyle and Patryk Dudek ensured I had to settle for third.

Jason Doyle had been so unfortunate in 2016 when he was poised to add his name to Australia's list of World Champions, after joining Tony Rickardsson and Jason Crump as the only riders to have stood on top of the podium at three GP rounds in a row in the same calendar year.

He led me by sixteen points going into the penultimate round at Torun, but spent the night in hospital after being the innocent victim of a serious crash with Chris Harris in the third heat, as I mentioned earlier. The cruelty of sport saw Doyley in intensive care and his season was prematurely over when he was on the cusp of being feted as World Champion.

I had the opportunity to cash in on his misfortune, but it was Greg who accepted the challenge, outpointing me twenty-five to nineteen over the last two rounds to claim his fourth world title, albeit in the most controversial of circumstances.

Greg led me by nineteen points ahead of Melbourne, the last round, so short of the biggest turn-up ever, the title was his and he quickly settled things, equalising my first heat win with a victory three races later that left it mathematically impossible to catch and overtake him.

What caused the uproar, though, was heat nine when the World Champion in waiting was adjudged to have deliberately slowed down to allow Chris Holder, one of the Monster Energy boys along with Greg and myself, to pass him and claim a vital race win that helped Chris on his way to the GP win.

Greg was furious that the FIM jury backed the referee's decision to exclude him 'for a breach of the sporting code' and, in protest, he withdrew from the rest of the meeting although, happily, a threatened boycott of his coronation was averted.

Doyley bounced back from his injuries and dominated the 2017 series, accumulating thirty points more than I did and eighteen more than runner-up Dudek.

He won two GPs – in the Czech Republic and Australia – and I won one, at Gorzow in Poland, but his consistency over the twelve rounds was unmatched.

Jason failed to make the top four only twice all season while I only got into the final three times in all, encouragingly including the last two rounds of the year, which at least was a satisfying way to round off an otherwise disappointing GP series.

* * *

I don't think anything particularly went wrong in 2016, it was just one of those years ... you can't be amazing every year!

And, of course, there were personal compensations, the crowning glory being our wedding a week before Christmas. Faye and I had spent three months planning it but that was plain sailing because we both knew exactly what we wanted as we have very similar tastes.

Both of us agreed it should be on the beach and it was such a very special day. A dream wedding, with thousands of petals all over the sand and our friends and family there.

We had a run-through a couple of days earlier with our photographer and celebrant, just to ensure everything would go smoothly. However, there was a fright because as the time for the ceremony approached it did look as if we might have to revise our arrangements because of the wind.

But at 11 am, the time for Faye to walk down the sandy aisle, the wind just died down. We all said it was Dad looking down on us and ensuring nothing could spoil the day. It was a bit freaky because as soon as the ceremony was over, the wind returned!

It will be a special memory for us, but perhaps some of our friends and family won't remember in quite the detail Faye and I do.

When my parents got married, Dad decided that he would give guests a special present, a small piece of cannabis, and we decided we would honour his memory in a similar fashion. We had hash-infused brownies baked especially for the occasion and, what should I say, some of the more elderly members of our congregation were more lively and spritely guests when the music struck up than we might have expected!

* * *

If there was no obvious reason why I couldn't regain my title in 2016, there were many reasons for my 2017 displays, if you can call third place a failure.

Faye sat down with me during the year and laid it on the line: I was wrecking my chance of the world title because I was working too hard on our new home. She reminded me: 'You've got to remember what got you to this place – you're taking it away from your racing!'

She had to tell me to calm down, I was flat out; as soon as I got home after riding in Poland or Sweden, I was on the house straight away. I wouldn't even sit down. I'd come home, work, go to sleep, wake up, work, go back to the airport, basically that was my life for the whole year, humping and knocking down.

We had to replace the roof and the windows, which kind of gives a rough idea of what had to be done. The house, an old farmhouse, is split into two, Faye's mum and dad live in one end and we are in the main house. We hardly had any electricity – Faye was showering by the light of her mobile phone – and there was no heat.

We moved in at the end of May 2017 after the owner had let us carry out renovations before we actually signed the papers and bought it in the July.

Part of the deal was that we could move in to start what we felt was absolutely necessary work. It was character building but it obviously affected my racing, although at the time I said it didn't.

Pete Adams also told me I was doing too much at the house, so did a few other people, and Faye didn't mince her words, but I wanted to get it done as quickly as I could.

I admit it got to the stage where my actual days off were when I was riding and if you have that sort of a workload you've got to be tired physically and mentally.

I was so full blown because Faye was expecting and I wanted to make sure it reached a certain standard before Rylee-Cru was born.

It didn't help that we got broken into a couple of weeks after we moved in while I was in Prague for the Czech GP. At the time Faye didn't want to tell me so I could fully concentrate on my racing, but she had to.

She had been watching the GP at her parents' home and when she arrived back at the house she discovered the break-in. They must have been watching the house and known we had moved in, maybe it was people talking at the pub, word of mouth stuff.

Her parents live about twenty minutes away so her dad jumped into his car to hotfoot it to the house to make sure she was okay.

The intruders had smashed a window and you'd expect them to ransack it but they didn't. Some people break into houses and take what they want, smash the place up and turn all the taps on, they do everything, but this was obviously a targeted job. They came in but they didn't take any laptops, iPads, none of that. They knew what they were coming for: they took jewellery, a bit of cash and some sovereigns I'd been collecting to give to Rylee when she's older. It looked like they knew exactly what they wanted and got away with probably seventeen grand's worth of stuff.

All of this contributed to things that were maybe on my mind in 2017. I'd be at a meeting in Sweden and be on the phone with someone in England working at the house.

Sean, Tracy's dad, would come home from work to do some jobs and call me to ask: 'What do you think about this?' I'm like: 'Oh, I'm just about to go off to my first race, dude. I'll call you back after.'

We had moved from a modern, recent-build in a village about twelve miles away and the big difference is when we did something there it would cost a few hundred quid here and a few hundred quid there; where we moved to it was a few thousand here and a few thousand there. For example, I planted 700 elders and 365 conifers.

Before we bought the farm we went to look at it a few times. It was a shithole but I could see beyond that, I can look at something and see the end product.

I literally came in, looked around and was going, 'Okay, put a fence there and there, separate the stables, fence that off, have a nice back garden there.' I'd walk through the house a couple of times and work out what I wanted to do. We were looking for space and land, land more than anything, and there's twenty-four acres, seventeen stables that we rent out, a floodlit manège and a lake.

When it was finished we had five bedrooms, two living rooms, three bathrooms, and an ideal location, close to East Midlands Airport so I could spend more time with Faye and the girls.

I got my smallholder's licence, so I could have sheep and pigs or whatever I might want. I drew a map of the property and segregated off the paddocks and said, right, that one will have sheep in, that one will have llamas, we'll have chickens and guinea pigs.

I loved every minute working on the place. Sometimes I look outside and I'm like *Wow!*

I built a roundabout so cars could come down the drive, and a barbecue pizza oven. I've got a red telephone box with a concrete floor with Rylee-Cru's baby footprints in it and the date she was born. But what twenty-eight-year-old buys a fucking red telephone box for his house?

The whole of 2017 was hectic, moving house, renovating our new home, getting broken into and expecting our first child. I was also away a lot of the time, the combination of everything making it stressful at times.

The baby was due on 10 November and we were both a little worried in case Faye went into labour early as I had to fly out to Melbourne for the Australian GP and obviously I was concerned about leaving her and possibly missing the birth.

But I did get back in time: Rylee-Cru finally arrived ten days after her due date. Faye was in labour for thirty hours and I was with her and her mum.

Our little one came into the world on 20 November 2017 – ideal timing as I could spend the first few months of her life with her, changing her, bottle feeding her, and helping Faye without worrying about aeroplanes or speedway meetings.

* * *

While work went on at the house, we all started 2018 with zero points, but the difference was I was ready for it again and confident that I could be the first Brit to be a three-time champ.

But, I admit, I must have been a nightmare to live with in the two weeks before the last Grand Prix of the year, the big one in Torun where the title would finally be decided.

Leaving Teterow's Bergring Arena a fortnight earlier, there were ten points between me and challenger Bartosz Zmarzlik.

I don't normally get rattled but, for probably the first time, I was feeling the pressure going into Torun.

Faye and I were bickering because of the pressure and she said that's the worst she had ever seen me.

The Polish and Swedish league fixtures were going ahead as usual and I'd get to a track and I'd be normal, I wouldn't be thinking about it because I was focusing on my job, but when you are sitting at home for two weeks thinking: *I have to do good at Torun, the championship comes down to me riding well in Torun*, it does play on your mind.

You think about it every day, and every day, and every day, you eat yourself up. When the pressure's on it doesn't usually bother me one bit, I actually like it because I perform a bit more under pressure and it hasn't normally affected my private life, just in 2018.

Other years I haven't actually thought too much about it, but this time I knew that the rider I was battling against is there, practising every day at Torun, while I'm sat at home.

People were calling me and saying: 'If there's anything we can do for you to win the championship, let us know.' All I wanted was to be left alone, I was actually outside, laying bricks to put a roof on the cesspit, and people were on the phone, being nice, offering their help, anything, whatever you need, and I'm thinking all I want to do is sit at home and relax.

It's those phone calls and conversations, people in my ear, that's why I always take a break from social media with something like four rounds to go. They are going, 'Oh my God, you are going to be World Champion', yet there are four rounds to go, there's another eighty-four points up for grabs, anything can happen.

I had a ten-point lead, but the week leading up to Torun there were so many people saying different things that I started to think about it too much.

I'd won the title in 2013 after being a fair way back on the leader board and in 2015 it had probably been as comfortable as it will ever be, wrapping everything up before flying off to Australia for the last round at Melbourne's Etihad Stadium.

That year (2018) was unique in that I started off well by winning the opening round at Warsaw's National Stadium.

I knew that the first Grand Prix champion of the year had

failed to go on to be World Champion seventeen times in twenty-two seasons, so the omens weren't on my side.

There were one or two little incidents during the season, like my having an argument with my old Wolves skipper Freddie Lindgren at Prague.

Over the last couple of years, I've broken him down.

I was getting a little bit pissed off about how he was riding, fiercely competitive, like over a three- or four-round period. It got worse and worse and then we collided in the Czech GP final and I waited for him to come off the track and I just pulled him on it.

I put my arm around his head and said, 'That's the last fucking time you do that to me, the last time', and got stuck into him.

I made sure I did it out of view of the cameras, none of the public at the Marketa Stadium or sat on their sofas at home saw anything, and hardly anyone in the pits knew what was going on because I made sure I did it in private.

I didn't hit him but I wanted to. He nearly dropped his trophy because he was getting all stressed. There were two people in between us and then he went, 'Fuck you, dude, fuck you' and I was like 'Why would you say it when you're like five metres away from me and there are two guys in between us?'

Ruling on the collision, the referee said I was in the wrong spot at the wrong time. I didn't really understand what he meant by that, so I waited till Freddie came back off the track and had a go at him, and since then, he's been very different with me.

I actually went on holiday before the Danish GP. At the end of June, Faye, Rylee and myself went to Crete for a week, it was a different approach to normal but I guess it must have worked as I won the meeting and opened up a ten-point lead.

A couple of rounds later, after Cardiff, that lead had doubled and then there was another bust-up with Nicki Pedersen.

He did everything he could to stop me passing him, I thought he had stepped over the line and we clashed on the way back to the pits.

The Grand Prix race director Phil Morris had to jump in to prevent what could have turned really ugly, managing to drag one of my pit crew away when he was hellbent on joining in.

Nicki clashed with Maciej Janowski in the following round in Gorzow. Magic had given Pedersen the finger after they clashed and as he left the circuit thumped him on the back and all hell broke loose in the pits.

Nicki got a 300 euro fine for insulting Morris but they came down heavily on Magic with a fine ten times bigger!

I was left dumbfounded in the Slovenian GP after being turfed out of a race for delaying the start. Neither Zmarzlik nor Janowski, who were also in the race, were ready either when the clock showed 0.00 but the referee, Artur Kusmierz of Poland, only penalised me.

Careful scrutiny of the video of the incident will show clearly that while I had gone over time, so had the two Poles, who were second and third behind me in the overall standings.

I looked at the footage and based on that put in a protest, but the FIM jury ruled that it was out of time and they couldn't reverse the official's decision.

I'd had what you might call a mini slump – Zmarzlik had chipped away at what was a twenty-eight-point lead at one time and closed the gap to nine – but came back with a bang in Teterow in the ninth of the ten rounds, and my German win meant I was, once again, on the brink of being World Champion.

There are guys who use a really ugly tactic that gets up my nose. They jump off and make it look like you've knocked them off, and I hate that. They see a back wheel coming towards them and they get off it. If you are smart with it, which some of them are, you turn your hand on the bike to clip the mudguard and then drop the thing. That's stupid – you should just get off the gas and do a cut back and race.

I'm a racer, in my heart I'm a racer, so when someone does that to me I get really frustrated. There's no point in getting up and whingeing about a particular incident that's happened. It doesn't matter how much you bitch about it, you're not going to stop it.

It takes a lot to wind me up. I'm so chilled, you'd have to swear and push me around a few times before I'd flip. I'm the calmest guy around but if I've got to go, I can go, but someone would probably have to hit me – they'd have to hit me, kick me in the balls and then run like fuck.

I think it can piss off my opponents, like in the last round of the World Championship in Torun in 2018 when I crashed. I could have been in an ambulance on the way to hospital again, the title lost, but I was able to walk off with a really big smile on my face, as if I'd just stepped off Nemesis at Alton Towers.

And it wasn't an act, that was legit. I was laughing about what I'd done. I was like, I can't believe it, I crashed like a junior, like someone in their first meeting.

When I walked up the pit lane, I know I turned to someone and joked: 'Just put my name on that fucking trophy!'

The crash was all my own fault. I was wanting to be a racer and trying to pass Jason Doyle. I wanted to pass him to get into second place but, five years from now, I might sit back and settle for the third place and an extra point if I was on the brink of winning the series again.

CHAPTER 12

ON ENGLISH TRACKS

Very few of the top riders, the Grand Prix guys, those I consider my rivals for world titles, race in the UK.

How times have changed – going back there was a day when every single rider with a dream of becoming World Champion HAD to race in Britain because it was the biggest speedway country in the world.

There were more teams, more riders, more meetings and more races and that's what everyone wanted.

I'm no historian but I've heard that every rider to be crowned World Champion from the very first World Final in 1936 until 1964 – Lionel Van Praag to Barry Briggs – raced for a team in the UK. And even the 1965 number one Bjorn Knutsson had spent five seasons at Southampton and moved to West Ham for the 1964 campaign after the Saints had closed down when their Banister Court stadium was flogged off for housing. So the Swede also learnt his trade on English tracks, more varied in size and shape than those on the continent.

Poland's Jerzy Szczakiel, who was a shock champion in 1973 when he beat Ivan Mauger, who crashed trying to pass him, in a run-off, became the World Champion even though he'd never ridden for a British team, but that was very much a one-off.

Right up until the last one-off World Final in 1994 and the launch of the Grand Prix series a year later, no one else claimed the biggest prize of all without the experience of British tracks and conditions.

There was a time, even going back as recently as 2008, the season before I made my debut for Wolverhampton, when virtually everyone raced here.

That year, eleven of the fifteen GP riders had a British team, and of the other four riders chasing the gold medal, only Rune Holta, who had been born and represented Norway before moving to live in Poland and taking out a Polish licence, hadn't any British experience at all.

The others, even Tomasz Gollob, who was such a hero in his own country that he was said to be Poland's highest-earning sportsman, had come to race in England. He spent three seasons at Ipswich and accepted that he'd become a better rider for it.

In 2019, of my fifteen GP opponents only Jason Doyle was turning out regularly in the Premiership, riding for Swindon. He was the only top rider competing in all three major leagues, the Polish Ekstraliga, the Swedish Elitserien and the Premiership in England.

To be honest, I have no idea how he managed to do that as well as the Grand Prix.

I can't speak for everyone but I'm pretty sure that my reasons for not racing where I lived were the same as most of the others.

Why didn't I do it? Why didn't I compete for England when I was based there?

Let's look at some of the reasons.

There are too many meetings for a start.

If you add them all together with nine, ten, eleven or even twelve Grands Prix a year, I would have been riding in eighty meetings or more a season and that's too many. I wanted fewer meetings rather than more, and that's also why I stopped racing in Sweden as well as Poland and the GPs.

If I crash in the UK because I'm tired and I've raced too many meetings, I would have to miss matches in Poland and that's my living.

So it's deeper than you know.

I'm at a level now in my career where I need to be racing against the fastest and best guys in the world every time I sit on a bike. England is a lesser league because the big names aren't there. The tracks aren't as good, as well prepared or as safe as those in Poland and Sweden, so my risk of getting injured is a lot higher.

We all know and accept that racing has its risks, but I'm minimising the risk. I'm getting rid of the poorer quality of riders and I'm racing in Poland where the rider quality is better, it's a harder league with tougher opposition, the tracks are always better and there are fewer meetings.

Riders generally make far more money in Poland than they do in the UK, at least six times more, so if you want to put that into perspective with someone who works a nine-to-five job in Asda – they can either work for ten pounds an hour there or sixty pounds an hour somewhere else – what would they do? If working conditions were also better and safe at the supermarket offering sixty pounds an hour, what would they do?

I'm not saying every track in GB is rubbish. Wolverhampton, where I spent six years between 2009 and 2014 and a couple of late season months in 2016, which was the last time I raced in the UK league, is a great track.

While I was there, there was a great guy, Alan 'Doc' Bridgett, who was amazing at doing the track and he always has been, but even so he still couldn't get the consistency of it being the same every week.

At a lot of meetings it was, but he was reliant on when the stadium owners would let him get on the track, whether it was at three o'clock on a Monday afternoon or four o'clock. Because it's a greyhound track he couldn't always get on it when he wanted and they always have bookmakers' meetings on a Monday and obviously you can't be trundling around the track in a tractor when the dogs are racing.

Who owns the stadium is totally different between England and Poland and Sweden.

Overseas I can't remember a speedway stadium being used for anything else on a regular basis. Every track in Sweden is a proper speedway track; they don't have anything else on it, no greyhounds, no stock cars, nothing. It's the same in Poland where almost every stadium is primarily a speedway stadium and, naturally, speedway gets priority.

If the track people in Sweden and Poland want to work on getting the best possible racing surface, they can spend as many days as they want doing that. At most places in England they have to fit in with something else, which makes it so much harder.

What time Doc could get on the track at Monmore made a massive difference because of how much water he could get into the surface. Sometimes he'd say, 'It will be a bit slicker today, boys, because I couldn't get on the track for an hour and a half after I was meant to.'

I know you can crash on a well-prepared track because that's the game we are in. There was a time at Wolverhampton when Coventry's Ryan Fisher came up the inside of me and couldn't get round the corner and ran into me, breaking my scaphoid, but out of all my crashes over a four-year period I'd say that 80 per cent of my big crashes were in the UK and most of the rest were in the Grand Prix.

The GP crashes are more easily explained because that is just all out. It's everything to the riders in it; you are trying to win a World Championship so there are going to be times when you crash.

The problem I've always had is that I will never ease off because of the conditions. I put the same effort into a meeting on a wet night at Eastbourne as I do in perfect conditions at a Grand Prix meeting in Torun.

You mustn't ease off because, in my eyes, that is when you crash, and I don't want to be the rider who turns up to meetings and tootles around at half-throttle and finishes third or fails to finish the race at all. I'm always there to win and I'm going to ride like I'm going to win, and I did that in every race up until I was sick of riding in the UK.

You've got tracks like King's Lynn, which was normally grippy but the last few times I went there it was not the same King's Lynn, although it was still a good track.

Every rider is always looking for a smooth track, a track where you know you can go as hard as you want and be safe. Not full of holes or bumps and places where you would hit trouble even though you did nothing wrong.

But then you had to go to places like Eastbourne and Poole. Poole stadium is great, Matt Ford, the owner, is great, and all the riders there were great, but that track could be shit sometimes. You go into the corner and you've got three fucking bloody jumps before you get to the corner! The best way to describe Eastbourne is like an egg. At the bottom of the egg you've got a nice big wide corner. Then you've got the other one, which is really sharp.

Tracks – you go on your track walk and your shoes can be ruined because you are walking on an inch of gunge. The tracks in Poland and Sweden are of a much higher standard than the English ones. It's like the hillbillies have done it in the UK and the professionals have done it in Poland and Sweden. That's the difference. You feel safer in the other countries, but it's not only that, there are other differences.

The first year I came over in 2006, the race format saw the number-one rider on each team have the inside start position in heat one. But in the winter the promoters decided it would be a good idea to change it so that the number one always had the outside gate in his first ride.

In Poland if I have my first race I'll be off the inside gates because I'm number one, so I'd be off gates one or two, and a lesser rider would be off three or four. When I say lesser rider, I'm not saying that those riders are bad, but that they aren't as good as the number-one rider.

In England in the first race of the night, your number one goes off three or four depending who won the toss and you put the lesser riders on the inside. That actually makes that first race in England more dangerous than the first race in Poland.

Well, you've got more chance of making it safer if your good riders are on the inside because they'll get around the corner, but sometimes your number twos will struggle, especially if conditions are a bit tricky. It's no fault of their own that they're on the inside, but you do have to go up the inside at one point.

I had a nasty one at Eastbourne where I broke my left hand in

August 2014 when I was defending my world title. I was lucky to escape with just one broken bone, it could have been a lot worse than it was, but it was caused by track conditions.

I made a start, was in front, drifted up to the corner and hit the dirt line that was like three inches tall, so when I hit it, the bike just took off and I crashed into the fence, and took out three panels; the whole thing looked a mess.

I was battered and bruised, I felt dreadful and my hand and wrist were badly swollen, but I knew I was a lucky man to walk away with nothing more serious. I thought I'd broken bones everywhere because the pain was so horrendous and I was so relieved when the X-rays came back and all I had done was broken a bone in my hand.

I wouldn't have crashed like that anywhere else in the world apart from England because nowhere else would there have been a three-inch line of dirt going into the first corner.

That crash ended my season in the UK. I'd ridden in twenty-five of Wolves' twenty-seven Elite League matches but I was sick of riding in England.

It's all about scoring points, the way it is about runs and wickets in cricket, or hitting the treble and finishing on a double top in darts.

My figures in 2014 told a story. In England: 205 points from 25 matches and 118 rides, an average of only 7.80 out of 12.

In the Swedish Elitserien for Vetlanda I had 12 matches, 125 points from 52 races, an average of 9.43, and in Poland, riding for Wroclaw, I averaged 8.83 in my 12 matches, scoring 139 points from 63 races.

The strength of teams in Poland and Sweden is a lot higher than the UK but look at the percentages (comparing how many points I score to what the maximum would have been).

I managed – Sweden 78.62, Poland 73.54 and England just 62.84.

You could see it from my scores that I was not performing anywhere near as well in the UK as in the two strongest leagues in the world.

Why? Because I didn't want to ride in the UK in 2014. I'd had my fill of England at that time.

Wolverhampton knew of my feelings, but Pete Adams, our manager and the man who had done so much to help me become World Champion, said: 'You can't turn your back on British speedway after you've won your World Championship.'

I didn't want to let him down but I shouldn't have done it and it showed because I rode dreadfully.

Coventry was one of the premier tracks in the UK, they had staged speedway there continuously since re-opening after the end of the Second World War in 1948, and survived several troughs when track after track disappeared as crowds went down and spectator interest waned.

Charles Ochiltree, who ran the track like a military exercise, sold out in 2003 after fifty-six years at the helm and new owners took over. It was first pick for the British Final in the seventies, eighties and nineties and I'm told that even though the meeting was usually initially held on a Wednesday night, the place was rammed with fans queuing at the turnstiles from early afternoon for a 7.30 pm start.

The main Rugby Road on which the stadium stands, was chockablock with cars parked on the grass verges as the big car park invariably filled up hours before the first race.

After the Ochiltrees sold up, the venue was refurbished but it never seemed to be the same and certainly wasn't the magnet it had been as the biggest domestic meeting of the season, aside from a World Final or British Grand Prix. Brandon hosted GP rounds in 1998, 1999 and 2000, but it began to lose much of its lustre and crowd appeal.

It staged its last British Final in 2002 (Scott Nicholls won the first of his seven national titles that year), four years before I started racing in the UK.

I went there for the first time in 2008. Even though it was still something of a showpiece arena, and there was an aura about the place with its big stand, bars and restaurant, the track was dreadful and I don't know how many times I crashed there. Certainly more than I wanted to.

It was not nice to ride, it wasn't somewhere I looked forward to going to. I remember one particular meeting where I made a blinding start and thought I had the race done, but I came up the back straight and was in the fence.

I came into the corner on the inside because it was really slick and they had just watered it. I went backwards into the corner and then hit a dirt line and it flipped me off the back and I landed on my head. The result: concussion and out of the meeting.

CHAPTER 13

ALLEGIANCES

I **can't call myself English or British even though the UK's where I was born and Faye and I own a fantastic house here.**

I didn't go to school here, I hadn't got any friends here and if I wasn't a speedway rider I wouldn't be here.

That's how it is and that's how it always will be, because Australia is my home and that will never change.

But when I slip into my Great Britain speedway team Kevlars I only have one thing in my mind... and that's to win for GB.

I actually had a call to ride, at short notice, for the GB Under 21 side in a mini-test match against club side Plymouth after I'd only ridden three meetings in the UK, so I was obviously on the radar very early.

For some reason, and I can't remember what, I couldn't make it and I then had to wait a little bit longer.

I've had approaches from Australia to switch allegiances: every year someone's saying, 'Why don't you come to ride for us, Tai?

Why don't you come and ride for us, Tai?' I'm talking about people who were involved; I'm not talking people who were fans or people like that. Motorcycling Australia don't really have anything to do with it. They leave it all to the boys in charge.

But I've never gone back on my word to ride for Great Britain and all I want to do is win a gold medal with GB. I've got to admit, though, it was hard seeing the Aussie boys getting ready for the World Cup in their green and yellow Kevlars.

It wasn't easy to become British; it's like me saying to someone reading this, 'You are British but you won't ride as a Brit, now you are South African.'

It wasn't easy because I only ever thought of myself as Australian.

I was too young when I arrived in Australia to even remember England. When I was growing up I didn't spend any time with my family still living there because they were on the other side of the world, so in England my family are my friends, whereas in Aussie it's different. Even Faye said when she was there for the wedding, 'I can't believe how close your group of mates are' because there was like thirty or forty of us that all hang out with each other at weekends. We all go out to do something together, and that's since high school.

My mates didn't care if I was going to be British because they didn't look at speedway, they didn't follow it, they still don't.

I'm just Tai, I'm not a speedway rider, I'm just Tai.

They came out to a couple of GPs (Grands Prix), they came out to Melbourne when I won the championship in 2015, and a couple of the boys, have come over to England to see me.

You're asking someone to say that they are something when they feel that they aren't.

I grew up with Australians, I went surfing with Australians. I went to school in Australia, I learnt about Australian culture.

We didn't learn about World War I or World War II, we learnt about Anzac Day and where the Australians went to fight.

So my whole childhood was Australia, Australia, Australia.

You could put me in the middle of the desert and I'll be able to survive because of what I learnt at school, because that's the stuff they teach you. Surfing, lifesaving, outdoor education. We would go surfing one day, the next we're out building a bonfire and learning how to cook food. That's how it was for me from as far back as I can remember, until I was fifteen and came over to England to ride speedway.

You can edit *Wikipedia*, and Josh Gudgeon, a mate of mine, was messing around on it one day, and, as a joke, edited it to read 'Tai Woffinden is Australian', but someone has changed it back now.

Oh yeah, I can understand fans saying Tai Woffinden is an Australian.

But I told them years ago, 'I'm riding for England, I'm representing England, this is the country I am choosing' and I've stuck by that, I haven't changed my mind.

My decision was made a lot easier than it might have been because of one man ... a guy called Andrew Altoft, from a company called Subspecies.

He was sponsoring Scott Nicholls, he backed 'Bomber' Chris Harris, and he wanted to help me but only wanted to sponsor British riders.

At that time we were broke, had no money, were living in a caravan. My dad was buying diesel from some bloke down the road because it would save us money. I know now if he wasn't buying it from a garage that it's not legit – but I didn't know it then.

Andy was talking about ten thousand quid.

Fucking hell, it was an absolute fortune. Ten thousand quid.

TEN THOUSAND QUID. We were living in a caravan. It was beans on toast, I ate beans on toast every day for eight months. Beans on toast with a bit of cheese on top.

We had a cooker in the van so I cooked it when we were on the way to meetings, cooked on the way home too. All we needed was tins of beans, a loaf of bread, and a block of cheese, and that's literally all I ate. I'm not lying. Dad was the same; Dad used to have curried beans though. The first year we lived at my nan's, there might have been a few cooked meals but definitely when we were living in the next caravan, on the rough estate, that was just beans on toast.

The first three years was pretty much on a shoestring, we couldn't do a lot. There wasn't any going out or anything, just speedway, workshop, speedway, workshop, speedway, workshop, that's all it was. My mum used to bring us meals to eat there as we didn't have time to stop working on the bikes and I'd get her into doing clutch plates for me. Pam, Uncle Dave's wife, would wash my Kevlars in the middle of the night if I needed them the next day.

So when Andy comes round and says: 'Right, I'm going to give you ten grand, we'll do all your bikes, your covers, your mudguards, I'll give you some Subspecies T-shirts,' I couldn't say no to that.

Obviously at that time ten grand would be my biggest sponsor, so he had all the helmets, the Kevlars, logo'ed up. He did me a pit bay when I was reserve at Cardiff and everyone was blown away.

* * *

Every year until the last few, I got closer and closer to going to Australia because of the shit I was going through, the shit that I get and the people who don't really know the half of it.

But if anyone says I don't produce the goods in a Great Britain race jacket they are way out of order.

As I've got older and more mature I have become a better rider. Every year, except 2017, I was always there, riding for Great Britain in the Monster Energy Speedway World Cup and scoring the points.

I have just got on and scored more points, just on a different level. I got 18 and 14 in 2013, 13 and 21 in 2015, 19 in 2016, and in 2018 in the Speedway of Nations, which took over from the World Cup, I got paid 15 out of 18 in the semi-final and 17 out of 18 in the final. I got 14 of our 23 in the semi and 17 out of 21 in the final. It's just doing my job.

I'd have been there in both 2019 and 2020 as well, if I hadn't broken my back riding in in 2019 and then fractured my hand in 2020, and I'm sure I'll be there again this year.

I'll go to the line and I don't even think about whether the guy next to me is Australian, or Polish or Russian. They are just three dudes I have to beat. Simple, isn't it? Some people could complicate it, I am sure they do. You just zone out and do your thing.

I know if I come to the track prepared, have worked on it during the winter and bring my A game on race day, it's good enough to win. I know what I have done prior to getting to the track, so being there is the fun part. The hard part now is being in the gym, training twice a day.

My first meeting for Great Britain was when Jim Lynch was boss, he gave me the opportunity. Everyone slated him for it. They said I was too young. Said I wasn't ready for it.

It wasn't even a test match, it was the World Cup, and you can't get a bigger stage than that. It was at Vojens, Denmark, 2008. In heat seven, I went from last to first.

In the team were Scott Nicholls, Chris Harris, Lee Richardson and Edward Kennett. They treated me as English, apart from me having an Australian accent, giving them shit and winding them up; but that created a good atmosphere, a buzz, because I was messing around.

If you type Tai Woffinden and 2008 World Cup into Google you'll see the race on YouTube. You'll see Jim Lynch, I'm off gate four, and look, he has his head in his hands, thinking, *Fucking hell, here we go*. You can see him thinking, *Come on mate, do me proud!*

It was obviously a big decision from him to put me in at seventeen years old. I probably wasn't riding at World Cup level then, but I find that through my whole career, when I've been given a challenge, I've stepped up to the plate.

You look back at all the World Cups. In 2008 I was too young, I shouldn't have been in it, but I got nine points. It was a couple of weeks before my eighteenth birthday, and nine points for me at that age, at that level, was really good for me, it was really good.

Jim invited me into the World Cup team and I just took it with both hands and went out and enjoyed doing my thing. It was cool to be part of it, it was the next step, another stepping stone, racing in the World Cup.

I was always there, I was always scoring the points, and as I have gotten older and more mature and a better rider, I've just scored more points on a bigger scale. I'm just doing my job.

We'd finished a poor third in the first qualifier at Coventry and Jim took me to Vojens in Denmark for the Race-Off three days later. Again we finished a poor third, we were miles behind Sweden and Poland with 36 points while they had 53 and 50 to go through to the final.

I can't remember any real planning or get-togethers or

anything like that. I think Jim gave a talk in the changing rooms before, but I can't remember anything else. Just rock up and race.

The final was a couple of days later at the same track and I'm fairly sure I stayed over for the final, but I think I was in the pits helping the Aussies. I had an Aussie shirt on as well, so I rode for GB in the World Cup on the Thursday and then was in the pits with the Aussies, with my Aussie shirt on, in the final. Gotta be involved, don't you?

How did I feel when I first raced against Australia?

Same as I feel now. It breaks my heart watching the team put an Aussie race jacket on. It does every year.

The World Cup and the Speedway of Nations is the worst week for me because I stand there and watch my mates put on the Australian race jacket, and I stand there and think, *I wish that was me.*

It doesn't affect me when I'm out on the track with my Great Britain race suit on though, because I can go out there and score nineteen points in the Speedway of Nations. It doesn't matter who I'm riding for, when I get on the bike, that's all irrelevant. I just get out there and do the job I am given to do.

The funny thing that year, Scott (Nicholls), Lee (Richardson) and Bomber (Chris Harris) were all keenly competitive with each other – and Scott and Bomber when they were both in the same team at Coventry as well – and, all of a sudden, they are having to become best mates for the week. They all spoke to each other, but they were fiercely competitive.

I might have actually gone to the first round, which was at Coventry with GB racing against Denmark, the Czechs and Sweden. I wasn't in the team even though Jim had put me in the squad. I think I was in the bar drinking with my Aussie mates, funnily enough, with an Australia hat on. Australia had already won their qualifying round in Poland.

Then Jim called me the next day to say he wanted me in the team for the Race-Off in Denmark, instead of either Simon Stead or Olly Allen, who were both dropped with Eddie Kennett and me coming in.

Jim parted company with the GB Speedway Team after that and Rob Lyon took over in 2009. I didn't know much about him at the time, but he organised a pre-season get-together at King's Lynn sometime in March.

It involved sitting in class and discussing things, practising, bonding together. It was looking like it was a step in the right direction although, personally, I wasn't at that stage because I was still living the dream, racing a dirt bike for a living and partying.

The first day we had a talk in one of the hotel rooms, when Rob went through a lot of things with us.

He showed us a lot of stats and asked if any of us knew when was the last time Great Britain or England had won the World Cup? I didn't have any idea and he told us it was in 1989, more than twenty years ago.

After we'd finished all that, someone asked if we could go ten-pin bowling in the evening and Rob said we could, although much later he told me he did that to test our attitude.

Rob and Chris Louis, who had been a world-class rider and was helping to run his father's club Ipswich, were sharing a room at the Butterfly Hotel, just off the A47, a mile or so from the track and a few miles outside the town centre,

They stayed at the hotel along with four or so of the dozen or so riders who were at the two-day camp: Lee Richardson, James Wright and, maybe, Olly Allen and Danny King. The rest of us,

Lewis Bridger, Chris Harris, Lee Complin, Ben Barker, Eddie Kennett, Adam Roynon and, I think, Simon Stead, ordered one of those stretch limos to take us from the hotel into town. We all jumped in and the drink was flowing, although I have a feeling Roynon stayed on the soft drinks. I was still in that partying stage.

We got back to the hotel and we were still messing around in the car park and somehow I managed to smash a couple of pot plants although I couldn't remember anything about it. No one said anything about it and we all rocked up at the track the following morning to practise.

Rob singled out four of the riders, the ones who had stayed at the hotel, and told them they could go and get ready to practise.

He took the rest of us round the back of the pits and gave us a fucking roasting! He was furious and said the hotel manager complained that there had been a disturbance late at night and some of the plant pots had been smashed.

Rob turned to us all and demanded: 'I want to know who smashed the plant pots?' I owned up and agreed to give him £20 for the damage I'd caused.

Rob then went on to explain why we were there and what he expected of us, how he wanted to make the GB set-up more professional before telling us: 'You don't get three chances with me – you have only got one chance and you have all used that up. Next time, it doesn't matter who you are, you will be out!'

He was clearly upset, especially because it was the first time we had been with him and he felt we had shown him a complete lack of respect. He made it clear that it was up to us whether we stayed or left and we could either work together or go home.

Rob was really organised and I started to see structure when he was involved. The hotels were booked when we got there, there weren't any issues, there was the pre-season testing at King's Lynn, stuff in the classroom. We discussed things, talked about how we could improve, about what we wanted to see. Rob was very professional, he was doing it how it should be done. He was, until Rob Painter's company took over the rights to the Great Britain programme in 2018, the most professional of them all.

It seems that Rob Lyon and the British Speedway Association did not have the same approach and they parted company. If they wouldn't let him do it his way he wasn't interested, because he knew what needed to be done to be successful.

At the end of 2016 I got a lot of grief for saying I didn't want to ride for GB any more. Whilst everyone just waved Rob goodbye – because it was me, they had a go at me, calling me every name under the sun. I could have worked with Rob, for sure.

After Rob Lyon, they went back to Neil Middleditch, who had already done one long stint back at the beginning of the 2000s. I like Middlo, he's a sound bloke, full of life and very busy.

It was different after Rosco, Alun Rossiter, took over from Neil in 2014.

Yes, we got a silver medal in the 2016 World Cup, but it was in Manchester, and we got seeded straight to the final as the hosts. If we hadn't been seeded, we wouldn't have made it because we hadn't got the team to secure a spot in the final.

I had a five-year plan that I put forward to the British Speedway Promoters' Association, but it was not approved.

Many of my suggestions have now been incorporated in the new GB set-up run by Rob Painter and partner Vicky Blackwell. Their blueprint is as close as you can get to my blueprint, and their professionalism has translated into the way the Great Britain speedway team is being run, like a business, as I wanted, and I am sure success will come along.

In the old World Cup you had to take your four best riders but we never had four who could have won it.

Scott Nicholls and 'Bomber' Chris Harris were in the Grand Prix series for years, but how often did they qualify in the top eight? Scott was in it for nine seasons and finished seventh in 2003 and eighth in 2007 but he wasn't in the top eight all the other years.

Bomber had nine full years in the GP series and was sixth in 2010, but out of the top eight every other year and only in the top ten once.

If they hardly ever finished in the top eight of the World Championship they weren't going to be good enough to win the World Cup.

GB relied on them for too many years, unlike Poland. The Polish team that won it in 2016 at Manchester, were part of Marek Cieslak's Under 21 team from five years earlier.

Rob wanted the same thing I wanted once I'd stopped my partying and took everything more seriously. Ten years ago, he wanted the same things that I want now.

After our dismal performance in the 2015 World Cup – we were knocked back into second place in the round at King's Lynn and then knocked out in the Race-Off in Denmark – I wrote to the British Speedway Promoters' with my vision of the future, a plan to turn us from also-rans into, hopefully, the best team in the world.

I wanted pre-season fitness tests for all the potential GB riders over the age of fifteen and for everyone to wear a Polar V800 fitness watch so they could send their personal training results every week to whoever was in charge.

There would be a second fitness test in the middle of March and the results from the first and second tests would give the manager a good idea of who had been working hard in the winter and wanted to be a professional athlete and, more important, who couldn't give a toss about being physically fit.

The records would help choose who should be in the squad, and if one rider couldn't be arsed about working hard in the winter then he shouldn't even be considered for the team. Training shows who is determined to be successful and the best and who isn't.

It might not be what other people wanted and the manager would probably take stick from fans, riders and the keyboard warriors and, short term, it might handicap the chances of doing well in the World Cup.

But it's all about having a real five-year plan.

I put forward a number of ideas to Rosco, but he did not adopt them.

In late March I set up a fitness test for thirty riders. I supplied a cost, address and a personal trainer, Kurt Gibbons at Derby College. I do not know whether the riders were made aware of the event or not, but not a single one turned up! It made me look a complete idiot as my personal trainer had taken time out of his busy schedule.

We all got together at King's Lynn for the World Cup round against Australia, USA and Latvia.

As a group we went for a Nando's in the town centre and I stood up at the end of the table and I told everyone what I thought. I'm saying, 'Mate, we're fucking nowhere. This is what we need to do, we need this, we need this, we need this.' I told them all the things that made me successful and I told them all how it needs to be done, how we're gonna do it, how we're gonna move forward.

One of the riders pipes up: 'Well, you don't have to be fit to ride speedway, you just have to have a good engine underneath you.'

I wasn't having it and let him have it: 'Well, I'm sorry, mate, a good engine didn't fucking help me in my 2010 World Championship from Cardiff onwards. That's a load of shit, I'm living proof that if you work hard, you can be successful.'

That's the kind of thing I was battling against. It's not good enough to be content riding Premiership and Championship (Elite and Premier League as it was then), aiming to be a British champion, if on the world stage you are shit. Why do I even waste my breath? I waste my breath because I want to be successful, I want to win a World Cup.

I've got my World Championship-winning bikes in the garage and I contemplated keeping my bikes from the 2016 World Cup and the 2018 Speedway of Nations but I'm not keeping them because I came second.

My gold medals are in the safe but I didn't even keep my silver medal from the World Cup. I gave it away to a young girl in the crowd. The enjoyment she might still be having from that medal means more to me, that she can be happy every time she looks at it because I've given her my medal.

I got slated for it, saying it was disrespectful, that I don't care about Team GB. Sorry, I just carried the team to a silver medal. It's just a medal? I saw her in the crowd, a beautiful little girl, and asked people to bring her down to the rostrum. The smile on her face, stood on the podium with my medal, priceless. Priceless.

Going back to my blueprint ... I wanted a riding/training camp in Croatia over the last week in February and the first week in March. Okay, we could have a good time together but that wouldn't mean getting drunk every night and eating the wrong food; you don't need to be out of your head to enjoy yourself.

I also wanted a one-week training camp, possibly in the French

Alps with Len Silver, my promoter at Rye House in 2007 and 2008 and a former World Cup-winning Great Britain manager who runs his own skiing travel business. It's great to train at high altitude because oxygen is thinner there, and we could also use it as a big promotional tool. It would be good PR and by that I mean with mainstream media and not the speedway media.

The other side of my blueprint was to take Team GB away from the club owners' control.

It should be run as a business, its own company with dedicated bank accounts.

The income could come from sponsors and we should be looking for an agent and PR company that doesn't have any current ties with the sport. They will only be in it for the money, which means they will work on getting bigger deals with sponsors so they have a decent percentage. It will benefit everyone as it is in their best interest to bring bigger deals to the table.

I'll never forget what happened at Vojens when we were there in 2015 for the Race-Off round.

I called Rob Lyon and told him: 'Mate, I'm stood outside a fucking kebab shop. Rosco's brought us to a fucking pizza and kebab shop, in between practice and racing, at a World Championship event.

'Do you know what I mean? And now they're on TV, calling us fucking athletes? Come on. I didn't eat anything. I went back to the van and had a fucking protein shake, while all the others fucking stuffed their faces with pizza and kebabs.'

That was after practice in the morning, and I said, 'Right Rosco, where are we all going for lunch?'

'We'll get in the van and go find a place.'

I think I took a car, because there wasn't room in the van, and then we went into the town. Vojens is tiny and we walked around and the best place we could find was a kebab shop. I was furious, I was fuming. I was so pissed off. The last time I'd had a kebab before a meeting was probably when I was seventeen or something like that.

Rosco is a nice guy, a real nice guy, and I get on well with him, but we have different views about speedway.

I believed Rob was the right guy. I wrote to the British Speedway Promoters' Association telling them: 'You guys need to make the decision about Rob Lyon ideally this month, this will give us enough time to plan and put together everything I have proposed over next month rather than October when the new Team GB manager will be voted for.

'If it is left until that point it will be too late to organise everything, especially with sponsorship as companies will start to spend their budgets in the next few months, and by then we would have already missed our fitness test, and riders will have an option to pull out as the contracts will not be ready to state it is compulsory.

'I am willing to work alongside anyone providing that it is done properly and professional as above.

'Contracts will be written up to all British riders and list events that will be compulsory, if they do not co-operate they will be penalised, which will mean they will not get the opportunity to ride in British Under 21s, British Championship or in the Team GB squad.

'Also they will have to pay a penalty which will be payable to the company that is going to fund Team GB.'

I added: 'I would just like to clear up any confusion with the comment I made after the World Cup Race-Off. It was not a threat or blackmail!

'I was simply speaking from the heart and what I said was

100 per cent true. If I cannot be a part of making Team GB a World Championship-winning team I don't want to be a part of it. This will not just benefit Team GB it will benefit British speedway as a whole.'

If you have a fitness test in October and another in March you can tell which rider has worked hard in the winter. That makes it easier when it comes to picking a team because you have irrefutable facts. There might be one guy who's a bit more talented but he spends the winter sat at home, watching TV, checking Facebook. Whereas the other guy is in the gym working his arse off. You narrow it down to those who want it and work for it and those who don't give a toss.

Nothing happened and towards the end of the 2016 season I'd made up my mind that I wouldn't carry on until there were dramatic changes.

I made my decision public saying: 'I've made a decision to sit out the 2017 World Cup but I remain proud to represent Great Britain in the Grand Prix.

'We'll see where we are at in 2018, who knows I may be back for that.'

And just to avoid any misinterpretation of my motives I added: 'I can also confirm I won't be looking to switch nationalities and ride for Australia, that's not part of my thinking.'

I wanted to kill that suggestion stone dead even though, in speedway, it's pretty simple to do so.

It wasn't only the way GB was organised, it was everything. Every year I had grief trying to get my expenses paid even though I do what's right.

I had problems from the first World Cup I did in 2008, trying to get paid, or rather trying to claim back my expenses, because we don't get paid to do the World Cup.

Riders from Poland, Denmark and Sweden, they get paid all their expenses and they also get points money.

When I race in Poland for a Polish club I get paid for however many points I score. It's the same in Sweden and it was the same when I rode for Wolverhampton, I got points money.

But when you race for Great Britain you get fuck-all. Why should racing for Team GB be any different?

I've never been paid points money, you get your expenses back but that's it. You spend a week riding for nothing, everyone does.

You will get the dickheads who say it shouldn't be about money and it should be about representing your country, but it's my job. It's how I pay for the shopping, it's how I pay my mortgage, how I pay for my food.

We used to take fruit and water, and packs and that, so we didn't have to buy stuff when we were out. So for those first few years, my expenses were really low.

Even so it was always a problem. They were always asking questions. 'Why have you invoiced us for this? Why have you invoiced us for that? Why are you claiming back this food?'

It cost me from the World Cup week starting to a World Cup week finishing and I'm not getting paid. I'm claiming back for all that, because I'm not getting any money. So if we stop at the BP and get a bottle of Coke and a bottle of water. I'm claiming back a bottle of Coke, a bottle of water. Because it's the World Cup and I'm riding for nothing. If I was at home, I wouldn't be buying that, so why should I pay for it? Why should I be out of pocket to ride for Great Britain. Every year it got worse and worse. They were asking more and more questions. What you have got to remember is, I'm growing as an athlete, as a businessman.

As a rider, my engine bills were getting bigger. I'm going to better tuners.

I've never claimed back an engine bill. To this day all the Polish boys get their engines serviced before every World Cup. Every rider. And the Polish people pay for that. I couldn't even imagine what would have been said if I sent in an engine bill for a service. I serviced my engine before the World Cup and the Speedway of Nations every year.

I sent them to Peter Johns who services them for me, so they're fresh for the World Cup. It works out to be 400 quid each engine, and you take three to the World Cup.

When Mum was doing my stuff, I was having hassle getting expenses back and explaining why we did this, and why we did that. All that shit. And she'd say: 'Oh Tai, I don't think we can put this through.' And I'd be like: 'Put it through because we spent that this week. And there's a reason why we're here this week. For them. So they can pay me back what we've spent. I'm not being out of pocket for something I'm not getting paid for doing.'

My expenses would be something like £2,700 for World Cup week. Flights, mechanics, food, diesel. I'm competing for them, I'm not getting any money for it.

My mum looked after me for twenty-one years and would buy the chicken and vegetables to feed me, and these guys haven't looked after me for two minutes, they never have. So why should I do anything for them? I'm competing for GB so the least they can do is pay me back what it has cost me to get to the World Cup.

We had the qualifying round at King's Lynn and finished runners-up so had to go into the Race-Off in Denmark in 2015. At the end of the King's Lynn meeting I took the engine out of the bike, washed it, went to the airport and flew the next morning with my mechanic and two of my engines, my best two engines, to ride and try and help GB reach the final.

I scored twenty-one of our forty-three points but we only finished second behind Poland and didn't get to the final and four months later they said: 'Why didn't you tell us that you were taking this mechanic and why did you send two engines on the plane?'

I told them: 'Hang on, I'm going to a World Cup, I scored twenty-one points out of twenty-one, didn't drop a single point, and you're questioning why I took my two best engines!'

I wasn't racing in England that season, I was only racing in Poland and Sweden and doing the Grand Prix. I had to go and race in two different countries, one of my vans had to be driven from Poland, where it was based, to Denmark to do the Race-Off at Vojens, and my Swedish van had to be driven to England for the King's Lynn round because I didn't have any machinery in England as I wasn't racing there.

All my stuff is in Poland and Sweden. The British Speedway Promoters Association are saying: 'We're not happy that you didn't tell us about having to bring your bikes from Sweden to England.'

What was I expected to do?

Every year I had to call my Wolverhampton promoter Chris Van Straaten to tell him I'd not been paid and every year he'd eventually sort it out. I'd have been better just sending the expenses to him and save a lot of time and hassle.

Over time it did get easier and the only beef I had in 2016 was when we were runners-up behind Poland.

As I said, I'd waive my expenses but I did expect a decent slice of the prize money for finishing second as I'd scored nineteen of our thirty-two points.

Instead, as I discovered to my cost, Rosco had decided that everyone would get an equal share, so even though I got almost half of our points, I got exactly the same as Danny King (five points), Craig Cook (five) and Robert Lambert (three), which I didn't think was fair. I couldn't understand why the total prize fund wasn't just spread in relation to what we had all scored.

I said that I might be back and as soon as Rob Painter won the franchise to run the GB team in 2018 he called me up. We had a meeting and he outlined his plans and his thoughts and I was back on board, totally committed again and determined to get that gold medal I still yearn for.

We came close in 2018 and we were the real winners, but because of the rules we missed out to Russia in the Speedway of Nations. I got gold and the Grand Prix World title and should have had another gold medal and world title for the Speedway of Nations as we scored more points than Russia, but the regulations said the title was decided on one last race and finishing second and third was better than winning the race. We should have won and would have done but for a ludicrous rule that saw Russia winning the gold medal despite scoring fewer points than us.

How can that happen? And would it ever happen in another sport?

Just imagine any country winning football's World Cup despite scoring one goal fewer than their opponents in the final, or a nation being crowned cricket's World Cup winners after getting less runs than the opposition. Wouldn't happen, would it? Yet it did in the Speedway of Nations final in 2018, when Russia scored forty-five points over the two days and we got forty-six but had to settle for the silver medal!

Normally I can't tell people how I really think, I can't speak my mind, because if I do I'll get shit. There's all those different words they like to use: arrogant, or cocky or big-headed.

But I'm not that person, I'm just passionate about what I'm trying to achieve.

CHAPTER 14

MAKING A DIFFERENCE

I **defy anyone to visit a hospital full of seriously ill kids and not be moved to tears.**

In the summer of 2014 I travelled down to London to Great Ormond Street Children's Hospital (GOSH) and left with plenty on my mind and with a burning conviction. I had only been there for ten minutes or so and I knew I had made the right choice: GOSH would be my 2014–15 personal charity.

After Dad died in 2010, I'd wanted to do something to help others suffering from the dreadful disease that killed him. Through the twenty-four hours before Dad actually passed, me and Mum felt we wouldn't wish that on our worst enemy. It wasn't even twenty-four hours, it was twelve hours, but it felt like the longest day of our lives, it actually felt like weeks.

It was so horrible to see how he was as his life ebbed away. Everyone prays that the end will come peacefully, but Dad was tormented with excruciating pain, so I thought if I could raise some money it could be put towards helping people not having to go through what we did.

The first charity I chose to support back then was Cancer Research UK. I decided that I would do a sponsored cycle ride from my home track at Wolverhampton to Cardiff in the week of the 2013 British Grand Prix.

I was joined on the final leg to Cardiff by the Welsh Paralympic cyclist Mark Colbourne, who heard of my plans after his father died from stomach cancer in 2012. He got in touch and said he would like to join me on the second leg and I was grateful to have his company.

Mark broke his back in a paragliding accident in 2009, which left him with paralysis in his legs, and he spent twelve months learning how to walk again.

He took up cycling in 2010, around the time that Dad died, and adapted swiftly enough to win two medals at the 2012 Paralympic Games in London, a silver in the one kilometre sprint and then the gold in the three kilometres individual pursuit. Mark joined me for the final 15-mile stretch of what was a 138-mile ride.

I set off from Monmore Green on the Monday night, after scoring thirteen, paid fourteen, from my five rides against Birmingham, disappointed that we had not only surrendered our 100 per cent home record but seen the Brummies, having ridden two fewer matches than us, close the gap at the top of the Elite League to three points.

I soon forgot about what had happened, though, when I got on the bike and started pedalling away with Cardiff's Millennium Stadium my eventual destination.

I wouldn't say I was a keen cyclist, but once I set myself a challenge, I don't think about anything apart from what I am going to do in that present moment.

There was one day when it started to rain a bit and when you are five hours into your ride, the last hour going up hills in the rain, it's a case of gritting your teeth and grinding away, getting through it.

I stopped off at a velodrome to meet up with Mark and he helped me during the last miles. When I'm doing something, whether it's a race or a charity cycle ride, I'm the type of person that when I'm in the zone, I'm in the zone – once I'm seated on the bike I'll get it done and you won't be able to stop me from doing it.

There was a proper feeling of satisfaction when I finally got to Cardiff. I'd raised around £30,000 when my original target was £20,000, and I was more than happy with my first fund-raising effort when I finally handed over the cheque at Scunthorpe Speedway.

I wanted to do something more for charity the following year and I thought, okay, adults dealing with an illness is one thing, but what must it be like for a child and their family having to deal with a cancerous tumour or other life-threatening or life-changing disease? That must be a lot harder, not only for the child but for the whole family; it's got to be a lot harder for kids to handle.

That's why I chose Great Ormond Street Hospital Children's Charity.

It's just a great hospital, it's very well known throughout Britain and they don't just take kids from the UK, they have them from different parts of the world as well.

I can't remember how I came to think about GOSH as my charity but maybe Pete Adams mentioned it when we first started discussing what I wanted to do. Whenever I had an idea, thought about doing something, I'd always talk to Pete about it.

One of his friends, Simon Ewins, was Business Development and Responsibility Director for Whitbread, and he was heavily involved in a major project by the company's Hotels and Restaurants group, which has more than 800 hotels and 421 restaurants country-wide, to build the Premier Inn Clinical Building within GOSH.

Simon had helped support my cancer-fundraising bike ride by offering me free accommodation and arranging for an ice bath at their Premier Inn in Ross-on-Wye about halfway between Wolverhampton and Cardiff.

Whitbread Hotels and Restaurants had announced GOSH as their nominated charity in 2012 and pledged £7.5 million to fund a major development programme. Simon and Pete helped arrange meetings with the GOSH fund-raising team and stepped in with advice on how we could maximise our efforts.

Great Ormond Street Hospital first opened on Valentine's Day, 1852, with ten beds, as England's first children's hospital, and today 619 children and young people are admitted for life-changing treatments. There's an old part of the hospital, where there are still three or four patients to a room and they are going through the process of changing to single en-suite rooms.

The Premier Inn Clinical Building, which embraces new operating theatres, intensive-care facilities for some of the sickest patients, and self-contained en-suite bedrooms, was officially opened in January 2018. It completed the seven-storey Mittal Children's Medical Centre that replaced the top four floors of the old cardiac wing, some of the hospital's oldest facilities, with a modern, world-class environment for staff and patients.

I visited the hospital and was able to meet patients, including the lovely little Ella Chadwick, in the Eagle Ward, which treats children with kidney problems.

She was probably six or seven years old at the time (2014) and was a beautiful little one who had spent most of her life in hospitals, much of it in the Royal Manchester Children's Hospital. She took a shine to me and I took a shine to her and we were photographed together during my visit. Ella was one of the patients I was allowed to spend time with, although there were some children in isolation that you can't go in and hug because they don't want you to possibly pass on an infection.

In November 2018, Ella featured in *Pride of Britain*, ITV's showing of the *Daily Mirror*'s awards of the same name, and was presented with a Child of Courage award by *The X Factor*'s Dermot O'Leary, Simon Cowell, Louis Tomlinson, Robbie Williams and Ayda Field.

Her inspirational story left millions of viewers wiping a tear from their eyes as they heard that Ella, who has had years of dialysis, had undergone more than forty operations, including kidney transplants. Yet despite her struggles, she has a generous heart, an infectious positivity and a zest for life, raising thousands for charity and putting smiles on poorly children's faces.

I was delighted to see Ella appearing on the show and, from my own experience, it's impossible to spend any length of time in places like the medical centre, see sick kids, and not leave determined that you will try to do something to help. Their courage resonates with you and is something you won't forget

It also motivates you to push that little bit harder to raise funds.

I was really inspired by the children I met, they all face tough challenges with amazing bravery, and I also saw, first hand, how important it is to have a modern bedroom with space for Mum or Dad to have a bit of privacy, to be alone with their son or daughter.

The cost of each bedroom, with accommodation so that a parent can stay overnight, was £100,000, and that became my target.

I'd raised around £30,000 for Cancer Research UK in 2013 but I wanted this to be a lot bigger. It's mad to raise that amount but I resolved that, with the help from a speedway community that is so special, I would do it. When I spoke to the guys at our meetings, from day one they said that I needed to do bucket collections. But they are not usually very successful. They still bring in money but aren't the ideal way to raise really significant amounts. Maybe a few hundred pounds, maybe even a couple of thousand.

I told them the speedway fan base is very loving and kind-hearted, and I was proved to be spot-on with my confidence in them.

I'd decided that I would do a sponsored cycle ride again, this time the much shorter distance from Newport to the Millennium Stadium, on the Friday, practice day. Fans from every club in the country were invited to come and join us on that fifteen-mile stretch between the two Welsh cities.

GOSH were out in force on the Saturday, they had collecting tins and buckets virtually everywhere you turned in Cardiff centre, including the Fans Zone, which had moved to a new location in Wood Street, virtually in the shadow of the stadium and at the heart of the city centre.

Their collectors were amazing but they were stunned at how much was raised from that day where I guess practically every person in the GP crowd must have put something into the collecting cans and buckets.

BSI, the GP rights-holders, did their part as well, allowing the announcer to publicise our efforts over the tannoy, and when all the monies were eventually totted up the total was close to £50,000.

The final tally was given an unexpected and major boost when a lady called Heather Vitty sent a message to Simon, who was at the meeting, asking if she could see him as she wanted to make a special donation to the fund.

She had been an avid Bradford fan until the Dukes dropped out of league racing at the end of 1997, but like so many other fans made the pilgrimage to Cardiff after it became the annual home of the British GP in 2001.

When she and Simon met up she revealed that she wanted to hand over a cheque for £5,000 and then offered to double it if, as a fortieth birthday present, her husband Ian could meet and be photographed with me and his favourite riders, Greg Hancock, who actually won the meeting, and Nicki Pedersen.

Heather was a director of a Leeds-based HR business and among their recently acquired clients was GOSH. She told me: 'It wasn't until I saw what you were doing that I thought it would be a very nice idea. You have got to do something for other people.'

Arrangements were made for us to all come together at the post-meeting press conference and the newly crowned British GP champ Greg and myself handed Ian an extra surprise when we penned a personal Happy Birthday message on the steel shoes we had worn during the meeting.

My fund-raising was always meant to be over a calendar year with the British GP, a focal point, and I always knew I would reach my goal.

There are hundreds, thousands, of ways to raise money for a charity and I used the bike ride, the collections and social media.

It can be hard work at times but when you do achieve what

you set out to do it's very satisfying and more so when you see the difference your efforts have made. You can never do it without the help of those generous people who have been involved, especially the speedway supporters who contributed so much, and you do get a warm feeling about it.

It's cool to think some of those kids who were three to four in a ward with no privacy other than being able to draw the curtains around their beds, are now able to be in their own room where their parents can have all the privacy they want and need.

Helping to make sure the families are as happy as they can be in their circumstances means a lot to me, especially now that Faye and I have Rylee-Cru and Calle we know how precious a child is.

When I started my challenge, I knew it wouldn't be easy, but I've met some amazing children whose lives have been saved by GOSH and I was delighted to be able to exceed my initial target and hand over a cheque for £105,501 at the Premier Inn in the centre of Birmingham.

At the formal handing-over Rachael Willis-Fleming, spokesperson at Great Ormond Street Hospital Children's Charity, paid her own warm tribute to the supporters who had made it all possible: 'We have been overwhelmed by the incredible generosity of the speedway community whose support will help us make a real difference.'

Each and every one of those fans who dipped into their own pockets can be proud of the new environment the kids have at GOSH.

I know that I can make a difference, even if it is only in a small way, and while I was having treatment at the Nottingham MS Therapy Centre – I was in the hyperbaric oxygen chamber in

June trying to help my broken back heal a little faster – I spotted that they were planning to build an extension.

There was a poster appealing for financial support, so I set up a JustGiving page online to try and get £2,000 and it didn't take long before we were close to the target.

I wanted to do another big charity effort and discussions were already in the pipeline about having a crack at something else for GOSH, but unfortunately the coronavirus outbreak took over, although I did finally think of a way I could help this year. Hopefully there might be an opportunity when our lives get back to something like normal again, but that didn't mean I couldn't do something to help during the restrictions we have all faced.

I got in touch with GOSH again during the 2020–1 winter after spending most of 2020 living almost in isolation in Poland. They told me that were making this Sight and Sound Centre and I felt it was my job to help them do that.

Life must be quite scary for a young child who can't hear anything or has problems with their sight. As a professional racer, I depend on my sight and hearing to give me a competitive edge, so I can't imagine how tough it must be for kids experiencing those conditions.

We raised £105,000 the last time and it was only fair to try to double that. GOSH is my charity and I thought it was time to do something else to help them again. We don't know what the future holds for any of us and I was determined to help if I could. One of my original plans was to get another two or three well-known guys involved and try to get half a million between us.

I'm friends with Alex Lowes, the former British Superbike champion and current World Superbike road racer, his twin brother Sam, who is racing in Moto2, and Motocross World Championship competitor Tommy Searle. Obviously, with the pandemic there was no way we could get together so I came up with an alternative which meant I didn't even have to leave my home!

I enjoy cycling, it keeps me fit and healthy and it gets me out of the house for a few hours – usually. So I plumped for a twenty-four-hour pushbike ride – riding twenty-four hours non-stop on a static bike in my own fitness studio, and to show it live, all twenty-four hours of it, on Facebook.

I spent the build-up to the fund-raiser, which was being done at the end of February, doing interviews with everyone I could think of – the weekly *Speedway Star*, *Cycling Weekly*, and other magazines as well as TV stations, and I managed to get quite a few of my celebrity pals to join me for periods of the ride, while at the same time I would talk to friends and fans from all over the world, hoping everyone would help to reach my £200,000 target.

I pushed the line that every little contribution would help, and told *Speedway Star*: 'People drive to work every day and grab a cup of coffee that probably costs a couple of quid or so. If they just give up that coffee for one day and donate that cost of a cup of coffee – if my ninety-odd thousand Instagram followers did that, there's your £200,000! If people like the story of what I am doing, even if it isn't a cup of coffee on the way home from work, it might be a chocolate bar for 80p, please don't have a chocolate bar and instead donate that 80p to GOSH. When I did the last one in 2014 there was one big donation of £10,000, but some people put in ten pence and at the end of the day it all adds up. It's all for the cause, every penny is to help these children.

'The speedway fans were tremendous and so generous, but this time, for me it's not just about asking the speedway fans for their support, it's about making this reach a wider audience than speedway. That's the direction I am trying to go. A lot of people think £200,000 is a lot of money to raise but it is do-able if we are getting close but not quite there, I'll stay on the bike till I'm there. I won't give up, that's not me.'

Between us, Zwift, the online cycling and running physical training programme that enables users to interact, train and compete in a virtual world, GOSH and myself managed to get a host of household sporting names to join in.

People like Watford and ex-England goalkeeper Ben Foster; former F1 driver Mark Webber (a long-time speedway fan); fellow Australian, motorcycle Grand Prix racer Jack Miller; Moto GP star Cal Crutchlow; recently retired Rotherham cycling brothers Dean and Russ Downing who had helped to plan the route when the Tour de France visited Yorkshire; another cyclist, Matt Stephens, who represented Great Britain in the 1992 Olympics road race in Barcelona; Isle of Man TT legend John McGuinness (another speedway follower, who rarely misses a meeting at Belle Vue); seven-times world motorcycle trials champion Dougie Lampkin; boxer Carl Froch, the former super-middleweight world champion; and a host of my speedway rivals all agreed to lend their weight to the project, either by riding or chatting as I pedalled away.

I started at 8.30 am on Monday 1 February and the plan was to carry on throughout the night, talking to guys in Australia when it was dark in England, and then finish at 8.30 am on Tuesday 2 February.

Unfortunately, problems struck some thirteen and a half hours into the ride at around 10.30 on the Monday night, and

I had to give up. That's the first time I have said I was going to do something for charity and haven't done it. I was very pissed off but I will do it again although it will probably have to wait until the end of this season because I won't have time to do it mid-year.

There's a difference between cycling for twenty-four hours outdoors, on the roads, and doing twenty-four hours on a static bike: it's a lot harder on a stationary bike.

What makes it more frustrating is that until about an hour before I had to step off the bike, I was cruising. I had a little bit of knee pain but nothing to worry about. But then my foot started hurting.

One of my legs, the right one, is shorter than the other, five millimetres shorter, and I have an insert in my shoe. When I stand up on the pedals while cycling, my ankle rolls in with every revolution, and a repetitive movement like that while doing 85 revolutions per minute on average is a lot of strain and it got to the stage where my ankle would have swollen up inside the shoe. I just could not go on.

One of my Australian cycling friends is Rohan Dennis, the 2018 and 2019 men's world individual time trial champion and currently a member of the UCI World Team Ineos Grenadiers and a four-times Tour de France participant, and I'm sure he will be able to give me some advice to make sure I can get through the full twenty-four hours next time.

There are still some adjustments I can make to my cycling shoes for when I get back on the bike to do the ride again. I'm not going to carry on from where I was forced to stop – I am determined to do the twenty-four hours again and complete the challenge for such a good cause.

CHAPTER 15

CONTROVERSIAL CHARACTERS

Every sport has its controversial characters – so step forward three-time World Champion Nicki Pedersen.

There's a video of Poland's Krzysztof Kasprzak fighting off his pit crew and track staff as he breaks into a sprint to confront Pedersen after he'd knocked him off in the final Grand Prix of 2014 at Torun that has been viewed 273,000 times.

There's another on YouTube of a race in Sweden in 2015 that has had close to 200,000 viewings and shows one of his furious rivals dashing down the track and hurling himself at the Dane as he sits on his bike, knocking him down to the track with a perfect body slam.

You'll almost certainly be able to find other clips that feature incidents involving Nicki, all you need to do is google his name and you can probably spend an evening watching a series of incidents in which he features in hairy moments.

But it is that video mentioned above that is the most astonishing because his attacker is four-times World Champion Greg Hancock, speedway's Mr Nice Guy, a gentleman and one of the most composed and calm-headed riders there's ever been on the world circuit.

Greg doesn't do red mist and no one could remember seeing him lose his rag, but the camera follows him as he finally lets it all out and hurls himself at his long-time GP opponent.

It caused something of a sensation, not because Pedersen was the victim and on the receiving end of an angry attack – but because the perpetrator was someone with an almost perfect record, especially when it came to fisticuffs. Greg would usually pick himself up and dust himself down after every track incident, and there are bound to be them, but this time he definitely blew his top.

I've found Nicki to be a proper Jekyll and Hyde. He's Dr Henry Jekyll when he's away from the track, someone who's easy to like and someone you would probably want to make friends with if you didn't know the other side of his character and personality.

But when he slips into his Kevlars, jumps on a bike and heads towards the tapes at every big meeting, he becomes fiercely competitive. On the track I find his riding unconventional and his attitude totally focused on winning. Not my favourite rival.

That night in Sweden, Greg got that frustrated with him, he ran after and tackled him off his bike – you should go and find it online.

The crowds either loved him or hated him in the GPs, a man controversially riding on the edge.

Yes, there is a flip side to him, you could be sitting in the pub, or at the airport waiting for a flight, and he's the nicest guy – when he's away from the track, he's really the nicest guy you could meet. You can have a normal conversation with him about anything. We've had our issues but, as I've said, away from the track he's good company. When you get to the track, no, I don't respect him at all, not a bit.

I do respect him when he's away from the tracks because he's a nice guy, he's very successful, he's done everything he needed to do: he's created a name for himself, he's made a ton of money and he's good at all his business stuff.

Me and Britain's Ben Barker had a bit of rivalry going through the ranks. We used to race each other and had a couple of crashes and a few words were exchanged every now and then.

Our careers have crossed a few times. Ben, who is a couple of years older than me, had started league racing in 2003 as a member of Oxford's Conference League side, and by the time I was ready to make my first appearance for Scunthorpe in the third tier, he was racing for Somerset in the Premier League as well as Stoke's second team in the Conference.

The following season he was in Stoke's first team in the Premier League and I had joined Rye House at the same level, so there weren't many years between us.

We got to Bydgoszcz, Poland, in 2010 and we were staying in the same hotel and having a few drinks down in the casino and Ben invited us up to his room. I'm with my mate Danny, and the pair of us went up and Ben orders room service, like three bottles of vodka and two bottles of Jack Daniels. I thought this was going to get messy with just the three of us.

I was right. It starts to kick off and, for some reason, we finished up outside the room and in the corridor.

By this time we are making so much noise that the hotel security have arrived. Ben is just stood there and the big security guard is stood there and I'm stood there.

I belted Ben with a big right hook. I'd had a few drinks and was a bit drunk and usually I can keep calm, but when I explode, I explode and I'd had enough of him.

I hit him, nearly took his chin off. I followed through with the punch, which was probably powerful enough to have knocked out Tyson Fury or Anthony Joshua, and as I followed through I hit the security guard as well as Ben.

I immediately thought, *I'm fucked here*, so turned around, ran down the corridor and, as I went, looked over my shoulder and saw the security guard had grabbed Ben. I didn't stop to see what happened after that and instead just went back down to the casino, where I kept doing my thing before going back to my room.

I didn't see Ben again that night but when I rocked up at the Grand Prix the next day, Ben turns up and he's got this massive black eye.

About three months, or perhaps even a year later, Ben's in the bar at Rye House and my aunty Helen, my mum's sister, is there because she was seeing somebody from down that way.

He was talking to someone in the bar and, as it happened, my aunty was sat next to him, although he didn't know she was my aunty. Ben didn't know who she was, probably thought she was just a supporter, and he's giving it the big one saying I stole £1,000 out of his bedroom. I don't need £1,000 out of Ben Barker's hotel bedroom and I didn't steal it.

Aunty Helen called Mum to tell her what was being said and then Mum told me and I took to Twitter to call him out and wrote that I was going to knock him out when he came to Wolverhampton where I was riding that year.

I think Ben might have been at Coventry and when he came to Monmore Green the referee pulled me aside before the start of the meeting and warned me: 'If you have a fight with Barker you'll be banned for two weeks and have to pay a fine.'

So I didn't get to have a good tussle with him and sort it out, but that day will come.

We've never spoken about it since, although these days we don't ride against each other, so there's not been many opportunities to pay him back.

A thousand pounds is a lot of money and I would never steal off anyone and I never have done.

There's nothing wrong with ordering your Big Mac, Chicken McNuggets, a crispy Garlic Mayo Chicken One, fries, strawberry milk shake and an Oreo McFlurry if that's what floats your boat and you aren't too worried about the calorie count.

But there's a time and a place for everything. And the time definitely isn't close to the start of a big meeting and the place certainly isn't the opening rounds of the Speedway World Cup.

Who in their right mind would think of it as being the ideal meal for any professional athlete just a couple of hours away from the first race of the biggest team event of the year?

Yet, that is what Ben thought was the right thing to do during the World Cup at King's Lynn in 2011. It was a generous gesture but hardly the most professional of actions.

I don't remember anything having been arranged as far as feeding all the team mechanics, and the rest of the team might have gone and eaten in a restaurant in the town during the break between practice and the first race.

All the Polish mechanics were there and laughing at us in our bay. They were all laughing and looking over at us as if to say, 'Look at those English idiots'. Fancy bringing McDonald's into the pits and eating that shit.

All their riders – World Champion Tomasz Gollob, World number two Jarek Hampel, Krzysztof Kasprzak, Janusz Kolodziej and Piotr Protasiewicz – were out, having proper meals.

We were made to look a laughing stock and no wonder the Poles took us apart once the meeting started, and finished thirteen points ahead of us. They qualified straight to the World final in their own country at Gorzow while we went to, and were eliminated from, the race-off and never even made the last four.

Thankfully, I don't think that would happen now, but it shows how unprofessional the British approach was at one time, and it's not really that long ago.

I don't think any other country would have done that and that episode was one that was talked about all over Poland as the mechanics' tittle-tattle spread from track to track.

By connection, everyone in the team that night were made to look foolish and it reflected badly on the entire GB set-up.

I could see the Poles sniggering and smirking and you couldn't blame them for using that as one of the reasons we hadn't won the major team trophy for thirty-odd years!

CHAPTER 16

FATALISM AND FEARLESSNESS

Friends have died and friends have been injured and even paralysed – that's the harsh reality of racing speedway, or any other form of motorsport, I suppose.

Ayrton Senna was the top F1 driver in the world but he was killed when he crashed while leading the 1994 San Marino Grand Prix. If it could happen to the Brazilian superstar, it could happen to anyone else and speedway isn't immune from tragedy.

I was at the meeting in Poland on Sunday, 14 May 2012 when Lee Richardson, riding for Rzeszow, crashed and suffered fatal injuries, dying in hospital in Wroclaw.

Lee had been one of the safest riders there has ever been, a former World Under 21 Champion, Great Britain international, and a permanent Grand Prix racer for four years between 2000 and 2006.

His father Colin, who also rode for England, had been a successful performer for a decade in the seventies and eighties, and his uncle, Steve Weatherley, rode in roughly the same era and was good enough to win international caps at Second Division level. His mum Julie had been an on-screen presenter for ScreenSport Television when they used to cover the sport live.

The family knew all about the danger because Steve was paralysed in a fatal crash at Hackney in 1979 in which one of his opponents, Vic Harding, lost his life. That was a black day for British speedway but Lee still wanted to be a speedway rider, and his parents didn't try and stop him even though they knew the risks.

I was standing in the pits that day, watching the race as he chased after my Wroclaw and Wolverhampton teammate Freddie Lindgren and his race partner Tomasz Jedrzejak, who was at Eastbourne that year after previously riding for Belle Vue and Lakeside. I saw him go in. I saw him hit the guy's (Jedrzejak) back wheel and just go flat out into the fence. Then I turned around, I didn't want to look.

Lee was only thirty-three and I could only think of his wife Emma and their three young sons, Josh, Jake and Jenson.

We'd both been with the same Polish side, Czestochowa, in 2008, and in for Vargarna in Sweden in 2011, and would often be on the same flight out of Stansted or some other airport. Even when you aren't at the same club, speedway is such a small world that you quickly get to know everyone and, by and large, we all rub along with each other.

We'd also ridden for Great Britain together. Lee was one of the mainstays of the squad when I made my Speedway World Cup debut in the 2008 Race-Off in Denmark and we were also both in the starting line-up for meetings in the 2009 Race-Off and the qualifying and final in 2010, the last time he rode in the team World Championship.

Did I get on well with Lee? Not really, we had a bit of rivalry and exchanged a few words, but you had to admire anyone who scored so many points for GB in the World Cup.

Yeah, I knew it was bad, you don't go into that fence that hard and come out of it okay. I say that, but it was the second time I'd seen him crash like that.

The first one was in a meeting, probably in 2008, at Czestochowa in Poland and he went straight through the fucking pits gate where the track doesn't go, demolished the fence – and he walked away from it. It was a real big crash, and I don't know how he got away with that one, it was very scary. He just missed the air fence by a couple of fence panels, so it was full force against something solid.

You know, when you see it and watch the paramedics picking him up and sending him off in the ambulance real quick, that it's serious but, no, you don't think he's died. You think, fuck, he's hurt. Lee went in so hard and on his head. He was leaning over the side of the bike, he was still on it and the fence was there as he went into it. If it had happened a few yards further on, he wouldn't have hit the solid fence, he'd have gone into the air fence, which is only on the bends, and who knows what would have happened if he hadn't been in the wrong place at the wrong time?

He didn't die at the track; he died in hospital of internal bleeding. It would have been even worse if he'd passed away on the track, at that time. I haven't seen that and that would be shit, wouldn't it?

I don't know how we go on after something like that, it took us a while, but you have to do it, don't you?

Perhaps Lee was never fully appreciated in England but he was like a god in Poland and there were incredible scenes when news of his death filtered through on the grapevine.

Supporters lit candles in front the new grandstand at Rzeszow and a Mass was held in Wroclaw Cathedral, not far from where he passed, in the city's main hospital. A Polish League basketball match was started with a minute's silence on the Monday night, too.

There have been other track fatalities since I first came over to England, but thankfully they are a rarity these days, with the added safety of the air fences, which must have saved lives over the years.

One of the direct consequences of Lee's accident, although it had no actually relation to the injuries he received, was that the world governing body ordered that every track should have cushioned barriers on the bends. It wouldn't have prevented Lee's death, but it was a great move that has played a huge part increasing the safety at tracks everywhere.

They were the brainchild and invention of the four-time world number one, New Zealander Barry Briggs, and we all owe him a debt of gratitude for developing the air fence and preventing so many of us suffering far more serious injuries.

What did surprise me was that our meeting at Wolverhampton went ahead on the Monday night. The match between Coventry and Rico's Lakeside was called off once the news of his death was confirmed, even though it was scheduled to be shown live on Sky Sports.

But Wolves' meeting, ironically the Gary Peterson Memorial Shield commemorating one of the club's ex-riders who was killed at Monmore Green in similar circumstances in October 1975, did go ahead as planned.

I knew that Sunday night that Lee wasn't with us any more and I didn't fuckin' sleep. I think I had about two hours of sleep in all, I couldn't get it off my mind.

I thought it was disrespectful to have the meeting. There's the old saying that the show must go on and that's how some people think, but respect is respect at the end of the day and I shouldn't have ridden.

I only did so because our promoter Chris Van Straaten wanted me to and it would keep everyone happy. That's what I've done, always kept everyone else happy, but now I would be a bit more selfish and if it happened today and I felt the way I did then I would refuse to race.

We had a minute's silence before the start, meeting after meeting after meeting, not just the one.

It was kind of the same as when Dad died, you get to the track and everyone goes, 'Ah, how are you, Tai? How are you?' Well, you fuckin know how I am, don't ask me. My dad's died and I don't really want to talk about it, and then they go, 'I know how you feel.' Some of them probably do, but people always asking how you are used to wind me up.

I think it was probably the same when Lee died – the riders would just keep riding, keep riding, it takes your mind off it. If you're sitting around thinking about it all the time then you'll think about it, but if you can keep yourself busy it definitely makes the healing process better I think.

I know it's hard to know how best to pay respect to someone who has died, but you do it on the Monday, and then a track on the Tuesday doesn't do it – and then a track on the Wednesday, they want to do it.

If you could only go back to having meetings one night a week in Britain, it would be done in one night, wouldn't it? Every rider doing it nearly at the same time and you could actually arrange it with all the tracks as 7 pm, minute silence, job done.

Everyone's different. I'm pretty shrewd when it comes to stuff like that. Is that the right word? Fatalistic, is that the word? I just fucking don't think about it.

I'm totally aware of what can happen because I have seen it too many times even though I've only been racing for a decade or so. I've always said when I get on that bike I can die, be paralysed, I can have a brain injury, I can come out of it a cabbage, you know what I mean?

When I get on that bike I know that, and I've accepted that, and that it could happen to anyone. I've been through the scenarios, I've imagined myself in a wheelchair, I've imagined myself not being able to fuckin' talk, not being able to see, like what it's like walking around the house blind and having to feel everything.

I went through all that shit when I was about seventeen or eighteen after I watched a video online, and I imagined it all happening and how your life would change and what you'd do and how you'd do it, and I accepted that that could happen and I know that these things can happen.

So when I get on the bike it doesn't even fuckin' cross my mind. When I see it happen, it's a sad moment, when I saw Lee crash, it sucked, I hate seeing people crash, but it's what we do.

What happened to Aussie Darcy Ward, you wouldn't wish it on your worst enemy, but it happens, doesn't it, you move on.

Darcy would definitely have been a real challenger for the world title.

In 2013, he was pushing for it, he was second in the standings behind Tomasz Gollob and two points ahead of me when he crashed in his second ride in the Swedish Grand Prix and was rushed off to hospital with a broken shoulder on his twenty-first birthday.

That was a big setback because it kept him out of the next

three rounds and there was no way he could come back and challenge after missing those vital meetings.

The following season, 2014, he could have won it but fucked up, partly through his own fault and partly through personal circumstances. His mum and dad had split up and that affected him and he had that night when the Latvian GP was cancelled because of the state of the track in Riga.

He went out for dinner with some of the Monster people, and, by his own admission, had too much to drink. He woke up the next morning and we all had to drive down to Daugavpils where they decided to run the round less than twenty-four hours after the previous night's cancellation. He still had a bit of alcohol in his system and failed a breathalyser test.

He was thrown out of the meeting, suspended for the last four rounds and then banned for ten months, so he never rode in another GP.

I think that was a big learning curve for Darcy and when his ban finally ended in June 2015, he came back a changed man and signed for Swindon on loan from his parent track Poole and was almost unbeatable.

You could never have suspected he had been banned for almost a year, I saw a different Darcy. I saw a fit and healthy, lean, watching-what-he-was-eating Darcy Ward. He was on a mission to show what he was capable of, and his riding and his scores when he came back were unbelievable.

In England I reckon he got double figures in ten matches in a row and was unbeaten in three consecutive away meetings at Wolverhampton, Belle Vue and Coventry.

The suspension looked like it had turned his life around. That sort of setback makes you hungry, you have that time off and come back and you're hungry for it, and as well as training and doing all the other things he was doing, he was on a mission, which was great to see.

It was a different Darcy, I hadn't seen that Darcy before.

Everyone saw a difference in him. He'd learnt his lesson from what had happened, been back to Australia, probably sorted things out and dealt with his situations and he came back.

He would definitely have been a big threat but it was all snatched away from him and, like Lee, it happened in an Ekstraliga match in Poland. He had joined Zielona Gora as soon as his ban was over and, as in England, he was immediately on fire, scoring ninety-nine points in only seven matches, and his form in the Swedish Elitserien for Piraterna was the same.

There was even talk of him getting a wild card for one of the late-season GPs, but no one ever had to make that tricky choice to bring him back or let him stew for another few months and pray for a permanent wild card in 2016.

Coming into the last race of their last match of the season, Darcy's Zielona Gora didn't have a lot to race for. They couldn't make the top four and play-offs but they weren't under any threat of being relegated.

However, there is no such thing as a meeting that doesn't matter in Poland because the fans are so tribal and the management so demanding.

There couldn't have been any real pressure on Darcy as he went to the tapes, as visitors Grudziadz couldn't win the meeting they needed to win to avoid being relegated.

Darcy had been beaten only once in his first four rides but admits he was desperate to finish the season on a high with a fourth win of the night. He lined up alongside his teammate Patryk Dudek, but the visiting Russian Artem Laguta was out in front and Darcy was preparing to pass him when he clipped his rear wheel and was thrown, bouncing off the track into the board fence.

No way was it as horrifying as the Lee Richardson crash I'd witnessed from the pits and it looked like the sort of spill that happens every now and again from which you get up and carry on.

Unfortunately, on this occasion the impact of hitting the track at around 50 miles an hour must have been like whiplash in a car crash. Darcy fractured his left arm, broke two vertebrae, damaged his windpipe and, most seriously of all, tore his spinal cord.

I like Darcy, I think he's a great kid. People will say other things but I know him personally. He's had a bit of bad publicity, but fuck me, the kid could ride a bike!

Darcy was one of them kids that you could put him on anything: put him on a set of skis and he could ski, put him on a snowboard and he'd be able to snowboard, put him on a mini bike and he rides it, put him on a motocross bike and he's quick. Flat track quick, speedway quick, a naturally talented kid.

Now twenty-nine (on 4 May), he has moved on, it's a new chapter of his life that he's got to understand and learn to deal with and he's doing that in his own way. Every time I see him in person he seems happier. He's getting better.

He was a patient at the Making Strides SCI Recovery Centre in Burleigh Heads, Queensland and has been one of their star pupils. He also married his sweetheart Lizzie Turner, who has been by his side throughout everything, at the beginning of 2019 and is rebuilding his life.

I don't see how you can fully adjust after something like that. I always see him at speedway time, and I feel like that can be hard for Darcy because that was his thing.

If I went to see him at his house in Australia I think I'd see a different side of him, because away from the speedway I wouldn't be talking about speedway unless he asked me about it as I wouldn't want to remind him of what he's missing out on.

It is what it is, he had the crash, and wrong place, wrong time, wrong track, wrong hospital, he nearly died. They didn't have the stuff to do the operation. They put a rod down his back to stabilise it and then he got out of there and had to deal with all the fucking aftermath of it all.

Imagine, you're laid in bed, you're paralysed from your neck down – because he was straight away, he was in pain, he couldn't move his arms, couldn't move his legs, all he could do was look up.

It was hard for him, I think they were trying to get the stem cell operation, but the same weekend that Darcy crashed, the only four doctors in the world that could do the operation, with stem cells of a cow's brain or something, to help re-grow your spinal cord, weren't available.

The same weekend that Darcy crashed, French motocrosser Mickael (Mika) Musquin, the elder brother of the two-time MX2 World Champion Marvin Musquin, had a bad accident in a Supercross race and was paralysed from the shoulders down.

I think there was someone else who also crashed that weekend and they were all trying to get the same thing, stem cell treatment, and of the four surgeons who can do it, one of them was on holiday, so that was down to three and you have to have the treatment within twenty-four hours of your crash for it to be successful.

In an emotional interview in the *Daily Mail*, Darcy described both the crash and the immediate aftermath: 'Me and Patryk were going into the corner chasing the guy in first. I think it was the end of the second lap. I was on the inside and I wanted to move out where there is more dirt and a better grip, but I could see my teammate was there so I thought, "Damn it, I can't go there." I came round the bend and must have hit a little hole which made me do a wheelie. I clipped the guy's back wheel and next I was rolling on the ground pretty fast and then it stopped.

'I could feel a bit of pain in my left arm but then thought, "I can't feel anything." The medic came over to me and I said: "I can't feel anything. I feel nothing." I panicked I guess.

'I woke up in an intensive care unit with other guys on the ward around me. I couldn't move as I was locked strictly into position but I was drowsy. There was a light bulb directly above me and I wanted it off so I could sleep a bit. I remember shouting "hello" to the nurses.

'My Polish is limited so I was rolling my eyes towards the bulb trying to direct them to turn it off. After a while they just ignored me, I think they thought I was mad with pain.'

* * *

If you're not prepared to take that on don't fuckin ride a bike, it's not your thing, you know if there's a hole on the track that scares you, don't ride. Just quit.

When the tracks are rough I fuckin' love it, just fuckin' hold on and go for it, attack it.

I remember watching an interview with Travis Pastrana, the American Motocross and Supercross rider who had been performing stunts on his bike even when he was still at school. He became one of the biggest names in freestyle motocross and was famous. Stunt performer Evel Knievel was his role model.

In the interview he said that when he did his double backflip he accepted the fact he could die or be paralysed.

I just thought, fuck that's like the best way to be, because if you can, it's almost like taking your brain out. Your brain, when you want to do something, if you're scared of what can happen, it stops you from doing it. But if you've accepted what can happen, and you're happy with that, and you can deal with that if it ever did happen, then no one can stop you from doing what you want to do.

No one, because the only person that stops you from doing something is yourself.

It's weird because I always think about crashing. I can go out for a race and be like 'Oh, imagine if I had a fucking massive crash on the first corner and cartwheeled into the fence.' That doesn't bother me, it doesn't change how I think; I can joke about it on the track walk or anything, it doesn't faze me at all.

One thing I have always wanted to do is get my certificate so I can skydive.

There's something called BASE jumping where you parachute or wingsuit fly off a cliff or some sort of permanent structure.

They say it's more dangerous than skydiving from a plane and it's something I want to do and I'm sure I will.

I want to go to Dubai, there's a building there, the Princess Tower that overlooks Dubai Marina. The *Guinness World Records* book lists it as the world's tallest residential building, 414 metres (1,358 feet) tall and there's a big platform on the 99th floor that's just for BASE jumping.

You run off the platform, you're metres and metres away from the building and you run off the platform and jump off it and you throw your parachute.

That would scare the shit out of some people, but I want to do it.

I've had people who know me ask if my lack of fear is one of the reasons I'm as good as I am? Fuck knows, that's the question everyone wants to know, but I don't know the answer to it!

Life's a risk and, the way I look at it, you are more likely to die on an aeroplane than a speedway bike, so enjoy it.

CHAPTER 17

'COME BACK IN. YOU BROKE YOUR BACK'

Eight fifty-five on the evening of Friday, 7 June 2019, and all my winter's effort was about to mean absolutely nothing.

I was happy to tell everyone I was going to retain my title, I was ready to rock and roll and I still feel despite the slow start that it was the accident that stopped everything.

I could have got halfway through the year and then in the second half of the year, after the Speedway of Nations, pulled the pin and just gone. I know how I felt inside myself, I worked my arse off in the winter, and I know I was the fittest I've ever been because my base fitness gets better every year.

I had never worked as hard to be physically prepared. I got Chris Neville, the Performance Specialist in the Great Britain Speedway Team camp, to come over to Australia. He arrived around eight days before Christmas and was joined by his wife Jo and their eighteen-year-old son Harry the day after Boxing Day.

Chris is an expert in his field. He has worked for football clubs Portsmouth and Blackburn Rovers, and was Conditioning Coach for the Football Association for more than four years, including the 2014 World Cup in Brazil and successive European Championships in 2012 and 2016.

A speedway supporter for most of his life, he regularly stood on the terracing at Swindon before getting involved with GB a few years ago and he also happens to be a great guy.

They stayed with Faye and me in our house in Perth and while I have my own ideas about how I want to train and know what's been successful for me, I am always pushing to be that little bit better and I wanted to start training earlier than normal.

Australia's a great place to train because of the climate and Chris and I work together well: he helped prepare food together and we also trained together.

We could do everything outside. He brought quite a bit of kit and equipment over with him and we'd be training as early as five-thirty or six in the morning, be done by seven-thirty or eight and then have some downtime with our families before a second session, starting again at four or five o'clock in the afternoon.

Generally it was strength based, down at the beach or local park, wherever we wanted to go.

Jo and Harry went home on 9 January and Chris left Perth a few days later and was also able to come along to a couple of race meetings at Pinjar Park with me. Having Chris over worked, it was cool for everybody because they lived with us and because they are beautiful people. We created a great friendship and even if I stopped riding today, I could still call Chris and ask if he wanted to go out for some food.

Chris calls me at least once a week just to see how I am, he's just a genuine bloke, the kind of person you need to surround yourself with in your life.

We'd go down to the park together, Rylee was playing, kicking balls around with him, it was good but then there was time to work, which we did.

During the season you have the pressures and time restraints, but Chris coming over to Aussie meant an opportunity to spend a bit of time together, working out a programme. I reckon I was in the best condition I have ever been and from the tests that we did, Chris said my body composition was the best he'd known it.

I even took on an Olympic distance triathlon, the Oceanic triathlon, down on the beach: a 1.5 kilometre swim, a 40k bike ride and a 10k run. It's not always idyllic weather in Perth and triathlon day was crazy stormy; the ocean was so rough they nearly cancelled the swim.

I love training, depending on what it is: I'll admit there's some things I don't really enjoy, but at the moment I'm into the distance stuff. Completing the triathlon showed how fit I was and I felt confident that I could be the first British rider to successfully defend the title and the first to do it since Nicki Pedersen thirteen years ago.

Confident enough that when I got back to the UK and discovered I'd been selected as the first speedway rider and seventh motorcyclist to be presented with the Royal Automobile Club's Torrens Award for my achievements in 2018, I told the guests, including Ben Cussons, chairman of the RAC: 'I have the best fitness levels I have ever had – so put some money on me to win again this year.'

I know I started the season slow in the GPs but that meant I was going to finish good.

The series changed and, in effect, became a two-day event this year with the introduction of timed practice on the Friday.

Everyone was intrigued to see what would happen on its launch at the opening round at Warsaw and I would be delighted if I could tell you what it was like, but I couldn't because I was forced to miss it, along with the 2018 silver medallist Bartosz Zmarzlik, and Max Fricke, called up to step into the shoes of the absent Maciej Janowski.

While thirteen of those who would compete in the round were able to get valuable time on the track, Bartosz, Max and myself had to report for duty for our respective Polish teams, Wroclaw and Gorzow, racing against each other in a re-arranged fixture.

Look at any other motorsport – for example, don't let Lewis Hamilton do F1 practice or qualification and see where he would finish on a track he's never been to before.

Warsaw isn't a permanent track, it's built afresh every year, so was I handicapped by not being able practice? One hundred per cent.

I believe they should make practice compulsory.

Take the second round, at Krsko, Slovenia. I had to race in Wroclaw instead of timed practice, with the fastest rider getting first pick on gate positions, and it must have been farcical because Janowski, Fricke, Niels-Kristian Iversen, Jason Doyle and Zmarzlik, like me, had a meeting in Poland so couldn't make it.

I was feeling ill but had to drive ten hours to Krsko to get there in time to sign on for the race. We drove all through the night, although I had nearly called the doctor the night before because I was vomiting all night on the way. I thought it might have been food poisoning but the mechanics got it a few days later so it must have been a bug.

If it had been compulsory to practise, as it should be, I could have flown in the night before, rested, done qualification, done the Grand Prix and been happy.

It's dangerous from a rider's point of view, it's dangerous from a mechanic's point of view. They have to work all day Friday, drive all night to get to wherever the GP is, work all day Saturday and then drive back to Bolton, or wherever they live, on Sunday.

Half the riders have practised and half haven't. How unfair is it on those riders who are forced to miss practice by their Polish clubs?

The reality is, the FIM should block out the whole weekend, they should say there will be no meetings in Poland, who now have matches on a Friday and Saturday, as well as a Sunday, on the same weekend.

They can't even argue that they don't have the necessary dates, because there were no meetings in Poland in July. Why have a month off in the middle of the year when it's the best weather?

If I was the FIM I'd go: event blocked, Friday, Saturday and Sunday; Friday, practice; Saturday, the GP; Sunday, a corporate day where riders come to meet the sponsors and then travel back home in the afternoon so they're home in the evening.

The new procedure allows the fastest in practice to have first preference on choosing gate positions in the meeting, but that doesn't concern me; the main thing for me is using practice to find the right set-up. I've won three world titles by getting the luck of the draw for gate positions, so what does it matter?

But that all went away in the opening heat of Wroclaw's Polish Ekstraliga match at newly promoted Lublin, which was quite a stormy affair from the off.

The first running was stopped after an elbows-out first turn saw me slip off. The referee warned Grigory Laguta, who had recently come back from a drugs ban, but allowed all four of us back into the re-run.

On the second lap, I went around the Russian and I could see him looking at me and knew he wanted to stop me getting through. Laguta was looking at me and because he was looking at me and not where he was going, he ran into his teammate Dawid Lampart's back wheel and then crashed into me.

The impact slammed me into the fence and I hit the solid fence, not where there was protection from the air bags, and broke my shoulder blade, bruised my lung and, I later discovered, broke my back.

I was lying on the track for a while, curled up in a ball, and left the track in the back of an ambulance that whisked me off to the local hospital.

Laguta, who was excluded from the race by the meeting referee, blamed his teammate for not being fast enough.

I knew I was hurt but I didn't know I'd fractured my back, because I was walking out of the hospital until the doctor ran out after me, beckoning and calling: 'Come back in, come back in. You broke your back.' I was like, *What?* Then he made me lie down on the flat bed.

I'd fractured my TH4 vertebra, just below my neck, in between my shoulder blades.

I checked myself out of the hospital and jumped in the car, in the passenger seat, and we drove the 400 kilometres to Wroclaw to see another spinal specialist.

I saw two there, went to the hotel, had a shower and was about to get some lunch when I was told I had an appointment at the spinal clinic at Wroclaw University, where I saw two more specialists who wanted to keep me in the hospital for a week on a bed, neck brace, all that.

Initially, I just thought it was an injury that I'd get over and be back quite quickly, but when they said it was my spine, I started to worry a bit more. Then both the specialists told me I'd be out for three months.

There was never any suggestion that I wouldn't race again or anything like that, but there were people in both Poland and Sweden asking if it was the end of my career. Just rumours.

I started having treatment straight away, in the hyperbaric chamber, low-frequency ultra-sound treatment, physiotherapy, laser treatment, magnetic-field therapy and ultrasound, some at home, some in Warsaw, Birmingham, some at Nottingham and some at Leicester.

It was hard work, it's hard mentally, to go in the oxygen chambers for an hour and a half. Some days, I did the hyperbaric chamber twice, depending on what slots they had. It was just a headfuck. One of the biggest disappointments being out was that I missed what I thought was a genuine chance of a gold medal. And I was just gutted that I couldn't go to Russia for the Speedway of Nations.

But you just do the treatments and then when you're healed, you just go back racing, that's the way it has to be if you are a professional athlete. Getting back to what I do best. So it's like I don't need to focus on why I'm doing it, I know why I'm doing it.

* * *

I was aiming to get back for the Wroclaw Grand Prix at the beginning of August and that is what I did. Or to be even more accurate, I was back in time for the previous afternoon's practice session, so that was mission accomplished.

By then, though, my chances of winning another world title had gone. I had missed two important rounds, at Prague, where

I usually go well, and at Hallstavik in Sweden. I was sixteenth overall and 32 points behind the three riders tied at the top of the standings; Emil Sayfutdinov, Patryk Dudek and Leon Madsen had all scored 47 points over the first four meetings and Bartosz Zmarzlik, who would go on to win the first of his back-to-back world crowns, had 44 points, 29 ahead of me.

While you never give up hope, in my head I knew that it would be an impossible task to catch and overtake most of them, especially having missed so many weeks of the season. I knew I couldn't retain my world title having missed two rounds but, one hundred per cent, I wanted to get into the top eight because I couldn't rely on being seeded. There were other riders outside the cut-off who had claims – after all, it is a world championship. I believed I could get in the top eight by the end of the year and that's what I was aiming at. I tried and tried, did my best but it wasn't to be.

I'd crashed on 6 June and I wasn't able to think about riding again until Friday, 2 August, the day before the Wroclaw Grand Prix. That had been my goal, my target, and there I was going into the dressing room at my home track, back on the GP trail.

CHAPTER 18

BACK IN THE SADDLE AGAIN

Sometimes you have to hide exactly how you are feeling and keep your true thoughts to yourself.

That's what I did when I was given the green light to start riding again after two months out with a broken back. The real truth, despite what I told the world, was that I believed I would miss the rest of the 2019 season, and once you have those thoughts at the forefront of your mind, no matter how positive you are in public, it is difficult to adjust.

Obviously, with the damage to my back, I had a lot of time off the bike, and I kind of expected to be out for the year. I was trying to come back as quickly as I could, but you don't know how long these things take.

I wasn't able to train properly, and thinking that I would probably be out for the season I thought I'd eat whatever I wanted. I got to the point where I was 7 kilos (15.5 pounds, or just over a stone) heavier than when I had last raced earlier in the year. You can't put on that sort of weight and be at the top of your game, even more so when you have been off the bike for a couple of months or so.

I was on the back foot, no doubt about it. It's the longest break I have ever had. You have two months out in the middle of the season and by the time you come back everyone else is sharp – they are race fit, both physically and mentally, and even if your fitness is on point, competing at that level is tough.

I was very, very, lucky not only to be racing, but lucky even to be back on my bike. The vertebra that I broke, the thoracic vertebra TH4, is the least bad option if you are going to break any of them. It snapped straight through the vertebra, fractured from front to back and all the way around, but fortunately it was held in place by the shoulder blades and the ligaments in my back. If the same injury had been three or four veterbrae further down my back, where the spine doesn't have the soft tissue, the ligaments and the shoulder blades, and all that sort of stuff around it, the whole vertebra would have been finished. That could have been far worse, and might even have seen me paralysed, but it is what it is. It's what we do: we race, and we face danger every lap we race. If you don't like the risks, then don't do it. I saw the season out and did the best that I could, and that's the end of it.

I was so happy to be back on the bike. It felt awesome to be racing again, and any points I got were always going to be a bonus. Since the accident, I had publicly always said that I'd expected to be back racing before the end of the season, even though some people had written me off. But despite the major handicap of having missed two rounds, my professed target was still to finish in the top eight – I didn't want to be asking for a wild card.

But I knew that even a top eight finish was going to be virtually impossible to achieve.

BACK IN THE SADDLE AGAIN

The truth is that although I hadn't made the best start to the season, I was convinced that I could have a major say in the medal races. Why shouldn't I successfully defend my title? Usually I get better the longer the season goes on. I'm someone who thrives under pressure, and I wasn't overly concerned when I only scored six points in the opening round at Warsaw because there were reasons, such as my having had to miss practice.

I'd been ill in the build-up to the second round in Slovenia, but I still finished in the top six and had climbed from twelfth overall to eighth. Then I broke my back. I missed rounds in the Czech Republic and Sweden, and so was sixteenth when I came back at Wroclaw. More importantly, I wasn't j ust sixteenth, I was 32 points off the leader Emil Sayfutdinov, and you can't make up that sort of leeway no matter how fit you are.

It's funny: someone texted me and asked, 'How hard are you going to try when you come back? Is it worth putting a bet on you winning the World Championship again?' I was like, 'Mate, I've missed at least two rounds and while it's not impossible, it's almost impossible, like other people are going to have big problems, aren't they?' The truth was that I'd have to win nearly every race for the rest of the season.

When I went out for my first timed practice at Wroclaw, a track I should have known as intimately as my own children, I hadn't been on a bike for two months, and coming back into a Grand Prix made me realise how good everyone is – the level at that stage of the season is so high. When you have been out for a couple of months, you certainly feel it more, and I struggled a bit with the bikes' set-up.

Even though Wroclaw was my club side in Poland, I'd never seen the track like that. But we did something pretty crazy with the bike at the end and I felt good in my last race, when I got a decent second behind Emil and ahead of both Artem Laguta and Jason Doyle.

I'd missed out on the semi-finals by a single point and it was cool to be on the pace and to be racing with some speed, so it was definitely a positive night overall, even if I didn't score loads of points. The half-dozen I did score was more than I would have got if I had not been there, but it was also a chance for me to get going again. Yeah, it was nice to be back.

It had been a long absence, and I was thankful that I could now race in front of all the British fans at Cardiff, although there were rounds in Sweden, Germany and Denmark before being back home at my favourite GP of them all. Apparently, so I learnt after the meeting, my second race at the Swedish GP at Målilla was my 500th heat – how about that for a piece of obscure trivia? It certainly didn't mean anything to me because the only statistics I'm interested in are the number of world titles I can win!

I was back racing in both Poland and Sweden and my league form wasn't too bad, but the competition is so different from the Grand Prix.

You always try to take at least one positive out of a meeting and while I again missed out on the top eight, and a semi-final spot, at the German GP at Teterow on 31 August, I did get my first race win since returning to the track. I also had the satisfaction of beating Bartosz Zmarzlik, who claimed second place in the final to join Denmark's Leon Madsen at the top of the leaderboard with seven of the ten rounds behind them.

With only seven points between the joint leaders and third placed Sayfutdinov, I was so far adrift going into the Danish Grand Prix at Vojens in September that I didn't have even an outside chance of squeezing into the top eight. I would have to rely on a wild card to contest the 2020 series.

Denmark would turn out to be the best result of my comeback as I picked up double figures in the qualifying stage but went out in the second semi, which ended my night's participation. At least I was on the up with the British GP at Cardiff on 21 September next on the agenda.

At every round I have a routine, but it is a different ritual at Cardiff. For the British Grand Prix, Faye and I always go out the evening before with our friends Darren Fletcher and his wife Lauren. Darren used to present the BBC Radio Five Live phone-in programme *606* with Robbie Savage before moving to become lead football commentator for BT Sport, and has been a speedway fan for years – he used to go and watch Long Eaton. In 2016, he dared me to wear a smart suit at Cardiff ahead of the GP, so of course I did and that certainly made heads turn when I walked into the pits all suited and booted rather than wearing jeans!

We always go to the same place, an Italian restaurant called Giovanni's, although we do have a pick of two different locations, both relatively close to both our hotel and the stadium. The owner, Giovanni Malacrino, a larger-than-life character, has three restaurants now, two in the city and a third, called Piatto Pasta House, which he opened earlier in 2019, on Cardiff Bay. We have had a couple of hair-rising nights at Giovanni's; one year there was a small fire in the kitchen when we were there. The previous May Giovanni went, unsuccessfully, looking for love on the Channel 4 TV show *First Dates* and certainly made quite an impression with the viewers. He and his former wife had separated in 2001 and she took their two kids to a new life in Italy, and everyone watching the programme was praying that he would find love after being moved to tears when he started talking about his children. It wasn't to be, though, and while he wooed the watching viewers he didn't win his chosen partner June's heart! Since he has previously appeared on *You Bet*, *Bargain Hunt* and *Come Dine With Me*, as you can imagine, life with Giovanni is never dull.

For once, Fletch and Lauren weren't at Cardiff. I think he was working at a game because the British GP, which was usually held in the middle of summer, had been moved to a new September date that clashed with the football season. But I still went to Giovanni's, his restaurant in Park Place rather than the one in the middle of the city centre at The Hayes, and, after the meal, he gave me a lift back to the hotel to save me walking. I hope I'll be there again when the British GP finally returns to being a midsummer round, after being cancelled in 2020 and 2021. And I hope Fletch and his wife can be with us.

Cardiff is the best GP of the lot, without a doubt. You can feel the whole buzz around the city centre, the fans' zone, and as it's a relatively small city you get to see all the people walking to the track and drinking in the pubs the night before the GP and afterwards. There's something about the place that is different, and not just that it's the GP that is always the loudest with the air horns. You get more people in Warsaw, but it's a different stadium to the Principality. The GP in Warsaw is bigger – there are 20,000 fewer people at Cardiff – but nowhere sounds as good or as loud as the Welsh capital.

If you talk to any of the riders they will probably tell you the same thing: Cardiff is the best of the lot because of the atmosphere. There is also usually a special riders' introduction before the GP, and you feel as if you are on stage at the Park Theater at the Las Vegas MGM because of the glitz and glamour of it all.

I've still not won the British Grand Prix, and I knew it was unlikely that I could fill that void, but my efforts weren't helped by an exclusion in the first race. Freddie Lindgren came into the corner and overcooked it, and as he did that I cut back and ran into him. There is no doubt about that, but he was kind of out of control going into the corner, which was the reason I hit him.

When we got back into my pit bay everything was bent, front wheel, forks, diamond (the main part of the bike's frame), so I jumped onto my spare bike for the next race, and it wasn't set up very well.

Some people were surprised that I took time to talk with the BT Sport pits reporter Charlie Webster about the incident. Perhaps others would have refused to do so, but I do everything I can for the sport, whether people believe I do or not. I never turn down any media, because I do everything I possibly can to publicise speedway, as I think I should. I didn't shout and scream that I'd been robbed, nor did I slate the referee for disqualifying me – it's the referee's decision and that's his job. My job's to ride the bike.

As far as I was concerned that was my year done. After that I didn't even care if I scored a point in the final round at Torun in Poland, I just wanted to get 2019 out of the way. Although I will never go into a meeting thinking that way, there was nothing on the end of Torun for me. All I could do was get out there and do what I could, and wait for confirmation of who would take over from me as world champion.

That cliché about something not being over till the fat lady sings doesn't often seem true, but there was still keen interest in what happened at the Marian Rose MotoArena. I've got good memories from there: I'd won the 2018 round to clinch my third world title; in 2015, that was where I scored enough points in the penultimate round of the season to let me fly to Australia for the final GP of the year in Melbourne with an unassailable lead as the world champion-elect; and in 2013 it was at Torun where I was crowned the world number one for the first time. You can't have any better memories of a track, a stadium or a city than that, can you?

So sixth place in the final GP at Torun didn't seem so bad in the end. Even so, I was relieved that the Grand Prix season was over, it was a season I wanted to put behind me and forget. It hadn't all been pain and disappointment, though. For me, the British Speedway Grand Prix in Cardiff is always a good one, by far the best GP of the year, and 2019 was even more special in a way, because I spent the morning of the meeting at a book signing in the Revolution bar and restaurant opposite Cardiff Castle.

One of my major sponsors are ATPI Sports Events, who are part of the ATPI group, a global travel agency that has a sports division which has been an official supplier of Olympic Games tickets for over twenty-five years. Their CEO, Ian Sinderson, is a long-time speedway fan and has given considerable support to me as well as other riders, and to Belle Vue as a club, and he's also a backer of the No Limits academy helping young British riders.

In Cardiff, ATPI took over the bar, rebranded it as #TaiRevolution for the Saturday and put on a series of events for supporters in the build-up to the start of racing. I autographed copies of *Raw Speed* on an upper floor and I couldn't believe how many people turned up to get a signed copy of my autobiography. The book signings were great, this one especially, with hundreds of happy people getting lots of photographs. It was a great morning for me.

I know Ian was planning to do something similar at the 2020 British GP but, of course, that never took place because of Covid-19, although with luck he might be able to do it again. He told me that more than 2,500 fans went through the door of Revolution on that Saturday, so it was a shame that he wasn't able to repeat it, on an even bigger scale, the following year.

The Great Britain Speedway Team also used the venue on the same day to announce officially the new joint team managers. Oliver Allen and Simon Stead spent an hour or so there answering fans' questions – an enlightened approach to involve supporters with the national team. I have never hidden my feelings about Alun Rossiter's time in charge of the Lions and my views haven't changed since he stood down a couple of weeks before Cardiff.

* * *

There are times when you have to look ahead and plan for the future, which is why watching the 2019 Speedway of Nations from the comfort of a chair in the BT Sport studio, was so hard to take.

I watched it all fall to pieces as GB made a disastrous start, Craig Cook crashing into teammate Robert Lambert in their opening race, which was a shame, but you learn from mistakes, and if you don't make mistakes you are never going to learn! I sent an email straight away to Rob Painter with my thoughts, and I am sure that Chris Neville, the Performance Director, and other members of the back-office team will have done he same.

One of the biggest problems about the whole set-up was that the British Speedway Promoters' Association (they are now known as British Speedway Promoters Limited), have franchised the running of the GB team to Rob and his partner Vicky, but still insisted that they picked the team manager.

That was something that was out of Rob's hands and it was wrong, but at least it now looks as if it has changed as he was backed in his choice of Rossiter's successors.

Rosco was the BSPA's pick, and he was manager: he chose which riders to take to the Final in Russia. Given his selections at the time my choices would have been different, and I still believe my team would have performed much better.

The other year when I didn't ride for Great Britain, 2017, I didn't watch it at all, but in 2019 I had to and it was tough viewing ...

First place is the only position I ever think about – being second doesn't mean anything to me, which is why I gave my 2018 Speedway of Nations silver medal to a little girl who was in the crowd. I've never kept any keepsakes or souvenirs from any event that I didn't win, my whole life and career is about winning, not finishing runner-up.

In 2018 the organisers scrapped the World Cup, in which the competing national teams had to field four riders and a reserve, for the new Speedway of Nations with three-rider squads.

For 2020 I wanted to go one further than in 2018, starting by winning our qualifier to lay down a bit of a marker with a big result. That first round was at Manchester's National Speedway Stadium in May and we went into it confident we would not only book our place in the two-day final in Russia – but give ourselves a psychological edge over our rivals by qualifying as the highest scorers. And that is exactly what we did.

We were a better team than we had been twelve months earlier. Robert Lambert was a year older and a year more experienced, while Craig Cook was a better rider than he had been in 2018.

Even though he'd had a testing year in the Grand Prix, he would have learnt from competing against the best riders in the world every fortnight or so.

I didn't practise because I rode at Belle Vue the previous year and my philosophy is that you still go the same way round and the shape of the track hadn't changed.

We sealed top spot with one race to go to join Russia, Sweden, Poland and Germany in July's World Final and could relax as Australia and Denmark also went through.

An indication of how comfortable it was for us was that I happily stood down from one of my races to give Robert, who was our Under 21 reserve, an opportunity to get a taste of the action as my replacement. I was also confident enough to give my race partner his choice of gates throughout the meeting – I let them choose because I'm the most experienced and we are a team. I didn't want to take the easy way; the team comes first, and if I can give my teammates confidence by starting off the worst gate positions, I will do it.

We all knew it would be tough at Togliatti in the final. The Russians were the favourites, not only because of having home track advantage, but also because they had Emil Sayfutdinov and Artem Laguta as their two senior team members, and both are among that select group of world-class riders. But I believed that we could give them more than a run for their money, and that as long as we got the breaks and didn't suffer any misfortune we could go one better than in 2018.

It wasn't to be, however, and by the time the final came around in July I was still a few weeks away from being able to get back to racing. With me being injured, it was the perfect opportunity to send a couple of kids over to Russia to give them the experience. I knew that Dan Bewley already had a visa so he could have gone, and if I had been in charge, he would definitely have been on that plane.

On TV, Rosco said that Bewley wasn't ready. He was in the five-man squad but not ready. I simply did not understand.

To me, that was Rosco trying to cover his own arse, saying that to justify his decision or make excuses for picking Bomber (Chris Harris). In fact, everything he said frustrated me. There seemed to be no thought process, as though he was saying things just for the sake of saying them.

It would have been awesome for Dan to go to Russia, to see how racing at that level works, to sample the atmosphere of a world final, riding in an environment where the first or second language isn't English, to see how the world's top riders prepare, to recognise the effort they put in – from every aspect he could only have benefited from being in Togliatti, instead of sitting on his backside up in Cumbria watching it on TV.

We already knew that we would need Dan as our Under 21 rider in 2020 as Robert Lambert would be too old, so why not give him that experience, without him being under any sort of pressure? I honestly believe that a team of Robert Lambert, Dan Bewley and me could have won a gold medal in the Speedway of Nations in 2020. Bringing Dan into the squad early would have given him invaluable experience and helped integrate him into the team.

That's in the past now, and it is pleasing to see that the new men in charge do seem to have a long-term plan, along the lines that I have been advocating for a few years.

It was while I was out injured and before my return from my broken back that I began to spend more time thinking about my future, and especially the number of meetings I wanted to do. I had been thinking for a long time about focusing more on the

GP and that is what I decided I was going to do in 2020. Having already cut out Britain as one of the leagues I was racing in, I now felt it was time to forget about Sweden as well. I wanted to be able to stay in better physical shape and to keep the same fitness and dietary schedule as during winter and pre-season.

Another big decision that I made after getting back in the saddle was that our second little one would be born in Australia. It meant that I had to miss the first test match under Simon and Olly, the new managers of the Great Britain team who had been chosen to replace Alun Rossiter.

I've made some of my views on what Rosco did, right and wrong, quite clear, and I welcomed the arrived of Simon and Olly from the moment their appointment was officially announced to the fans at a public meeting at #TaiRevolution ahead of the 2019 British Grand Prix.

Rosco had stood down – some of the people in the know told me it was before he was pushed – after what happened at the Speedway of Nations in Russia, although he was quick to issue a statement, part of which read: 'This isn't a knee-jerk reaction to what happened in Russia although I do have to say the criticism was over the top.

'I've always been prepared to put my hands up when I make a mistake, but a lot of what I read and heard criticising myself and the team as a whole wasn't made with knowledge of the facts.

'If you're already without the world champion and then your next two riders crash, no manager is going to be able to change that.

'But as I say, this isn't purely about Russia, I've had a lot of things to consider and I do believe when you're not entirely comfortable with things, that's when you have to look to move on.'

He probably included me among those critics, because I did

have my say while working with the commentating team on BT Sport for the 2019 Speedway of Nations. I spent some time in the studio as one of their analysts and I was openly disparaging about some of the things Rosco had done and said during his six years in charge of the national team.

I know my outspoken views as one of the BT Sport pundits, along with Scott Nicholls, upset some of the watching supporters, but that was only because I was telling it how it was in my eyes.

Bomber Harris had given terrific service to GB over the years but he was thirty-seven that year and no longer at that level. So why did he go while Dan was left at home?

I like Craig Cook, but if we want to make strides in a five-year plan we had to bring on the kids. Cookie's older than me, nearly four years older, and, while he's riding good in the British leagues, when he was in the Grand Prix series in 2018, he finished sixteenth out of sixteen riders, and for GB to win a World Championship event, you need riders who are more successful than that.

As captain, I wasn't involved in picking the team. I had given my opinion, but I'm not a decision maker and all I could do was say what I thought should be done; it was up to other people to decide.

We were unfortunate that Robert and Cookie were injured in the first race in Togliatti, but in my view we had no chance of being able to win. That was obvious.

There's me at the level I'm at, Rob is a little bit under me but can go and beat the best guys in the world in a given race while the rest of the British speedway scene is that far behind us two and, until our young hopefuls start riding in Poland and Sweden regularly instead of being happy riding in two leagues in Britain, it won't change.

BACK IN THE SADDLE AGAIN

I got Bewley a team spot in Sweden last year and I'm willing to do whatever I can for any of the youngsters. Over the years you build up friendships with people at different clubs in different countries and it's not hard to do that.

In the 2019–20 winter I helped to arrange for a couple of young lads to go out to Australia to ride and get fit and I was there to help them. I've also given my time to help on the No Limits youth programme and we do have some talented young kids, but they will need the experience of racing in other countries before they can ever think of reaching the level Rob is now at.

We have seen what happens when I'm not in the squad. In 2017, when I took a year out, we won the opening round of the Speedway World Cup ahead of Australia, America and the Czech Republic but that was at King's Lynn, a British track in front of a patriotic British crowd.

We went to the final at Leszno, Poland, a week later and finished last, 35 points behind Poland, 27 behind Sweden with Russia, who only had four riders after Grigory Laguta was banned for a drugs offence, 3 points ahead of us in third.

Cookie apologised for his display, admitting: 'I feel embarrassed', and Bomber put his finger on it, saying: 'Obviously we were good at home but the riders aren't used to Poland, it's a different kettle of fish as the boys found out!'

I don't want to sound like, it's me, me, me, but Bomber was right: it is a totally different level racing in Britain than it is in Poland, Sweden or Russia.

Rob is practically there. He's in the 2021 Grand Prix series and he's European champion, which is great for us, and as long as it's the Speedway of Nations we have a chance of a medal. But it's not always going to be that way and if they go back to the

World Cup with five-man teams then we are fucked unless we bring on the kids.

If we go on ignoring the young riders and keep going back to the old hands who haven't made it at the very top, then that's me done!

But as long as there's growth and we are focused on the kids and bringing them up, I am there 100 per cent. I want my spot to be taken from me by a kid riding better than I am, and the only way that can happen is if we give them the chance to show it.

Lots of things have changed for the better since I came back into the team, but not enough. We've had a couple of years' building and I feel GB is now established in the Speedway of Nations competition and we could have had another good crack at it. We won in 2018, but because of the stupid rules the losers, Russia, were declared the winners, which was also frustrating.

As luck would have it that's the only season in which I've been fit enough for the competition. I missed 2019 and 2020 but, hopefully, everything will be okay this year and, with the final at Manchester, then we have to be confident we can finally end that long wait for a gold medal, all those years since we won the World Team Cup in 1989, when Kelvin Tatum was the captain. I want to do what Kelvin did and I'm still desperate to get that win, but I just hope they keep the competition as a pairs championship for as long as possible, because if they put it back into fours then we're fucked again.

From what I understand, the plan is to keep the format as it is for the old World Cup, with five-rider teams, as an intermittent competition, maybe like football, once every four years. But there's a new guy running the FIM world championships after Eurosport Events won the rights from 2022 onwards, and when new people come in, then things can change, and you just have to roll with the punches, as they say.

Simon and Olly can do it their way and they will have my support. They are both ex-riders, so from a rider's point of view we can probably relate to them more than someone who hasn't been a rider or someone who has not had experience at a certain level.

Olly did a lot of elite level racing in Sweden and Poland, he spent five seasons in the Swedish ElitSerien with Vargarna and Getingarna and he also raced in Poland for Gniezno and Krakow, so he knows what it is all about. Steady was out in Poland as well, and they both represented Great Britain internationally.

Olly was in the Speedway World Cup not so long ago, having been chosen by the then managers Neil Middleditch and Jim Lynch in 2007 and 2008 respectively, which is recently enough to give him a real insight into what it is like to be racing today.

Simon has had even more experience in the World Cup as he was in the national team for five years in six seasons between 2005 and 2010, and again as recently as 2014. Middlo, Lynch, Rob Lyon and Rosco all had him in their starting squads and that sort of experience is priceless when you are managing the team. Steady scored double figures in three of his eleven appearances, which included the finals in 2005, 2007, 2010 and 2014, so he really knows what it is all about. It will be interesting to see how it all pans out over the next few years.

Simon is only eight years older than me and Olly is a month younger than him; they are from the same era and that should be an advantage. They are the guys in charge now and we will see how they help the boys improve in certain aspects and move forwards with the squad and try to have a proper long-term plan for the national team. It's all about the younger guys, they are the riders who need to get out and race in Poland and Sweden, start mixing it with the world's fast guys.

The Speedway of Nations is a three-rider tournament and at present that means it's me, Robert and Dan. We are the top three, but the next guys, unfortunately, are still a couple of rungs down the ladder, too far to make any real impact at the moment. Put it this way, if we went back to the old four-team tournament World Cup it would be a struggle but if it is the current Speedway of Nations, we have as good a chance as anyone.

Some of the young British riders signed Polish contracts in the winter and that's great, a step in the right direction. It's just time they need, but you can't buy time.

They are not going to progress by racing in the Championship or the Premier League, whatever you call it. They need to be following fast people and losing, learning from mistakes. They will never do that just racing in the UK, the competition isn't there. I doubt if anyone could come through just racing in the UK now. It's got to the point where you are winning, scoring 15, 15, 15 every week at, say, Wolverhampton on a Monday night and go to Poland's top league and all of a sudden you are racing all the guys in the world championship. It's good that the youngsters are wanting to do it. I did it when I first started – I think I had my first season at Czestochowa in 2006, when I was sixteen.

* * *

Once I'd had my final meeting of the season in Poland at the end of 2019, a year that I won't want to remember for the racing, we went back to Australia. Faye was expecting and we wanted our second child to be born in Australia, so we didn't waste any time getting over there.

We moved in to our newly built single-storey, five bed-roomed house, which is only a kilometre from Catalina Beach at Mindarie, near Perth in Western Australia. It's also about five minutes from where I was brought up as a kid. We started building it when we were in Aussie the winter before. We bought a plot of land and I project-managed its building from Europe. All we had to do when we got there was get all the furniture while I worked on the garden. It was cool – we had somewhere we could call home. We didn't bother to have a house-warming as such, but it was Rylee's birthday while we were there and we had a party and all my mates came. Every year since I first met Faye in 2014, we have gone to Australia and either stayed with friends or in an Airbnb place, spending more than four months there without having somewhere of our own.

Faye was pregnant when we went to Australia the last time, in 2019, so we needed somewhere and we had to make it happen. Airbnb is super expensive when you are looking to stay for four and a half months so we had our own place and it was really nice. We spent a lot of time at the beach. I took Rylee for swimming lessons, and Calle was born out there, on 1 December 2019.

That was an exciting, if anxious, time. After Faye's waters broke Calle had some problems and had to stay in hospital for four days following her birth, during which they had to pump her stomach out. She weighed 3.7 kilos (8 pounds 2½ ounces) and being present at her birth was just amazing. When the baby comes out and you hold her for the first time, you can't explain the feeling till you do it. People used to say to me 'Wait till you have a child' and I didn't know what they were on about. It's hard to put into words, but it's the best feeling in the world.

It was stressful at the time, though, and I have a picture of Calle in hospital with a tube down her throat and lines into her little arms and you feel so helpless, just waiting and seeing that tiny baby and all you are thinking is whether she is all right. Thankfully, she was.

Both Faye and I wanted two and they are both healthy and that's us done. When you think about it, it's easier to have only two; for instance, when you travel somewhere one of you can have one and the other has one as well. You have got all your attention on two kids, but if you have three you can get middle child syndrome, the second one is not going to get as much attention as the oldest or the youngest.

I'm a bit selfish, I'll admit. There are other things I want to do, and so does Faye. If we had three it would make it a bit harder, little things like being in the car where Faye can chat to one of them and I can chat to the other. If we had a third we couldn't do that, could we?

CHAPTER 19

POLAND – AND THE PANDEMIC

Wroclaw has been my home track in Poland since 2012, but I never expected the city would become the Woffinden family home. Yet that's how it turned out last year after the world was hit by the Covid-19 pandemic.

The Polish city is only a two-hour drive from the German border and, at one time or another, has been part of Germany (when it was the largest city east of Berlin and known as Breslau), Bohemia, Hungary, Austria and Prussia. Set on the banks of the Oder River, it's famous for its Market Square, embraced by elegant town houses and boasting a Gothic Old Town Hall with its outsize astronomical clock, a must-photograph-it attraction for sightseeing visitors.

And ... its speedway track!

The stadium was the backdrop to an unique speedway occasion; it was where Ivan Mauger became the first and only rider to win three world titles in a row. He'd claimed his first in Sweden, at Gothenburg's Ullevi Stadium in 1968 and retained it at Wembley twelve months later. No one had ever completed the hat-trick and even the mighty Mauger wasn't favourite because, in those days, Poland was very much under the iron fist of the Soviet Union and their leagues weren't open to foreigners from the West. To outsiders it was an alien country and Wroclaw an alien track, but Mauger did complete another successful defence to achieve what no other rider has ever equalled.

Twenty-two years later, in 1992, Wroclaw was again the dramatic setting for another outstanding performance when Gary Havelock became only the sixth Briton (and fifth Englishman) after Tommy Price, Port Talbot-born Welshman Freddie Williams, Peter Craven, Peter Collins and Michael Lee to win an individual World Championship gold medal. I was only two at the time so have no memory of it but, from what I have read, it must have been one of the toughest World Finals for anyone to have won.

The start was delayed for about forty minutes because of heavy rain, and then before the halfway stage there was one of the biggest thunderstorms Wroclaw has ever witnessed. Thunder, lightning, torrential rain – the works. There was a delay of over ninety minutes, waiting for the storm to pass and then the track staff had to go to work on a flooded track. Throughout it all, Havvy kept his cool. He won his first World Final race, but crashed in his second and collapsed on the centre green before the medical team rushed out to help. The crash coincided with more flashes of lightning illuminating the almost jet-black sky. There was no way the meeting could continue, giving Havvy time to receive treatment. He managed to make the re-run, nearly two hours after the crash, got a second place and then won his next three races to claim the biggest prize of all on his big-night debut. Later, I would get to know him as a rival, for he was still riding right up until he was forced to retire through injury a few weeks before the start of the 2013 season. He had dropped down into the second tier in 2006 and he was in the opposition Redcar team on my Premier League debut for Sheffield on 10 August that year. Havvy was twenty-three, approaching twenty-four, when he became world champion, and I was a few months younger (twenty-three years and fifty-six days). Imagine: my Dad had been in the same Middlesbrough team as Havvy's father Brian in 1983!

The Wroclaw stadium, which also hosted the first ever Grand Prix round, is known as Stadion Olimpijski which even someone without any knowledge of the Polish language could accurately interpret as the Olympic Stadium. Yet, curiously, there is no record that it has ever been used for the Olympics, either the Games or an individual event. There is a mythical tale that the equestrian events at the 1936 Games in Berlin were held in Breslau (as the city was known then), but there is no evidence to back that up, and Germany's clean sweep of the six dressage, eventing and show jumping gold medals occurred 350 kilometres away in Berlin's Olympic Stadium.

Since 1945, the university city has been known as Wroclaw, and that's where I put down my Polish roots in a year that no one will ever forget.

* * *

Early in 2020, February, we were relaxing in our new house in Australia when the phone rang. It was Faye's parents, Tracy and Sean, to tell us that our farm on the borders of Leicestershire and Derbyshire was under water. Storm Dennis wreaked havoc over most of the country and Chez Woffinden didn't escape. The house is on a flood plain and we knew it could happen; it happens every year, but usually it's confined to the top of the garden and the water is never that high. But this time, when they opened the dams, the Trent and the Derwent both burst their banks within about three hours of each other, and Faye's mum and dad sent us a picture of the kitchen and the living room under water.

We all lived together, in different areas of the converted farmhouse, but sharing a communal drive and the expansive grounds. The flooding blew all the electrics and they had to have a sparky in. Our part of the house was about two steps higher, I would say about six and a half inches for sure, than their kitchen and living room. Faye's car was flooded up to the middle of the footwell, and she drives an SUV, so it's quite high off the ground. The driveway was completely under water and of the outbuildings and storage units were flooded, but, by the time we got back, it was like it never happened – Sean and Tracy had cleared everything up.

That was the way the year started, but that widespread flooding was nothing to the havoc that a bug from China was to cause as the entire world was hit by coronavirus ...

This was different, nothing any of us had ever experienced before, except, perhaps the handful of centenarians who, as babies, had lived through the 1918 influenza pandemic, which by most estimates cost north of 50 million deaths worldwide.

As I told the weekly *Speedway Star* magazine at the time, it was becoming obvious that the speedway season was not going to be what I expected: 'What's happened will make people think. It will be interesting to see what the world does. Will everybody go back to how it was or will people change? It might make people think, like little things, taking anti-bacterial bottles everywhere and spraying the handles on the supermarket trolleys every time you use one. How many hundreds of people have handled those trolleys after they've been to the toilet and not washed their hands? I know things are dirty and I always wash my hands and use soap but now it's a bit of a different story. It makes you actually think. If someone is coughing, I will avoid them. Before you used to just walk past them without thinking or worrying.

'We wipe down everything now. Between me, Faye and the girls, I touched only one handrail throughout the journey from Australia back to Europe. We didn't touch anything to be safe and to protect everyone. Not everyone will do that but, at the end of the day, it's their own safety and if they are happy to do what they want, other people won't be.'

I had planned the year around having more time at home, spending more time with the girls and the way it happened it looked like it was going to be the complete opposite to what I was wanting to do.

Speedway riders have their commitments, not only to their families and friends but also to the people they employ as mechanics. Maybe people don't think about it, but I did. I employ my crew fifty-two weeks of the year, that was in my mind a little bit when we first began to understand the effect that Covid-19 would have on not only their own lives but the lives of everyone. They have been loyal to me in the years they have worked for me, I was determined to be loyal to them.

The Polish authorities had to delay the 2020 season, but they were still the first country to announce they would be staging a league season even though they demanded that all the riders took a huge cut in their contracts. They said the only way they could start the season was by making savings to counter the lack of fans, and not even their £4.6 million-a-year TV contract (the next deal which begins next year, 2022, is worth nearly £47 million and goes through to the end of 2025) was enough to cover the loss in revenues. You can imagine how keen the clubs were to ensure that there was racing and, as a rider, what do you do? In my mind there was only one thing I could do, and that was to accept the situation, even though it meant I had to leave Faye and the girls behind in England and base myself in Poland, living in Wroclaw and staying there for as long as there were travel restrictions and quarantine rules in force. I had to take a big pay cut – the best-paid riders had to accept major reductions, and even the lowest-paid were asked to accept 30 per cent less than they had agreed previously.

It was one of those seasons, with everyone doing what they could just to get by. Obviously, there were a lot of restrictions and not all sponsors were able to pay riders, probably about fifty per cent of them, and there were pay cuts there as well. I was in the lucky position that all of my sponsors stayed with me, which made it work.

Was it a terrible year? It was – and it wasn't! We still got to race, and that was all I wanted to do. My first problem, however, was working out how I would get to Wroclaw. After struggling to get a flight confirmed, I then decided the next option would be to drive out there, but the day before I was due to travel, I received a reply from the French immigration liaison officer confirming that when I got to France, I would be refused entry and would have to return to the UK.

Luckily, Ian Sinderson and ATPI came to the rescue. They booked a six-seater private executive jet to fly myself and Wroclaw teammates Max Fricke and Dan Bewley out to Poland in May, leaving from East Midlands Airport, only a few miles from my home, and taking us direct to the Polish city. The airport was closed, but ATPI obtained a letter from the Polish government saying that we could have a landing slot, for which we had to get permission from the airport. We were quarantined on arrival, and also had to provide the authorities with notice of where we were staying, our email addresses and contact phone numbers. The police told us that they would check that all the information was correct, and even though I didn't have anyone knocking on my door, Max got checked the first morning he was there. The police told us we would be in trouble if we didn't abide by the regulations, and that once we were able to go out we would have to continue to adhere to all the rules.

It was up to us to sort out somewhere to stay. I found a new apartment and the other boys were in other places in Wroclaw. Without ATPI's support none of it would have been possible – they made it all work. Because we had so much to take between the three of us, we even had to remove two of the aircraft seats out so that we could fit everything in. I took essentials with me in the plane, including ten boxes of coffee capsules, vegetable gravy granules, protein bars, stock cubes, my favourite-flavoured toothpaste and a push bike, mostly things that I didn't think I would be able to get there. In the apartment I had a washing machine, a cooker, a vacuum cleaner, pots and pans, everything I needed. I like cooking, so I was happy preparing my own food. The first Sunday I was there I had pancakes for breakfast and made myself a sweet potato curry in the evening; I even made enough to put some in the fridge for another day!

I had Apple TV in the apartment, including Netflix, so it felt a little like home. Looking after myself was never going to faze me. It's a funny old life, and this was just another little chapter in it, wasn't it?

I quickly settled into the apartment, FaceTimed the girls every day and missed them. Originally, the plan had been to stay there on my own, but it was just too long to be away from the family I love. I wanted to have them with me. After I had been there for a month, I suggested to Faye 'Why don't you come out and stay for the year?' She said she was up for that and suggested I should just book the tickets, but again ATPI hired a private jet to get the girls over.

The apartment only had one bedroom and all year the four of us slept in that one room! We had me, Faye and Calle in one bed and Rylee had a little bed next to ours but if she wanted to jump in with us we let her. Sleep was pretty minimal, as you can imagine with four of us in a double bed! It's all part of the journey.

It was a beautiful apartment, an easy walk to the famous Market Square, down by the river. Wroclaw is a beautiful city, I'd say one of the nicest towns in Poland. We could walk to the Galeria, go down to the shops, or stroll around the square. Whereas England had been locked down when I left, there was a bit more going on in Poland. I had to undergo two weeks of quarantine when I first got there, and constantly trained from the first; it was like a training camp. In fact, it was better because I got a longer pre-season so I enjoyed it more. The season didn't start until the middle of June but I got there about a month earlier.

There was considerable doubt about whether the Grand Prix series would even take place and the first eight rounds were called off because of the pandemic. The scheduled calendar was torn up with the opening round at Warsaw scrubbed and then rounds in Germany, Britain, Sweden, Russia and Denmark all cancelled.

In the end BSI, the rights-holders, and the FIM came to a decision that the series would be chopped back to eight rounds, run over four weekends between 28 August and 3 October.

Their solution was to have a series of back-to-back rounds, on a Friday and Saturday night, six of the rounds in Poland and the other two at one of my favourite tracks at Prague's Marketa Stadium in the Czech Republic.

Wroclaw's first Ekstraliga match was against Lublin on 12 June and the Grand Prix wasn't due to get under way until around three months later so I had plenty of time on my hands, which was another reason why I wanted the girls to join me.

Heat thirteen of the opening meeting of my strange season turned out to be unlucky after I'd made a great start to the year, unbeaten by a Lublin rider in each of my first four races. By the time of my last ride the dirt was building up against the fence and as I ran up into it my right foot folded the wrong way where it shouldn't have gone. It damaged the ligaments and then I did it again when we were away to Lublin at the beginning of August. I was riding into the pits, slowing down with my feet out as brakes, and there's a step of about two centimetres and I hit that and did the same thing!

The meeting at Lublin was much closer to the start of the GP series and I didn't feel super-quick in the first one on my home track at Wroclaw. There wasn't really any home-track advantage because it's an easy track to ride, everyone rides there in the league and it was the first GP round back. Things weren't helped when I needed medical treatment after laying my bike down in the opening GP on the Friday night to avoid my fallen ex-Wolves teammate Fredrik Lindgren.

After the crash, the track doctor put some ice spray on my ankle so I could get my boot back on because we didn't want it to swell too much, and overnight I had to put ice on it every hour, for fifteen minutes, to keep the swelling down. I was able to enjoy home comforts in the fifteen hours between the end of round one and having to be back on duty on Saturday afternoon. By then Faye and the girls were over and we had some family time together, so that instead of sitting in a hotel and FaceTiming each other, we were able to be together at home. The apartment where we were living was a ten-minute cycle ride from the track, so I rode my bike in and back home on both days. I found one thing really strange: I had three injuries racing in 2020, but I was able to train on my push bike regardless because when I was cycling the ankle was stable and didn't move. It only hurt when I walked, when my knee got over the foot.

It was nice to get the first two GPs out of the way, and it definitely gave a little boost to my confidence. It was also good to make the final in both meetings, although I knew there was a lot of room for improvement.

I actually enjoyed these back-to-back GP rounds, but the Sunday, racing in a Polish league match, was quite hard; not mentally, not physically as far as tiredness went, but because of pressure. Normally, practising on a Friday, racing in a GP on the Saturday and then Polish League on a Sunday, there's no stress. You are just out there riding your bikes and that's not a problem, but doing GP, GP and Polish League on consecutive days, it's three high-stress meetings. Some people talk about this being the way to go, with GPs on a Friday and a Saturday, and it wouldn't matter to me, but it's not good for fans to watch two GPs one day after another at the same track. I'd much rather see us go to Thailand, Malaysia, Australasia – that would be a world championship. Last year it was pretty much a Polish championship or, at best, a European championship.

On to Gorzow for rounds three and four on 11 and 12 September. It's such a specialist track, as it's super-sandy now and a great home track for anyone. Bartosz Zmarzlik rides it every week and goes really well around there, and it's a perfect home track, but for someone going there as a visiting rider it's a tough nut to crack, whether for a league match or a Grand Prix. No surprise that Bartek came out on top on the Friday and even though he was only fifth on the Saturday, he got thirty-two points while I only managed a sixth and a seventh, collecting twenty-one points.

The GP bosses had decided they would adopt a new scoring system in 2020 which made a round victory more valuable than it had been in previous years. Instead of accumulating points throughout the meeting, there was a premium on the finishing order in both the night's semi-finals and final. So you could go through the qualifying races without dropping a point but if you were then last in your semi-final you wouldn't go home with more than ten points. On the other hand, you could get into the semi with maybe eight or nine points, finish in the first two in your semi and then win the final and you would have twenty GP points!

I should have had a second and a first in the GPs at Prague, but I made a mistake in my set-up for the final on Saturday. As soon as I was pushed off that inside line, Bartek was through, pushing to find that extra 1 per cent. This was the first year of having that points-scoring system, and next time, if it stays as it is, I'd do exactly the same because you have to win the final; you didn't have to do that before, second or third was okay. It changed the dynamic, and so the one thing missing from my season was a GP win. Looking back on my career, I haven't won that many GPs, and we know that moving forward I have to win more under this points system. I did well at Prague, and apart from that mistake on the last bend everything else was on point.

Even so, the title was still up for grabs, I think it might have been the first time there were three guys going into the last round who could still win the championship but, at the end of the day, Bartek was better, and had been more consistent throughout the year. The points system was new but he would have won it under the old system. He was on it a bit more, and he, not I, won the GPs (four of them).

People often look too much into results, and analyse everything more than they need to. Some will say that if I had won the three rounds where I was runner-up then I'd have been world champion for a fourth time and Bartek wouldn't have two gold medals. The fact of the matter, however, is that he was the best over the season. It wasn't a straightforward season, the injury to my foot was definitely a hindrance because I needed rehab, recovery and physio. I moved countries, I was living in an apartment and, with the injuries, it was a tough year. But we know what comes with racing motorbikes and, over the season, Bartek was the best rider.

I've gathered a nice collection of gold medals over the years, having won three world titles, and the league in both England and Sweden. But there are still two gaps in my cabinet: a Polish league championship gold medal, and a gold for riding for Great Britain. I had hoped to be getting onto the podium and having the medal put around my neck in both competitions.

My main hope had been that I could lead the Lions to victory in the Speedway of Nations, especially with us being seeded to the two-day final early in May because we were the hosts. I fancied our chances, but the coronavirus pandemic put paid to that. First of all the final was rescheduled for late October, but with the difficulties of international travel in and out of the UK, it was eventually moved to Poland and, by the time the meeting came around, I was nursing a broken hand so, for the second season in a row I was a spectator, for both the Speedway of Nations and the Ekstraliga play-off semi-final!

During a league race at Wroclaw in early October I was chasing Gorzow's Niels-Kristian Iversen, the Denmark captain, when he slid off in front of me on the last bend. There was no way I could miss him. I ran him over and hit his bike and went flying across the track into the air fence. I could have got away with it unscathed, or I could have had a worse injury than a broken fifth metacarpal in my left hand. That's the way it goes – and that was the end of my season, for I had to have surgery to piece the bones together.

So it's going to this autumn as the 2021 Speedway of NationsfFinal is again pencilled in for the National Speedway Stadium. I'm looking forward to doing the two meetings in England, but Manchester in October, it's not the greatest of decisions in my opinion. Manchester in October? It's going to get rained off, isn't it?

We definitely have a good chance. I have been waiting for a team gold medal for quite a while. I have got gold medals to show from three world championships, three different leagues in England, and the league in Sweden, but I'm still without the two for my collection – Polish league gold, and the Speedway of Nations world championship.

CHAPTER 20

MY SPEEDWAY DREAM TEAM

There is one question that I am always being asked: who would I have in my Dream Team?

It's a game we all play at one time or another, picking your favourite sportsmen, whether it's footballers, cricketers, Australian Rules stars or, in my case, speedway riders.

Normally, you never get the chance to have a say in who your teammates will be. That's down to the club's hierarchy, to those who hold the purse strings or, in some instances, perhaps, the team managers who have the power to make the decisions.

So I'm going to play at being the big boss and choose my own Tai Woffinden Dream Team. It's a hand-picked side that brings together some of my oldest mates, big rivals, great teammates and, in my first choice, someone I believe was the greatest of them all.

One thing I can guarantee: we would win matches but, more important on this occasion, we would have a fantastic time sharing the same dressing room!

RAW SPEED

1 TONY RICKARDSSON

The greatest of them all.

Only two riders have ever won the world championship six times and Tony is the only one who has done it during the Grand Prix era, although he became world champion for the first time in 1994 in what was the last of the old traditional seasons in which there was a one-off event (or on one occasion, in Amsterdam in 1987, when it was staged, like the Speedway of Nations, over two days).

I didn't really know him too well because he retired in the August of 2006, when I was only fifteen and riding in the Conference League for Scunthorpe, but when I raced for the Swedish team Masarna in 2017, I met him a few times because he lived in the nearby town of Avesta.

I can't remember having seen Tony race but there's no doubt that his commitment and application was second to none because of what he achieved in quite a short space of time, winning his titles between 1994 and 2005. So how can you consider him anything but the greatest rider of all time?

He was totally professional, and for him there was no expense spared in the quest for perfection – you only have to talk to anyone who either saw him race or raced with or against him to know he occupied a pedestal above other riders. He did everything a professional racer should do, and did it very successfully.

He came down to watch a few of the Masarna meetings and while he didn't help me as such, I did get to know him a little bit as a person and we would chat normally about everyday things rather than speedway.

I went to see his workshop, which was as immaculate, as you might expect, even though he had by then been retired for ten years or so. He did a little bit of car racing after he quitspeedway and took me out for a drive in his Tesla electric car, which was quite an experience.

2 GREG HANCOCK

The first time I ever met Greg was before I started riding in England and when I was with my family on a holiday in Europe. We decided we would go and watch the Czech Grand Prix in Prague and, as luck had it, we stayed in the same hotel as him.

Greg knew my dad from when he had been riding and, like us, he was very friendly with the late Darren Boocock and his family, so there was that link between us.

When I signed for the Polish Ekstraliga club Czestochowa in 2008, Greg was already riding for them and we spent two seasons as teammates. We were paired up together for a lot of that time, and as one or both of us was riding Marcel Gerhard-tuned engines we had something extra in common. We had a brilliant partnership on track – we smashed it that year and that was cool.

The first year I came to race in Britain was 2006 and Greg had a testimonial meeting at Hallstavik in Sweden and invited me to take part. I was too young to ride in the meeting proper because I was only fifteen, but he arranged for a race against Maciej Janowski, who is almost a year younger than me, and we ended up crashing into each other and Magic went over the fence!

After we had the couple of years at Czestochowa, I obviously started racing in the world championship regularly on a fortnightly basis during the GP season.

I never think that Greg is twenty years older than me, old enough to be my father, and I don't think anyone else does because he's just a cool dude. When you see him at the track, getting ready to race or coming in from a race, he's exactly the same person that he is in an airport, in a restaurant or hanging out together, travelling to and from the races. He's just a genuine dude who goes about his life and enjoys everything. It's refreshing because he knows who he is as a person and he's happy being himself and racing a dirt bike.

We have that respect between us even though we spent six or seven years as big title rivals and whenever we met on track we gave each other room. If you can race against someone knowing you can both go flat out and the other won't try and fence you, that's the most enjoyment you can get, even if you sometimes lose. I don't mind racing someone and being beaten by them on a given day under those circumstances.

My respect for Greg is on and off the track, and even if he hadn't won four world championships, the first in 1997 and the most recent in 2016, he'd have to be in my Dream Team because of our friendship. We were both in Team Monster so have shared many occasions, meeting the fans before a big Grand Prix, at private parties after meetings. I've been to his house in Sweden on numerous occasions to hang out with him and he's a cool guy, has a cool family, cool kids. Mr Cool.

3 JASON CRUMP

Again, I only really raced against Jason at the highest level as he was coming towards what I thought was the end of his career and our relationship is more of a friendship than a racing rivalry.

He made the last of his 145 Grand Prix appearances at the end of 2012 and I didn't become a regular in the series until the following year, although we had, of course, both been in it in 2010 but I was nowhere near his level that year.

We had quite a lot in common in that we were both born in England, although in Jason's case his father Phil was an Australian speedway international and former world finalist and the natural thing for Crumpie to do was represent Aussie.

I think the first time I ever raced against him was at Czestochowa, I remember getting to the track and it was so grippy that I thought to myself *How am I going to get around here?* Crumpie would have had no such doubts and although I can't remember, he probably went out and cleaned up on the night.

Jason's career was starting to taper off as mine was growing. I was very much at the start of my career while his was tailing off and he was a different kind of guy to some, he always kept a little bit more to himself than some of the others. Some people say he was arrogant, and a lot of people say I'm arrogant, too, but that comes from the desire to win and nothing else.

He had a very aggressive style of riding, so different from Greg, but he was so professional and so successful. He always gave 110 per cent on the track and the combination of his aggressive style and desire to win worked hand in hand, and that's why he was a three-time World Champion.

He's back home in Australia now and we don't often bump into each other because he lives on the other side of the country, but we would see each other when there was an Australian Grand Prix in Melbourne because he usually worked for the TV guys.

He was over in England in 2019 when his son Seth was riding in a support race at the World Superbike Championships at Donington Park, which is virtually on my doorstep. I had arranged to pop along to catch up with him, but I couldn't make it because it was within days of the Polish crash in which I broke my back.

I admit that I was as surprised as anyone when Jason announced that he wanted to race in Britain again in 2020, and while he only had three meetings because of Covid-19, he is back this year and riding in both leagues, with Ipswich in the Premiership and Plymouth in the Championship.

It won't be the Crumpie of old, he has admitted as much himself, but what an unexpected boost for British speedway that the fans will be able to see him on track again.

4 EMIL SAYFUTDINOV

I can still recall the first time I ever met and raced against Emil – it was in the world Under 21 Championship round at Rye House in 2007.

I was riding for the Rockets and a few weeks before I was talking with Rene Aas, a former rider who had been born in Tallin, the capital of Estonia, but settled in the UK after racing here for quite a few clubs between 1993 and 2001. He settled in Sheffield and we met up one afternoon for a coffee at the city's Jeff Hall Motorcycles and he told me: 'Don't worry about the Russians, mate, they won't do anything.'

Won't they?

Emil (who is Russian) won three of his five races, got thirteen points out of fifteen and won the semi-final while I got eleven points and fourth place on the night. That was the first time I'd ever heard of him. He had a cool style and smashed it that day and went on to win the first of his two Under 21 world titles.

I rode against him at Under 21 level a few times but it was at Vetlanda in Sweden that I really got to know him and how he works. I enjoyed that time with him and at the end of the season we partied together all the time.

A bloke at one party grabbed hold of Faye's bum a couple

of times and when I saw him walk outside I followed him and knocked him out with one punch. This is how nice I can be: when he was lying on the floor and coming round I got him some water, even while Emil was telling me 'Leave him alone mate, he's drunk!'

We've been friends for a while and if I am at a meeting where Emil is also riding he will be the first person I go and talk to. He hasn't yet won the world title, but I definitely think he will win one.

5 CHRIS HOLDER

Just a dude, man. I like Chris a lot and I tried really hard to get my former Swedish club Indianerna to sign him in 2019, but it didn't work out.

The reason I wanted him at Kumla, the Indianerna track, was because I thought he could get back to the Chris Holder who won the world championship nine years ago. We go back a long way, longer than anyone else, since we were paired up together in the Australian junior championships when I was still at school.

Chris has been one of my biggest rivals in the fight for the world championship ... but he never stops reminding me about the day we first bumped into each other! And he always rips into me for my total lack of professionalism when we were partners in the Australian Under 16 Pairs Championship way back in 2003.

Most years the solo and pairs championships are held on the same junior track, over the same weekend with the individual meeting on the Friday or Saturday and the pairs event the following day. I was only twelve and hadn't had more than half a dozen races when I got a letter from Motorycling Australia saying I'd been selected for the 125cc Under 16 Championship.

Bibra Lake, the venue, was only some 30 kilometres (19 miles) from where we lived, and was the only proper speedway track in Western Australia after Claremont Speedway in Perth had closed down. The track, which was built on land at Jandakot Airport, had opened in 1963 and the club ran car and bike events there from day one and also built a small junior track on the infield of the main oval. It had staged four previous Under 16 championships and was always a big opportunity for the Western Australian riders to compete on their own doorstep.

It was such a big thing among the parents, who would spend a small fortune getting their kids from the other side of the country to Perth, involving a near 4,000 kilometre (2,485 mile) trek for anyone, like Chris, living in New South Wales.

I didn't have a chance of winning the meeting as I had only just started riding a bike, but I was told that if I could do a start I would be in it, basically to make the numbers up. I was only a little kid while all the others were big kids, three or four years older than me.

I'm not really sure how they picked the pairings for the second meeting but I know that Chris didn't have a partner so he got lumbered with me, probably because I was another of those without someone to ride with. Chris was only fifteen and had come across with his dad Mick from Sydney. We'd never met each other although his father knew of my dad because he had been a rider.

They paired us up, but we were parked on different sides of the pits and Chris went to the tapes for the first race and didn't know what had happened when I didn't appear!

I missed the race altogether, and after it Chris comes up to me and goes 'Where the fuck was ya?' I'd missed it because I'd gone off to get myself a hot dog or an ice cream, something like that, and he's never let me forget it.

That was the first time we had come across each other and he often reminds me now and we have a laugh about it. Poor Chris had no chance of winning the title being paired up with me. It would be a little different now and we often say we wouldn't mind racing with each other in a pairs meeting today.

He was a deserved world champion in 2012 but there have been a few things going on in his life – things that he has spoken to me about as a friend – which is not for me to talk about. Thankfully, those personal things are over now and he has started a whole new life and is working on getting back to where he was.

With all the stuff that's been going on, I want to see my mate back to where he belongs and I'm sure he wants it as well.

6 DARCY WARD

I'm mates with both Darcy and Chris but their friendship is on a totally different level. Fans nicknamed them the Turbo Twins and that's appropriate because they were like twins.

I'm sure that Darcy would have won a world championship if fate hadn't decided otherwise. He had his ban for failing an alcohol test at the Latvian Grand Prix in 2014 but he came back from that, sorted out his life and the form and speed he was showing before the accident in Poland in 2015 that left him paralysed would definitely have given him a real chance of being World Champion.

He and Chris used to hang out together all the time. They lived close to each other down on the South Coast, they rode together at Poole and at Torun in Poland, they travelled together; I have never known two riders as close as they were. How cool is that?

Darcy became a promoter early this year when, in January, he took over the running of speedway at the Mick Doohan Raceway in Banyo, North Brisbane, Queensland. Who knows, maybe I'll get the chance to race there!

Darcy was a great rider and he is a great guy and the three of us had some wild nights together. We got up to some of the craziest things and, at the end of the day, that's what life is about – finding people you like, racing bikes together, and having fun together. It's so unreal.

7 STEVE JOHNSTON

He's a legend! For me, he goes back to when I was a kid, for I was only a couple of years old when Steve stayed with us in Scunthorpe.

There are so many stories that I can't remember them all, although I've been told about them, like the time he dangled me over the balustrade at the house by my ankle, threatening to let go to scare Mum.

He was pretty much my favourite uncle, my 'adopted' uncle, even though I've only ever called him Johnno. Even now – he's back in Australia working in the mines – he texts me every week. We still keep in touch, and we always catch up when I am back home in the winter.

I was so happy when he got the chance to ride in the Australian Grand Prix at Sydney's Olympic Stadium in 2002, that was the first GP I ever went to because Dad took us along to watch him.

The first year I was riding at Scunthorpe, I'm fairly sure he was racing for Arena-Essex that year but he came along to help me in my first meeting against the American Dream Team. He sorted out my first sponsorship with Rock Oil, got a helmet deal for me and has always been around.

He's got such a personality that you can't not have him in your team. He's one of those guys who will lift everyone, everything is always a laugh with him, everyone is his friend and he's everyone's friend.

He probably wasn't as professional as you need to be to be at the highest level, but my Dream Team wouldn't be right without him.

He has a heart of gold, and what a character to have in any team.

CHAPTER 21

CONFIDENCE AND CONSISTENCY

A *few years ago, after I won my second world title, I was asked what I wanted to do next. It was one of the easiest questions I've ever had to answer and I replied: 'I want to win as many titles as I can. I don't have a number where I'd sit and think "Right, I've done it – I'm happy with that," I just want to keep winning.*

'I have two now, and that's awesome, but my focus is on number three. And if I win a third, I'll start thinking about a fourth, then it'll be a fifth – that's just how I am. You look at the best sportsmen ever, they're guys who win four, five, six world titles in whatever it is they're doing. I want to be one of them.'

I have looked back at the records of both Ivan Mauger and Tony Rickardsson, the two greats who won six world championships each. Mauger was thirty-nine when he stepped onto the top of the podium at Katowice, Poland, to collect his sixth World Championship gold medal. He'd won his first in 1968, so there were twelve years between his first and him breaking the all-time record, which until then he had held jointly with Sweden's Ove Fundin. Tony was thirty-five when he made it six and there were eleven years between his first and his sixth world title, so there is still time for me.

I won my first in 2013, my second in 2015 and my third in 2018, so I still have a few years in which to win another three to catch them up. I won't be thirty-one until August 2021, but what does it matter what it says on my birth certificate if I can put that framed sixth FIM World Champion parchment up on the wall? After all, Greg Hancock was still winning world titles well into his forties.

I got my third one in 2018 and while I haven't won the World Championship for a fourth time yet, there have been reasons for that, injuries being one of them. I had the broken back in 2019 which wrecked any chances I had, and last year I missed out and had to settle for the silver medal behind Bartosz 'Bartek' Zmarzlik.

I'm always confident. I trust my ability. I was fourth in 2014 after crashing out in the Gorzow Grand Prix; runner-up, nine points behind Greg Hancock, in 2016; third in 2017 when an on-fire Jason Doyle was totally dominant; and second again in 2020.

Bartek's had a couple of good years – a couple of amazing years, in fact. It was good to watch him lift the title first time, and back that up by doing it again last year. There's never disappointment on my side at seeing someone else lift world titles because I know what it takes, I know the effort you have to put in to become World Champion, and I am ready to put that effort in again.

Everyone in the championship is good enough to win the world title, it's just a question of putting the performances together over a full season. It is clear that, over the years everyone can win a Speedway Grand Prix round – I think the record books show that there have been forty-three different riders to have won at least one GP in the championship's twenty-six years.

If you want to count them, here they are: Jason Crump leads the way with 23 wins, then comes Tomasz Gollob (22), Greg Hancock (21), Tony Rickardsson (20), Nicki Pedersen (17), myself (11), Bartosz Zmarzlik (10), Andreas Jonsson (9), Leigh Adams (8), Maciej Janowski (7), Emil Sayfutdinov (7), Jason Doyle (6), Billy Hamill (6), Jarek Hampel (6), Hans Nielsen (6), Chris Holder (5), Niels-Kristian Iversen (5), Freddie Lindgren (5), Matej Zagar (5), Hans Andersen (4), Ryan Sullivan (4), Krzysztof Kasprzak (3), Tommy Knudsen (3), Antonio Lindbäck (3,) Leon Madsen (3), Martin Vaculik (3), Patryk Dudek (2), Rune Holta (2), Peter Kildemand (2), Mark Loram (2). Brian Andersen, Kenneth Bjerre, Martin Dugard, Max Fricke, Chris Harris, Michael Jepsen Jensen, Janusz Kolodziej, Artem Laguta, Adrian Miedzinski, Piotr Pawlicki, Bjarne Pedersen, Martin Smolinski and Darcy Ward have all won one!

Of those forty-three GP winners, only eleven have ended a GP season as World Champion – Gollob, Hancock, Rickardsson, Pedersen, Zmarzlik, Hamill, Nielsen, Doyle, Holder, Loram and myself – which means there's thirty-two riders who were capable of beating all their opponents in a one-off meeting who haven't been able to show the consistency needed over a full season.

Mark Loram has been the exception to one of the rules – the year he was crowned the best rider in the world, 2000, he didn't actually win a round that season, which only goes to prove that it is consistency over six, eight, ten, eleven or even twelve rounds that is important.

Under the system that was used for the 2020 season, with finishing positions having a major bearing on how many GP points you scored, I targeted at least a semi-final in every round and achieved that, but missed out on the final in both rounds at Gorzow. Getting into the final, and then winning it, can give you a big bonus as the difference between winning and being fifth is now eight points, so a rider requires a slightly different approach to the series.

Bartek will be aiming to be only the second rider ever to win three world titles in a row since Ivan Mauger did it between 1968 and 1970. No one else has ever completed a hat-trick of title victories so it will be some achievement if he can do it.

Realistically, Freddie (Lindgren) can probably win a world title; he's been third twice in the last three years. Emil (Sayfutdinov) can probably win one; he got the bronze medal in 2019 but was only six points behind champion Bartek, and that's the smallest gap there has ever been between the top three since the world title came to be decided under the Grand Prix format twenty-six years ago.

Looking at my rivals in 2021, only three of the permanent field, Anders Thomsen, Oliver Berntzon and my GB teammate Robert Lambert, haven't experienced the high of standing on top of the box and hearing his own national anthem blasting out over the stadium tannoy at least once in his life. As I've said, everyone, or at least the majority, of the riders in the series is good enough to win the world title, it's just putting the performances together. But equally, everyone is beatable.

I look after myself. I keep the weight down, which is the most important thing, and I stay healthy. I do a pretty good job – I'm in a really good way, I do everything an athlete does, which is probably pretty much the same for all athletes so I don't think too much about it. I wake up in the morning, train, eat breakfast, play with the girls. I just do everything: cycling, running, gym work, all the standard stuff to keep fit. I've got a gym at home. I'm surprised people still go to the gym, but maybe some people need to keep their motivation.

I know what level of rider I am with my performances since 2013. I'm a top-three championship rider, barring injury or mishaps, and I'm just trying to put the pieces of the jigsaw together again.

And I know that I can.

TAI WOFFENDEN GRAND PRIX RECORD – THE FIGURES

2010

April 24	European GP (Poland)	1 point, sixteenth.
May 8	Swedish GP	4 points, sixteenth.
May 22	Czech Republic GP	5 points, fourteenth.
June 5	Danish GP	5 points, twelfth.
June 19	Torun GP of Poland	7 points, seventh.
July 10	British GP	6 points, twelfth.
August 14	Scandinavian GP (Sweden)	3 points, fifteenth.
August 28	Croatian GP	6 points, tenth.
September 11	Nordic GP (Denmark)	2 points, fifteenth.
September 25	Italian GP	6 points, fourteenth.
October 9	Polish Grand Prix	4 points, fourteenth.

Ranking: Fourteenth, 49 points

2011

| June 25 | British GP [reserve] | 2 points, sixteenth. |

Ranking: Twenty-fifth, 2 points.

2013

March 23	New Zealand GP	9 points, seventh.
April 23	European GP (Poland)	14 points, fourth.
May 4	Swedish GP	12 points, fifth.
May 18	Czech Republic GP	19 points, first.
June 1	British GP	7 points, ninth.
June 15	Polish GP	12 points, third.
June 29	Danish GP	11 points, sixth.
August 3	Italian GP	18 points, second.
August 17	Latvian GP	15 points, third.
September 7	Slovenian GP	17 points, second.
September 21	Scandinavian GP (Sweden)	7 points, tenth.
October 5	Torun GP of Poland	10 points, sixth.

Ranking: WORLD CHAMPION, 151 points.

2014

April 5	New Zealand GP	7 points, ninth.
April 26	European GP (Poland)	5 points, eleventh.
May 17	Finnish GP	16 points, second.
May 31	Czech Republic GP	18 points, first.
June 14	Swedish GP	17 points, first.

June 28	Danish GP	9 points, sixth.
July 12	British GP	18 points, second.
August 17	Latvian GP	8 points, seventh.
August 30	Gorzow GP of Poland	did not ride, injured.
September 30	Nordic GP (Denmark)	7 points, tenth.
September 27	Scandinavian GP (Sweden)	7 points, eight.
October 11	Torun GP of Poland	9 points, sixth.

Ranking: Fourth, 121+2 points. Lost run-off for third place.

2015

April 18	*Polish GP	5 points, seventh.
May 16	Finnish GP	17 points, second.
May 23	Czech Republic GP	18 points, first.
July 4	British GP	15 pts, fourth.
July 18	Latvian GP	8 points, seventh.
July 25	Swedish GP	17 points, second.
August 8	Danish GP	11 points, fourth.
August 29	Gorzow GP of Poland	18 points, third.
September 12	Slovenian GP	18 points, second.
September 26	Stockholm GP	16 points, first.
October 3	Torun GP of Poland	8 points, ninth.
October 24	Australian GP	12 points, sixth.

*Abandoned after 12 races, track unsafe.

Ranking: WORLD CHAMPION, 163 points.

2016

April 30	Slovenian GP	10 points, fourth.
May 14	Warsaw GP of Poland	14 points, first.
June 11	Danish GP	15 points, third.
June 25	Czech Republic GP	9 points, seventh.
July 9	British GP	15 points, second.
August 14	Swedish GP	8 points, tenth.
August 27	Gorzow GP of Poland	15 points, second.
September 10	German GP	10 points, sixth.
September 24	Stockholm GP	11 points, sixth.
October 1	Torun GP of Poland	8 points, tenth.
October 22	Australian GP	15 points, second.

Ranking: Runner-up, 130 points.

2017

April 30	Slovenian GP	8 points, ninth.
May 13	Warsaw GP of Poland	13 points, fifth.
May 27	Latvian GP	9 points, seventh.
June 10	Czech Republic GP	7 points, tenth.
June 24	Danish GP	11 points, sixth.
July 22	British GP	9 points, ninth.
August 14	Swedish GP	14 points, fifth.
August 27	Gorzow GP of Poland	18 points, first.
September 10	German GP	5 points, eleventh.
September 23	Stockholm GP	6 points, thirteenth.

October 1	Torun GP of Poland	15 points, second.
October 22	Australian GP	16 points, second,

Ranking: Third, 131 points.

2018

May 12	Warsaw GP of Poland	15 points, first.
May 26	Czech Republic GP	16 points, fourth.
June 30	Danish GP	18 points, first.
July 7	Swedish GP	16 points, fourth.
July 21	British GP	16 points, second.
August 11	Scandinavian GP (Sweden)	10 points, eighth.
August 25	Gorzow GP of Poland	12 points, third.
September 8	Slovenian GP	5 points, fourteenth.
September 22	German GP	16 points, first.
October 6	Torun GP of Poland	15 points, first.

Ranking: WORLD CHAMPION, 139 points.

2019

May 18	Warsaw GP of Poland	6 points, twelfth.
June 1	Slovenian GP	9 points, sixth.
June 15	Czech Republic GP	did not ride, injured.
July 6	Swedish GP	did not ride, injured.
August 3	Wroclaw GP of Poland	6 points, tenth.
August 17	Scandinavian GP (Sweden)	6 points, thirteenth.
August 31	German GP	8 points, eleventh.

September 7	Danish GP	11 points, sixth.
September 21	British GP	5 points, twelfth.
October 5	Torun GP	9 points, sixth.

Ranking: Thirteenth, 60 points.

2019

August 28	Wroclaw GP R1	14 points, fourth.
August 29	Wroclaw GP R2	18 points, second.
September 11	Gorzow GP R3	11 points, sixth.
September 12	Gorzow GP R4	10 points, seventh.
September 18	Czech Republic GP R5	18 points, second.
September 19	Czech Republic GP R6	18 points, second.
October 2	Torun GP R7	16 points, third.
October 3	Torun GP R8	12 points, fifth.

Ranking: Runner-up, 117 points.

TAI WOFFINDEN – LEAGUE STATISTICS

BRITISH CAREER

		M	R	Pts	BP	TPts	Avge
2006 CL	Scunthorpe	35	169	377	45	422	9.99
2006 PL	Sheffield	4	15	23	2	25	6.67
2007 PL	Rye House	40	175	372	33	405	9.26
2007 CL	Scunthorpe	20	106	291	10	301	11.36
2008 PL	Rye House	35	169	430	24	454	10.75
2009 EL	Wolverhampton	37	162	303	33	336	8.30
2010 EL	Wolverhampton	38	181	328	15	343	7.58
2011 EL	Wolverhampton	25	114	233	9	242	8.49
2012 EL	Wolverhampton	19	90	198	11	209	9.29
2013 EL	Wolverhampton	23	112	262	19	281	10.04
2014 EL	Wolverhampton	25	118	205	25	230	7.80
2016 EL	Wolverhampton	10	47	100	9	109	9.28

RAW SPEED

Key: CL – Conference League (3rd tier). PL – Premier League (2nd tier). EL – Elite League (1st tier).

POLISH CAREER

		M	R	Pts	BP	TPts	Avge
2008 EL	Czestochowa	11	35	26	5	31	3.54
2009 EL	Czestochowa	17	86	125	16	141	6.56
2010 EL	Czestochowa	14	60	65	7	72	4.80
2011 L1	Gniezno	12	60	124	8	132	8.80
2012 EL	Wroclaw	14	71	115	13	128	7.21
2013 EL	Wroclaw	16	87	203	12	215	9.89
2014 EL	Wroclaw	12	63	128	11	139	8.83
2015 EL	Wroclaw	18	94	220	7	227	9.66
2016 EL	Wroclaw	18	95	223	6	229	9.64
2017 EL	Wroclaw	18	94	178	16	194	8.26
2018 EL	Wroclaw	18	95	195	17	212	8.93
2019 EL	Wroclaw	18	72	151	8	159	8.83
2020 EL	Wroclaw	18	83	167	13	180	8.67

Key: EL – Ekstraliga (1st tier). L1 – First League (2nd tier).

SWEDISH CAREER

		M	R	Pts	BP	TPts	Avge
2008 AS	Vargarna	5	27	52	7	59	8.74
2009 ES	Vargarna	19	95	150	18	168	7.07
2010 ES	Vargarna	8	30	32	5	37	4.93

2011 ES	Vargarna	9	42	55	10	65	6.19
2012 ES	Dackarna	5	22	36	1	37	6.73
2014 ES	Elit Vetlanda	12	53	113	12	125	9.43
2015 ES	Elit Vetlanda	14	63	138	14	152	9.65
2016 ES	Elit Vetlanda	14	72	140	15	155	8.61
2017 ES	Masarna	14	68	150	14	164	9.65
2018 ES	Kumla Indianerna	15	77	165	8	173	8.99
2019 ES	Kumla Indianerna	10	51	118	4	122	9.57

Key: ES – EliteSerie (1st tier). AS – AllSvenskan League (2nd tier)

Statistics up to and including Thursday, 1 April 2021.